PRISONERS AT THE BAR

PRISONERS AT THE BAR

An Account of the Trials of
THE WILLIAM HAYWOOD CASE
THE SACCO-VANZETTI CASE
THE LOEB-LEOPOLD CASE
THE BRUNO HAUPTMANN CASE

By FRANCIS X. BUSCH

Biography Index Reprint Series

BOOKS FOR LIBRARIES PRESS
FREEPORT, NEW YORK

DEDICATED TO
THE IDEAL IN THE ADMINISTRATION OF CRIMINAL JUSTICE
"A TRUE DELIVERANCE BETWEEN
THE STATE AND THE PRISONER
AT THE BAR"

FOREWORD

THE out-of-the-ordinary criminal case enlists universal interest because it is usually a threefold drama: the crime, the identification—apprehension and accusation of the suspect—and the trial and its consequence.

But the public interest in the trial of a defendant for a shocking crime has something in it far more significant than the high drama usually involved. Courts are established and their procedures regulated by basic constitutions or by the executive or legislative branch—whichever happens to be dominant—of the government. The administration of criminal law necessarily mirrors the government of which it is a part.

Crime itself through the ages has changed little or not at all, but the attitudes of particular societies toward persons accused of crime and the methods of dealing with such persons have changed, even in our own time, and are constantly changing. It has, therefore, been said with truth that the degree to which the ordinary citizens of a commonwealth are sensitive to wrongdoing and the degree to which, by their institutions and practices, justice is arrived at is a just measure of the civilization of that commonwealth.

And here one calls to mind Charles (Lord) Russell's masterly argument to the jury in defense of Mrs. Maybrick in which he thus accounts for the peculiar interest which Anglo-Saxons, under free and beneficent governments, have in the occurrences in their criminal courts:

There is no more striking scene to the reflective mind than that which is presented on the trial of a criminal case where the charge is a grave one—a judge who tries with certain hands fairly to hold the scales of justice, and a jury calm, honest, dispassionate, with no desire except to do justice in the case according to their conscientious belief. . . . In the language of the officer of the Court giving the prisoner in charge to you, he informed you that the prisoner at the bar had "put herself upon her country" which country you are.

The four American criminal trials presented in the succeeding pages have been selected not only because their dramatic quality attracted nationwide attention, or because they were major forensic battles in which great advocates displayed their skills and wits. In each of these trials the scene is laid against a background peculiar to American life, and each trial possesses a special social significance. Taken together, the trials described in this book can be said to typify the administration of criminal justice in the United States of America.

The plan followed in the work has been influenced to an extent by that most excellent series of seventy-five volumes of *Notable British Trials* (William Hodge & Company, Ltd., London, Edinburgh and Glasgow). Each volume of that series is devoted to a single case. An "Introduction," which briefly describes the crime and the suspected criminal, is followed by a verbatim transcript or full abstract of the trial proceedings—the opening statements, the evidence, the summations, the Court's charge and the verdict. Because of their resulting technical character, the appeal of *Notable British Trials* is largely to the legal profession. In the cases treated in this work, an introduction on the English pattern is followed by a nontechnical narrative condensation of the court proceedings and their consequences. The result is a fairly brief but accurate account of four notable American trials, specially designed for the general reading public.

With one exception the accounts of the trials which follow are based on the stenographic record or the printed appeal record in the particular case. The exception is the Steunenberg case which includes the trial of William D.

Haywood and others. In that case no stenographic record was discoverable and, in view of the acquittals, there were no appellate records. In the absence of such a primary source, the author was fortunate in securing copies of *Mc-Clure's Magazine* for the years 1907 and 1908, which contain Harry Orchard's confession in full and on-the-spot reports of the trial by that keen and meticulous observer, George Kibbe Turner. Other secondary sources, used for comparison and verification, were Clarence Darrow's *The Story of My Life* (Charles Scribner's Sons, New York and London, 1932), Irving Stone's *Clarence Darrow for the Defense* (Doubleday, Doran & Company, Inc., Garden City, New York, 1941), and contemporary newspaper accounts.

My acknowledgments are due to the clerks of the courts and other officials and librarians in public and private libraries and newspaper offices in Chicago, Washington, New York and Indianapolis for courtesies extended in making records available; to Mrs. Marian A. Hodgkinson and Mrs. Virginia Weissman and my daughter, Mrs. Frances Busch Zink, for library research, copying, comparing and proofreading manuscript; and to my wife for her valuable suggestions, encouragement and inexhaustible patience.

FRANCIS X. BUSCH.

CONTENTS

I

The Trials of

WILLIAM D. HAYWOOD
and
GEORGE PETTIBONE

for the Murder of

EX-GOVERNOR STEUNENBERG
of Idaho (1907)

The William D. Haywood Case

IT IS NOT ALONE *the prominence of the victim and the unusual means employed for his destruction that make this case unique. As a climax to fifteen years of bitter strife between the Western Federation of Miners and the Western Mine Owners' Association it has left a startling record of the illegal and violent methods all too often employed by organized employees and organized employers alike in the 1890s and early 1900s to gain their objectives: for labor, a fair share of the rewards of the labor employed in the great and growing industries of America; for capital, the maintenance of the* status quo.

It also furnishes a striking example of the triumph of superb advocacy over a strong case skillfully presented and the apparently insurmountable barriers of local prejudice.

CALDWELL, IDAHO, in 1905, was not unlike a score of other towns scattered through the sparsely settled Northwest. It boasted a fairly well-ordered community, a daily newspaper, a solvent bank, several "modern" hotels and a thriving business district which supplied the needs of its 4,000 hard-working, contented residents. Most of these derived their sustenance directly or indirectly from farming, sheep raising or mining—the state's principal industries.

In the late evening of December 30, Caldwell's most distinguished citizen, Frank Steunenberg, might have been seen walking slowly, as was his habit, from the Saratoga Hotel to his near-by modest home. As president of the

Caldwell Bank, he had spent a busy afternoon with his fellow directors clearing up the institution's year-end problems. He had stopped briefly at the hotel to join a circle of old friends who gathered in the lobby daily to discuss the current news—business conditions, Federal aid for irrigation and politics.

Steunenberg had been concerned in the state's politics. He had come to Idaho from Iowa in the late eighties. He was a printer by trade and, with his brother, acquired and published the Caldwell *Record*. He was solid, unpretentious, friendly and good-natured. His paper was strongly pro-labor, and Steunenberg himself carried an honorary membership card in the Boise Typographical Union. He was caught up in the Democratic-Populist coalition which swept the Northwest in 1896 and, to his own as well as to everyone else's surprise, was nominated on that ticket and elected governor. The term was for two years. In 1898 he was re-elected.

The test of his moral fiber came during his second term. The Western Federation of Miners called a general strike in the rich Coeur d'Alene mining district. The mine owners' association, following the custom of that day, promptly imported a horde of strikebreakers and put them to work under armed Pinkerton guards in the important Bunker Hill and Sullivan mines. The lawlessness of the strikers was matched by the lawlessness of the strikebreakers and hired thugs of the operators.

Tension increased. Finally the miners, in a riotous open meeting, voted to blow up the mine. A mob of over a thousand gathered and proceeded to carry out the mandate. The Bunker Hill and Sullivan mines were blasted with dynamite and rendered unworkable. Two men were killed. The mineowners and the disinterested citizenry called on the governor and demanded that he restore order. There was no state militia available. The guard was on duty in the Philippines. Steunenberg took the only course he could have taken—he asked the President for Federal troops. He knew what the action meant: his branding by union labor as a traitor to the cause of those who had put him in office.

The handling of the situation by the Federal troops was unnecessarily brutal. The affected area was declared under martial law. Hundreds of union miners and suspected sympathizers were arrested, herded into barbed-wire enclosures and kept incommunicado for months under conditions not unlike those of the odious concentration camps of a half century later. Hundreds of others fled the state to escape arrest. The governor was then induced to give his sanction to a "permit system" which, as it turned out, meant that no man could work in a mine or mill unless he had a permit approved by the military authorities, and this he could not get unless he renounced his membership in and allegiance to the miners' union. It was this act, more than the calling in of the troops, which brought down the storm around the governor's head. He was denounced by every union organization in the West. His life was repeatedly threatened and, during the remainder of his term as governor, he was under constant guard.

But all of this had happened in 1899. A truce was finally patched up between the miners and the operators. Order was restored and, after an eighteen months' occupation, the Federal troops were withdrawn. Steunenberg's term expired. He retired to his home and business affairs at Caldwell and for six years had enjoyed the uneventful life of a successful, small-town businessman, a highly esteemed citizen and a well-liked neighbor.

As Steunenberg approached his home in the gathering darkness of that winter evening there was nothing to awaken in him a sense of danger. There was the old wood and woven-wire fence that separated his front yard from the unpaved street. There was the creaking, in-swinging gate which opened upon the plank walk that led to the broad porch. Supper was awaiting him, and he opened the gate as he had done uncounted times before. The pushing open of that gate on December 30, 1905, was the last act in the ex-governor's life.

To use the language of some of the witnesses, who testified in the labor trials of Haywood and Pettibone, there was an explosion so terrific that it "shook the earth and could be heard for miles around." A bomb had been attached to the gate in such a way that it would be detonated when someone opened the gate or tripped over a string stretched across the gate opening just above the ground. The fiendish device had proved completely successful. The unsuspecting victim sprang the trap, and the resulting explosion so mangled his body that he was almost instantly killed.

The cold-blooded murder of their ex-governor aroused the people of Idaho as they had never been stirred before. The immediate question, *Who would want to kill Frank Steunenberg?*, drew a common answer, *The miners' federation*. The succeeding question, *Who did the killing?*, was answered within forty-eight hours. One of the murdered man's closest friends had been Joe Hutchinson, who, in 1896, had been elected lieutenant governor on the ticket with Steunenberg. Immediately after the explosion he examined what was left of the gate and fence, and in the debris found some pieces of plaster of Paris and a piece of fish line. He rightly concluded that the line had been used as part of the trap to touch off the bomb.

Naturally, every stranger in the town fell under suspicion. Among these there was one—a ruddy-faced, mild-mannered, pleasant chap—who called himself Tom Hogan and posed as a sheep buyer. He had lived at the various hotels in Caldwell more or less constantly for four or five months and, so far as known, had made no particular efforts to buy any sheep. He seemed well supplied with money and mingled freely with the lobby and bar loungers. After the explosion it was recalled that he had made frequent inquiries about Steunenberg—his business and social activities and when he was expected to return from his out-of-town trips.

Hutchinson's friends told him of their suspicions of Hogan. Hutchinson acted quickly and boldly. He induced a couple of maids at the hotel to let him search Hogan's room during his absence. The hunch paid off. In a chamber pot he found a piece of fish line matching the piece he had found at the gate of the ex-governor's home and particles of plaster of Paris similar to that which had been used to make the bomb.

Sheriff Moseley was called in, and he took charge. Through a baggage check picked up in the room, Hogan's trunk was located at the depot, broken into and searched. In it was a complete set of burglar's tools and a motley assortment of clothes evidently designed for various disguises. It also revealed that Tom Hogan more commonly went by the name of Harry Orchard. It was late afternoon of New Year's Day when Harry Orchard, alias Tom Hogan, was arrested, charged with the murder of Steunenberg and lodged in the Caldwell jail.

While Orchard stoutly denied his guilt, the evidence against him was accepted by the public as conclusive. To this verdict was added the conviction, trumpeted in the regular and special editions of every paper in the state, that Orchard was merely an instrument which the Western Federation of Miners had used to punish Steunenberg for his supposed betrayal of the union cause.

The demand for the apprehension and punishment of the real murderers of Steunenberg—the higher-ups—was not confined to Idaho. Excitement and popular feeling in Colorado ran nearly as high. The general offices of the Western Federation of Miners were in Denver, and the principal officers of the association lived there. Colorado had had its own war with the federation. The record of the fifteen years before Steunenberg's murder was one of a continuous succession of strikes, strike breaking, killings, Federal intervention, martial law, wholesale arrests and deportations. As recently as June 1904, the railroad depot at Independence had been bombed, killing fourteen non-union miners. The outrage was charged to the federation, and Orchard was repeatedly named as the perpetrator of that crime.

For ten days the local Idaho authorities tried unsuccessfully to crack Orchard. On the twelfth of January it was given out that James McParland, manager of the Pinkerton Detective Agency at Denver and long-time representative of the mineowners in their battles with the federation, had been placed in charge of the investigation. Subsequent events made it quite evident that governmental and other agencies in Colorado had as much to do with McParland's appointment as the law-enforcement officers of Idaho.

The only hope of the State to implicate the so-called higher-ups lay in getting a confession from Orchard. McParland, because of his first-hand experience with the activities of the federation and the Western Mine Owners' Association and his long experience in dealing with criminals, was an ideal selection for the job.

To the orthodox police methods McParland added some original touches. Orchard was immediately removed from the Caldwell jail to the Idaho State Penitentiary at Boise. While in jail he had been treated like other inmates—three plain but adequate meals a day and a fairly comfortable bunk in a small, barred cell. He was allowed a period of exercise under guard and communicated freely with his jailers and other persons who called to see him. When he reached the penitentiary he was placed in a dark cell in "murderers' row." There was no other prisoner within hailing distance. No one was permitted to talk to him and, except for the turnkey who three times a day pushed a meager plate of unappetizing food through the bars, he saw no one. This was kept up for ten days.

At the end of this softening-up process, the warden took him out of solitary and introduced him to McParland. Orchard tells of that first meeting in his *Confessions and Autobiography*[1] published a year or so later. "I think at first he asked me if I believed in a hereafter and a God. I think I told him I believed in a Supreme Being or something like that. He also told me that he believed I had been used as a tool. . . . He spoke of what an awful thing it was to live and die a sinful life and that every man ought to repent for his sins and that there was no sin that God would not forgive. He spoke of King David being a murderer, and also the Apostle Paul . . . who was then called Saul, consenting to the death of Stephen and holding the young men's coats while they stoned him to death. . . . He also told me of some cases where men had turned state's evidence and that when the state had used them for a witness, they did not or could not prosecute them. He said further that men might be thousands of miles away from where a murder took place and be guilty of that murder and be charged with conspiracy, and that the man that committed the murder was not as guilty as the conspirators, and, to say in a word, he led me to believe that there was a chance for me even if I were guilty of the assassination of Mr. Steunenberg, if I would tell the truth; and he also urged me to think of the hereafter and the awful consequences of a man dying in his sins."

Except as Orchard tells it in his *Confessions and Autobiography,* there is no source of information as to what took place between him and the master detective during the next thirty days; but on February 19, 1906, it was given out that Orchard had made a "full and complete confession." The publication of the fact that the confession had been made—the full text of it did not become public until much later—was accompanied by a sob story in the best

---

[1] The full text of Orchard's confession appeared in his *Confessions and Autobiography*, published serially in *McClure's Magazine*, July, August, September, October and November 1907.

American newspaper tradition. The following from the *Idaho Statesman* of February 20 is typical: "With tears rolling down his cheeks, with bowed head and thoughts of his early religious training, Harry Orchard broke down and made a full confession. It is believed that every word spoken by the conscience-stricken man is true."

Orchard's confession charged that he had been hired by the officers of the Western Federation of Miners—Charles H. Moyer, its president, and William D. Haywood, its secretary-treasurer—to kill Steunenberg, and that he had been assisted by George Pettibone, an active member of the union, and Jack Simpkins, a member of the executive board of the federation. He named also a certain Steve Adams as one who had plotted with him the killing of Steunenberg. Adams, said Orchard, had been his associate in other outrages, including the dynamiting of the Independence, Colorado, depot, to which Orchard also confessed.

An immediate search was begun for Simpkins, but he was never apprehended. Adams was promptly arrested and lodged in the same penitentiary cell with Orchard. Orchard and McParland both went to work on him. He was without legal counsel and, between threats of hanging and promises of immunity, was induced to confess a participation in the Independence depot and other bombings. Also, as the result of information furnished McParland by Orchard, Adams confessed that he and Simpkins had killed a couple of claim jumpers in northern Idaho some six or seven years before.

Immediately following Orchard's confession, a formal requisition on the governor of Colorado for the extradition of Haywood, Moyer and Pettibone was placed in the hands of the Idaho officers. They proceeded to Denver and presented it to Governor McDonald. The Colorado executive issued a warrant for the arrest of the three men. The presence of the Idaho officials and the action of the two governors was kept a close secret. The warrant was placed in the hands of Colorado officials on Thursday, February 15, but no attempt was made to serve it until Saturday, February 17, at 11:30 P.M. The three men were then arrested and lodged in separate cells. Their requests to communicate with lawyers or members of their families were denied. Before daybreak Sunday morning they were taken from jail, hurried to the railroad station and, under an armed guard of Pinkerton's, Colorado and Idaho officials, loaded on a special train which sped over cleared rails out of Colorado, through Utah and Wyoming and into the State of Idaho.

Within the week petitions for writs of habeas corpus on behalf of the three men were filed in the Supreme Court of Idaho. The Court, in a long opinion[2] handed down in April, held that the fact that the prisoners were not given an opportunity while in Colorado to apply for writs of habeas corpus was a question for the consideration of the Colorado courts alone. The motives of the governor of Colorado in acting as he had were not a subject of judicial inquiry, stated the Court, and whether the Colorado warrant for the men's arrest was legal or illegal became a moot question once they were in Idaho and held there under due process issued by a competent court of that state. That the fundamental rights of the men had been violated in Colorado was no reason, said the Court, why they should not be made to answer to a crime properly charged against them by the State of Idaho.

The prisoners' petitions in the Federal courts fared no better. On an appeal from an adverse decision in the Circuit Court of Appeals, the Supreme Court of the United States, with one dissenting voice,[3] held that—even assuming the arrest of the three men and their forcible removal to Idaho had been effected by fraud and connivance be-

---

[2] *In re* Moyer, 12 Idaho 250, 85 Pac. 190.
[3] Pettibone v. Nichols, 203 U. S. 192 (Justice McKenna, dissenting).

tween the governors of the two states, and the accused thereby deprived of the right to test the legality of extradition by writs of habeas corpus in Colorado, and even if it should be further assumed that in such a proceeding they would have been discharged on the ground that they were not fugitives from the State of Idaho—the courts of the United States were without jurisdiction once the prisoners were brought within the jurisdiction of the courts of Idaho and formally charged with the commission of a crime against that state.

Whatever hope the prisoners may have entertained of avoiding trial in the prejudice-infected atmosphere of Idaho was destroyed by this decision of the Supreme Court which was handed down in December 1906. It was then that Clarence Darrow was called from Chicago to take charge of the defense. Associated with him were Edmund Richardson of Denver, general attorney for the Western Federation of Miners, John Nugent and Edgar Wilson of Boise, and Fred Miller of Seattle.

Darrow's first concern was over the confession of Steve Adams. As an experienced criminal lawyer, Darrow reaiized the importance of Adams as a witness for the prosecution. The case for the State depended on convincing a jury of the truth of Orchard's confession. Because it is elementary law, it could be assumed that any court would have to instruct the jury that the confession of an accomplice was to be received and scrutinized with caution, and that a verdict of guilty could not be supported by his uncorroborated testimony. While the full texts of Orchard's and Adams' confessions had not yet been made public, it was known that Orchard had charged that Haywood, Pettibone and Moyer had hired him and Adams to blow up the Independence, Colorado, depot, and that Adams had confessed that fact as well as other associations with Orchard and the defendants. Adams' testimony, therefore, was an important, perhaps a vital, link in the prosecution's chain of evidence. Darrow set to work to remove that link.

The prosecution held Adams and his wife and children in pleasant confinement, under alert and numerous guards. It was impossible for anyone connected with the defense of Haywood and his codefendants to obtain access to him. It was learned, however, that he had been visited by his uncle, one Lillard, who lived in Oregon. Darrow and one of his associates sought out Lillard. Lillard told them that Adams was penniless and could not afford counsel, and had been frightened into confessing to "something he knew nothing about" under a promise of immunity from prosecution for the trouble he had got into in northern Idaho some years before. Lillard told them he felt sure Adams would repudiate his confession if he was assured of being furnished with competent defense counsel in the event that he was prosecuted for this old crime. Lillard was given that assurance, and shortly afterward Adams repudiated his confession. He was promptly removed to Wallace, Shoshone County, and indicted for the murder of Fred Tyler in 1899.

The case against Adams was rushed to trial. The State's strategy was obvious. The conviction of Adams would give the prosecutors of Haywood and his associates a club over Adams which would insure the performance of his supporting role to Orchard. James H. Hawley, one of the special prosecutors of Haywood, Moyer and Pettibone, and probably the best criminal lawyer in the Northwest, was appointed by the State's attorney general to prosecute Adams. Darrow and his associates, together with a local attorney, John Wourms, appeared as counsel for Adams.

The case came up for trial in February 1907. Darrow shouldered the burden of the defense. The evidence was weak, but a vigorous prosecution made the most of it. Everyone, including the members of the jury, knew that, while the case was nothing more than a belated prosecution for the murder of an obscure claim jumper by an equally obscure defendant, the verdict would have an important consequence in the "big trial" in Boise. The jury heard the evidence and the arguments and, after being out for two days, disagreed. It was rumored that the jury had stood seven to five for acquittal. An attempt was made by Adams' defenders to have him released on bail on any bond the Court might fix. The application was denied, and Adams remained in jail. The defense, however, had scored its first victory. Adams would not be a State's witness to corroborate Orchard's confession.

The public was now clamoring for the trial of the murderers of Steunenberg. Nearly a year and a half had passed since the explosion at Caldwell had ended the life of the ex-governor. The second trial of Adams would have to wait.

The prosecution had long since decided to try Haywood first. For this decision there were sound reasons. The evidence against him was stronger than that against either Pettibone or Moyer. Haywood, in addition to being secretary-treasurer of the miners' federation, was a member of the executive board of the Socialist party, had been the party's candidate for governor of Colorado in 1906 and was an organizer of the militant and generally discredited Industrial Workers of the World—the "wobblies." In these associations and in his trade-union battles he had outdone all his associates in the open advocacy of armed force and revolution, if necessary, to obtain and secure what he deemed the rights of labor. He had figured prominently in every violent episode in the long war between the miners and the operators. For the average citizen he personified the lawless element in union labor. Moreover, he was known to be temperamental and highly emotional, and it might reasonably be expected that these characteristics would be manifested and prejudice his testimony should he be called to the stand.

The case of the State of Idaho v. William D. Haywood came on for trial on May 9, 1907. Appearing for the prosecution were William E. Borah, elected the preceding November to the United States Senate,[4] James H. Hawley,[5] District Attorney Owen M. Van Duyn and his assistant, Charles Koelsche. Darrow, Richardson, Wilson, Nugent and Miller appeared for the defense. Wilson was a former law partner of the presiding judge, Fremont Wood—a fact, as it turned out, which injured rather than aided the defense.

The first order was the selection of a jury. Under Idaho state practice, the respective counsel were allowed a wide latitude in questioning veniremen to determine their competency and desirability as jurors. The selection made slow progress. Everyone called had heard about the case. Some had formed fixed, and therefore disqualifying, opinions. Many declared their reluctance to convict on the uncorroborated testimony of a confessed accomplice. The first venire was exhausted without final agreement on a single juror.

At this stage there was an extraordinary development. Representatives of the press, with the permission of the governor, were permitted to interview Orchard in the penitentiary. Up to this time only the barest outlines of Orchard's confession had been made public. Now, with the trial in progress and counsel and Court engaged in the vital process of selecting impartial citizens as jurors, there suddenly appeared in the Idaho papers and every big-city daily from New York to San Francisco a substantially complete account of Orchard's confession. The reports of the confession were accompanied by the opinions of well-known special correspondents who had been invited to be present at the sensational release. Without exception they took the expected line: Orchard, the reclaimed and repentant Christian, was a changed man, tell-

---

4 Borah did not take his seat until after the conclusion of the trial.
5 Hawley was later elected governor of Idaho.

ing the full and awful truth as a measure of atonement for his sins; and his story was convincing.

Coming as it did during the examination of prospective jurors, the publications and their attendant publicity were a flagrant contempt of court. That was Judge Wood's first reaction. He summoned the attorneys for the prosecution and asked for an explanation. They solemnly declared they had no previous knowledge of the intended release. The Court called on the district attorney of Ada County to investigate. That was the end of it; no action was ever taken.

It is questionable which profited most by this extraordinary proceeding—the State or the defense. In all probability the publicity aggravated the already overstimulated community prejudice and affected the temper of talesmen who took their places in the jury box. On the other hand, the defense was definitely aided by the knowledge, theretofore scanty and uncertain, of what the testimony of the State's key witness was going to be. With unlimited funds put at their disposal by the miners' federation, the defense counsel engaged and directed an army of hastily assembled investigators to check every detail and follow every suggested lead in the reported confession. Every indicated corroborative witness who could be located was interviewed. Every record which could throw any light at all on Orchard or his story was examined. The results gave the defense the most valuable of all weapons in the trial of a lawsuit—a foreknowledge of an opponent's case and facts in hand on which to base effective cross-examination and prepare opposing witnesses to counter or avoid the State's evidence.

Orchard's confession was an amazing disclosure of murders committed and contemplated and a score of lesser crimes all effectively commingled with his recent repudiation of the devil who had prompted his acts, his acceptance of God, and his declared belief that, though a sinner, he had been saved, "through no good merits of mine, but through the blood of Jesus Christ, our blessed Savior and Redeemer."

Specifically, Orchard confessed to eighteen murders which he declared he had been hired to commit by Haywood, Pettibone and Moyer. Thirteen of these were victims of the Independence depot explosion[6] which Orchard said he suggested, planned and, with the help of Steve Adams, executed; two were the unintended victims of an explosion of dynamite, which he set off by a gun-trigger trap, in the Vindicator Mine in Colorado; one—shot in cold blood by Orchard who was aided by Pettibone and Adams—was an employee of the mine owners' association who had made himself particularly obnoxious to the officers of the miners' federation; one was a man named Walley, the victim of a time bomb intended for Judge William H. Gabbert, chief justice of the Supreme Court of Colorado; the eighteenth victim was ex-Governor Steunenberg. The price for these killings—mass or individual—ranged from $100 to $300.

Orchard, according to his confession, began his career of crime in 1895, when he burned down a cheese factory, to which he had got title through borrowed money, in order to get the insurance. After collecting the money he deserted his wife and infant daughter and went to British Columbia. He was followed there by the wife of a friend of his, whom he had seduced. He soon drifted to Idaho, where he became a miner and a member of the Western Federation of Miners. He helped carry the dynamite to blast the Bunker Hill and Sullivan mines. When the federal troops came in he fled to Colorado and went to work in the Cripple Creek district. In Colorado he "married" Mrs. Ida Toney. He justified this marriage on the ground he had not heard from his other family for a long time and they would never know of it.

He became a "high grader" in the Vindicator Mine. He

---

6 As a matter of fact, fourteen men were killed as the result of this explosion.

confessed to secreting high-grade ore on his person and selling it to assayer-fences—to the detriment of his employers and for his own enrichment by $5.00 to $50.00 a day. His successful dynamiting of the Vindicator Mine established his reputation with Haywood, Moyer and Pettibone as a dependable operator, and they put him to work on arson jobs and helping to frame alibis for other operators who were jailed and awaiting trials on charges of wrecking ore trains and other acts of violence.

Pettibone, who was an amateur chemist, taught him to mix "hell fire," a combination of phosphorus, bisulphide of carbon, benzine, alcohol and turpentine, which in arson jobs would create an unquenchable flame. Together with Adams and Pettibone, he stalked mining officials and public officers designated by Haywood and Moyer, seeking a chance to murder them and make a sure get away. Among these were Governor Peabody, General Sherman Bell, Justice Gabbert and Judge Luther M. Goodard, all of Colorado. Governor Peabody had miraculous escapes from two well-planned attempts at assassination. The bomb planted for Justice Gabbert found an innocent victim, who had no connection whatever with either the miners or operators.

Orchard told of being sent by Haywood and Moyer to San Francisco to "get" Fred Bradley, former superintendent of the Bunker Hill and Sullivan mines. Orchard was only partly successful. His attempt to poison the entire Bradley family by opening a bottle of milk on the Bradley doorstep and putting strychnine in it failed; and the explosion of the trap bomb which he set for Bradley, while it inflicted serious injuries, did not kill him.

Orchard confessed the assassination of Steunenberg and two previous unsuccessful attempts in one of which Jack Simpkins participated. All of these recitals were embellished with a wealth of detail, implicating Haywood, Pettibone, Moyer, Simpkins and Adams. There is more in this remarkable document of Orchard's activities and of crimes suggested and planned but not executed. Among these was the unsuccessful plan to kidnap the young children of August Paulson of Wallace and the suggested "silencing" of Steve Adams because he knew too much, drank too much and "talked in his beer."

The tedious process of selecting the jury dragged on. Venire after venire was called and exhausted. Practically everyone called had known with varying degrees of intimacy either Steunenberg or one or more of the local counsel. Many of these were excused for "cause." Then there were those who, for one reason or another not constituting cause, were not wanted either by the prosecution or the defense, and these were excused until both the prosecution and the defense had exhausted their peremptory challenges. Finally, after more than three weeks of examination and elimination, a panel of twelve was agreed on. Eleven were ranchers, and one was a resident of Caldwell who had been a close friend of Steunenberg. All swore they were impartial and would "a true deliverance make between the people of the State of Idaho and the prisoner at the bar."

Mr. Hawley made the opening statement for the prosecution. He was an impressive figure—six feet, two inches in height—with a fine carriage and a strong but well-modulated voice. Long years of trial experience had given him courtroom ease. His language was pointed and picturesque, studded with the colloquialisms of the Northwest. Dramatically and forcefully he pictured the death of Steunenberg, the discoveries that led to the apprehension of Orchard as the actual perpetrator of the crime, his conversion and "voluntary" confession.

Hawley made no attempt to defend or excuse Orchard, but insisted that the completeness of the confession, extending, as it did, to an admission of a list of crimes unparalleled in the history of a single criminal, was the guaranty of its truth. He declared that Orchard's confession would be fully corroborated, and the evidence would show beyond the peradventure of a doubt that the leaders of the Western Federation of Miners had been responsible for the death not only of Steunenberg, but of scores of others. An objection to the reference to other crimes and their victims was sustained, but the prosecution, despite the ruling, repeated the charge throughout the trial.

Orchard was the first witness for the State. Slowly and with deadly emphasis Hawley led him through every line of his confession. Orchard had been well rehearsed. He was cool and well poised. He took his time to consider each question put to him and answered it responsively in a minimum of well-chosen words. His manner of expression was that of a disinterested narrator of a remote event rather than of something in which he had been the principal actor. The general impression of the spectators, some of them men of eminence[7], was that he had told the truth. Mr. Hawley had every reason to feel satisfied with his direct examination of the State's star witness.

Prior to the trial it had been determined that Mr. Richardson should cross-examine Orchard. This was a grievous mistake. Darrow excelled in the two principal departments of the trial game—cross-examination and argument. Great as was his skill in argument, there are many who knew him well (and this includes the author) who would say that because of his remarkable intuition, knowledge of human nature and accumulated experience, his skill as a cross-examiner was even greater.

Mr. Richardson conducted what lawyers commonly call a hammer and tongs cross-examination. His manner was threatening, his voice loud and his questions insulting. He examined Orchard on every detail of the confession, giving it an emphasis by repetition. Orchard had been prepared for just this type of cross-examination. He refused to get

---

[7] One such was Professor Hugo Muensterberg, famous Harvard psychologist and author of *On the Witness Stand* (London: Clark Boardman Co., Ltd., 1923).

excited, repeated his direct testimony with accuracy and, in some instances, under vicious proddings, amplified and embellished it. There is no doubt that the cross-examination was a great disappointment to Darrow. The most tolerant of men in his judgment of others, Darrow's comment in his autobiography[8] that Richardson was "somewhat lacking in subtlety" can be accepted as a gross understatement of his real thought. The cross-examination did accomplish one purpose: By using the results of the searching pretrial investigation of the defense it laid the foundation for the contradiction and impeachment of Orchard's testimony in many respects by credible and disinterested witnesses.

Realizing its necessity, the State did everything within its power to corroborate Orchard's testimony. It did produce a large number of witnesses who supported him in some of his admissions concerning his activities in behalf of the miners' federation. This, however, was corroboration of collateral matters, and the legal competency of much of it was, to say the least, dubious. There was no corroboration of the vital charge that Haywood and his associates had hired Orchard to kill Steunenberg.

Following the general practice in all trials, civil as well as criminal, where the defense conceives that the prosecution has failed to prove its case as the law requires, the attorneys for Haywood, after the State had rested, moved the Court to direct the jury to return a verdict of not guilty. Judge Wood overruled the motion, but in a later comment on the case stated he had done so with grave doubts and had been influenced to a degree by fear of criticism which might have followed such a direction because his former partner, Edgar Wilson, was one of the counsel for the defense.

The defense, in addition to Haywood who took the

---

[8] *The Story of My Life* (New York & London: Charles Scribner's Sons, 1932).

stand in his own behalf, called nearly a hundred witnesses
to impeach Orchard in one or more of the details of his
testimony, or to testify that his reputation for truth and
veracity was bad and they would not believe him under
oath.

The prosecution's hope that Haywood would destroy
himself on the witness stand was disappointed. Prepared
by the careful coaching of the defense, he was cool, mild-
mannered, serious and soft-spoken. He gave his direct testimony clearly and convincingly—a specific denial of every
one of Orchard's charges so far as they involved him and
a general denial of any previous associations or connections
with Orchard. His testimony was unshaken by Hawley's
vicious cross-examination. Moyer and Pettibone took the
stand to corroborate Haywood and made good witnesses.

Mr. Hawley made the opening argument for the State.
It was an unqualified defense of the truth of Orchard's
testimony and a slashing, bitter and inflammatory denunciation of the miners' federation and its officers. Darrow
followed with what, in the opinion of many, was his finest
effort in his long list of forensic battles. He spoke without
notes and for eleven hours.

No attempted summary is adequate to convey to the
reader the power and persuasiveness of this masterpiece of
logic and emotional appeal. Only verbatim excerpts can
reveal its quality. The appropriate lines of argument were
obvious: to destroy Orchard and build up Haywood and
the cause of union labor which he represented. In Darrow's presentation his assault upon Orchard came first.

Who is this fellow Orchard? Take his own story. A man
who was bred to cheat and to lie; a man who, as a young
man in the first blush of his manhood, gave his soul to
Christ. I don't know about these second conversions—
whether they are more solid than the first or not. He was

a member of the church. He was superintendent of the Sunday school. He was a Christian Endeavorer. He isn't endeavoring any more; he has got there. That was when he was a young man. But that didn't help him then.

Maybe he has religion for keeps this time. If I were the Governor, and thought he had, I would kill him quickly, before he got a chance to get over it, and then make sure of his soul. I don't think Harry ought to trust himself. But he had it before and he commenced to cheat and steal and to burn down his own cheese factory to get the insurance money; and he must have made a false affidavit in order to get it. It shows that he could lie under oath, too, at that time. He ran away with his neighbor's wife—left his wife and little child without a penny, and they did not hear of him until recently. He went out into the world . . . not to work—oh, no, not for Harry. He knew a better game than that and he commenced a better game still. He came West to grow up with the country.

He never did a courageous thing in his life; not one. If his story is true, he was with a thousand men when he touched off the fuse at the Bunker Hill mill. If his story is true, he sneaked through the dark passages of the mine and fixed a box of powder when he blew up the Vindicator. If his story is true, he sneaked back in the darkness and put the box of powder under the station and ran away in the night when he killed fourteen men. If his story is true, he laid a bomb at Goddard's gate that he might open it and be killed. If his story is true, he met a man coming out of a saloon, drunken, at midnight, and killed him without a chance or a word or an act. If he has told the truth, he sneaked up the back stairs and poured arsenic or strychnine in milk to poison a man and his wife and little babe. If his story is true, he planted a bomb outside of Bradley's door to kill, not Bradley, but the first human being who might happen to open that door. If his story is true, he went up in the night and laid a bomb at Steunenberg's gate, and then he ran back in the darkness and had nearly reached the hotel before Steunenberg was dead.

Will you show me the act that was not the act of a sneaking, craven coward in this man's life? Will you show me where he has ever met bravely man or beast? Has he even taken a chance in his miserable life? Has he ever met a foeman where that foeman had a chance to shoot or a chance to strike? Has he ever gone into a court of justice and stood his ground?

And yet you are asked to believe him. You are asked to give him immunity and every one of his kind. You are asked to say to the old and to the young: "You may kill, you may burn, you may lie, you may steal, you may commit any crime forbidden by God or man, and then you can turn and throw your crimes on some one else and your sins on God, and the lawyers will sing your praises." All right, gentlemen. If, in your judgment, public policy demands it, go ahead and do it. Don't stop for a little matter like Bill Haywood's neck.

The most effective point made by Darrow in his denunciation of Orchard concerned a detail which might well have escaped a mind less alert. In his confession and his testimony Orchard had revealed his real name—Albert E. Horsely. Here is how Darrow utilized this casual item of testimony.

Again, gentlemen, I repeat that until Harry Orchard had confessed and had been forgiven by Father McParland, he had some spark of manhood in his breast. Listen. There have been other great criminals in this world. Our penitentiaries are full of criminals whose names are unknown. Men have mounted the scaffold, they have fallen through the trapdoor, they have been strangled to death, their bodies have been eaten by quicklime inside of the prison walls, and they have protected their names. Their names were the only sacred things left to the criminals. Look at Orchard. Who is he?

He left Ontario a young man. His record was bad. It wasn't infamously bad. His name was not Harry Orchard; his name was Albert Horsely when he left. He went to Detroit with another man's wife. When he reached Detroit his name was Harry Orchard. He lied, he stole, he burglarized, he committed arson, and became a murderer, and his name was Harry Orchard. His best friend never knew any name but that. The name of Horsely was buried deep in this criminal's heart, and he protected it as the one thing that bound him back to his childhood days. He wasn't totally depraved—he protected his name. He had gone away from Ontario; had taken the name of Orchard and had covered it with infamy and slime, but he had left the Horsely name comparatively pure in the little Ontario town.

This is the picture of Harry Orchard that comes to me. You may picture him a saint if you want to, or if you can; and if you can, you may take away the life of a fellow being on his testimony, and I will say to you as the judge does to the condemned murderer: "May God have mercy on your soul." You may picture him as you think he should be pictured. But here is this man; here is a little rural town off in Canada; here is a country graveyard with a white fence around it and a church by its side. Here are two old-fashioned Quaker people who read their Bible and who love their God, and who live in the sight and in the fear of God, a quiet, peaceful, honest life, rearing their children and hoping that they will follow in the footsteps of that Quaker couple. They die, are buried in that old graveyard in the country town; the names on the marble headstone are never heard of beyond the limits of the little town where they lived and where they died; but they lived an honest, upright life; and, when it was done, they laid their burdens down to sleep the peaceful sleep of the just, and their names were honored and respected.

They bore two sons and six daughters. One son went out into the world. He married; a child came. Temptation overcame him. He left his wife to toil for herself. He left his child and baby girl, unprotected and unaided, to grow up alone without a dollar or a penny or a father's love; he went out into the world and covered himself with mud and dirt and crime until he was revolting in the sight of God and man. The brother stayed at home, a quiet, peaceful, honest man, having children to bear the Horsely name to generations yet unborn. The sisters married. They had children in whose veins flowed the Horsely blood. They are quiet, honest, peaceful citizens. The little girl, growing up neglected, uncared for, has been struggling alone until she is nine years old. The Horsely name is all she has. The honor of the grandfather and the grandmother sleeping in their Quaker graves is all she has. She has nothing from her deserting father.

Suddenly there comes back a story that the monumental criminal of the ages is Albert Horsely; that this man who went out from this quiet town covered himself with crime and with infamy; and every neighbor who goes through that quiet churchyard can point to the graves of this old Quaker couple, and say, "There lies the father and the mother of the greatest criminal of modern times"; and the world can point to the brother and the sisters, living and toiling as best they can with the burden of the world upon them, and say, "There is the brother, there are the sisters, of that monster who has challenged the civilized world with his iniquities and his crimes"; and the nieces and the nephews can be pointed at, and the deserted wife, and, above all, the little girl—flesh of his flesh and blood of his blood.

Gentlemen, I want to know what any of you think of this miserable wretch who blighted the life of this deserted girl to save his miserable neck? Am I still crazy? Are the men of Idaho different from other men? Does not the same sort of blood flow through your veins as flows through the veins of all men who ever lived? Can anybody look upon this act with anything but horror? Think of that girl! Gentlemen, every act of this villain's life pales into insignificance compared to the crime committed against that child. The blowing up of the Independence depot was a sacrament compared to the running of that poisoned dagger into the heart of his nine-year-old babe, a dagger that couldn't kill, but would fester and corrode and leave its pain and sting, and leave the fingers of the world pointed at her and the voice of the world raised against her as long as her offspring should remain upon the earth.

Why did he do it? You know why he did it. He had protected this one thing through all his crimes; and, until he spoke his name upon the witness stand, nobody knew it except that "inner circle" to whom he had confided it. He had kept it through all his crimes and through all his wanderings, and the character of his dead father, the name of his brother and sisters and the helpless babe, and the honor of his wife—these at least were unassailed. It was left for McParland to help him commit the crowning infamy of his infamous career. Why did he do it? Not to give glory or luster to his family name. No, not for glory, not for honor. He did it, gentlemen of the jury, because the miserable, contemptible Pinkerton detective had persuaded him that his story would gain more credit with the jury if he gave his real name; because McParland had persuaded him that if he would give his name, it would help to tie the rope around Haywood's neck.

To discredit Orchard utterly, it was necessary to do more than remind the jury of the long list of sordid crimes to which he had confessed, and that until he had been caught and faced with the evidence which would surely hang him he had been a ruthless and cowardly killer. It was imperative that Darrow should destroy the prosecution's contention, adroitly propagated in and out of court, that, whatever had been his past, Orchard had repented his sins and by his repudiation of the devil and acceptance of Christ his confession took on the cast of an atonement and was entitled to credence.

This posed a difficult problem for Darrow. He was a notorious agnostic. Boise, while not bigoted, was an orthodox Christian community. To have scoffed at the Christian religion and scouted the possibility of faith in its teachings to redeem even so great a sinner as the State's star witness would have been a fatal mistake. Darrow realized this. His masterly handling of the situation offended no one and served its purpose: to raise a reasonable doubt in the minds of the jurors of the genuineness of Orchard's eleventh-hour sanctification by grace.

Now, gentlemen, like Brother Hawley and Brother Richardson and Senator Borah, I, too, have a profound regard for religion. Mine may be the broader. I don't want to say to these twelve men that I think the Christian religion is the only religion that the world has ever known. I don't believe it for a moment. I have the greatest respect for any religion or any code of ethics that does anything to help man, whatever that religion may be.

And for the poor black man who looks into the black face of a wooden idol and prays to that idol to make him a better man and a stronger man, I have the profoundest respect. I know that there is in him, when he addresses his prayers to his wooden idol, the same holy sentiment and the same feeling that there is in the breast of a Christian when he raises his prayer to the Christian's God. It is all one. It is all a piece of ethics and a higher life, and no man could have more respect for it than I have.

In the ways of the world and in the language of the world I am not a professed Christian. I do not pretend to be. I have had my doubts about things which to other men's minds seem plain. I look out on the great universe around me, at the millions and millions of stars that dot the firmament of heaven in the nighttime; I look out on all the mysteries of nature and the mysteries of life, and I ask myself the solution of the riddle and I bow my head in the presence of the infinite mystery and say: "I don't know." I cannot tell.

But for that man who understands it all and sees in it the work of a Supreme Being, who prays to what he honestly believes to be this Higher Power, I have the profoundest regard; and any communion of that poor, weak mortal with that Higher Power, which permeates the universe and which makes for good, any communion that lifts a man higher and higher and makes him better, I have regard for that.

If Orchard has that religion, well and good. I am willing that he should have it; I hope that he has it. I wouldn't deny that consolation and that solace to him for a moment. But I ask you whether he has it and what it means to him. I have no desire to injure Orchard, despicable as I think he is. I have no desire to take his life. I am not responsible for his being. I cannot understand the purposes of the infinite God who fashioned his head as He saw fit to fashion it. I am willing to leave it to Him to judge—to Him who alone knows.

I have never asked for a human being's life, and I hope that I may never ask for a human life, to the end of my days. I do not ask for his. If the time should ever come when somebody pronounced against him the decree of death and nobody else would ask to save his life, my petition would be there to save it.

I don't believe in man's tinkering with the work of God. I don't believe in man's taking away the life of his fellow man. I don't believe that you and I can say in the light of heaven that, if we had been born as he was born, if our brains had been molded as his was molded, if we had been surrounded as he was surrounded, we might not have been like him.

After this brilliant presentation of the abstract—a profound respect for *all* religions as an inspiration to higher living and the declaration, voiced almost as a regret, that in the presence of the "infinite mystery" he was bewildered about many things that to other men seemed plain—he proceeded to the concrete. Had Orchard belatedly got into communion with "that higher power which permeates the universe and lifts a man and makes him better," or was his latest pretension a pose, another twist of his facile, perverted, criminal mind, a dodge to escape the consequences of a crime in which he had been caught redhanded and shift the blame to others?

It is not for me to pass condemnation upon Harry Orchard, but simply to discuss his evidence and to discuss him as he and his evidence affect this case. Let us see whether he is changed. I do believe that there is something in the heart of man which, if rightly appealed to, may make him better. But I do not believe in miracles. I don't believe you could change in a minute a man's very nature. I don't believe it was ever done or ever can be done. You can't take Harry Orchard's face or his form and make it over again in a second, and you can't take his crooked brain and his crooked, dwarfed soul and make it anew in a minute.

If you, gentlemen, are going to bank on that in this case, then you are taking a serious responsibility with Haywood's life. I might have a little more confidence in this if Orchard had not confessed to the Pinkertons before confessing to the Savior. You might have a little more confidence in this if he had not sought to save his life before he turned to save his soul. . . .

Let us see, gentlemen, what Orchard has got, and then we can tell whether or not it is religion. There are certain qualities which are primal with religion. I undertake to say, gentlemen, that if Orchard has religion now, I hope I may never get it. I want to say to this jury that before Orchard got religion he was bad enough, but it remained for religion to make him totally depraved. I am measuring my words and I am going to show it to this jury so plainly that I believe nobody can doubt it. I say that there was some spark of honor and integrity and manhood about that depraved man before he got religion, but that after he went into McParland's hands he became totally depraved.

What does religion mean? It means love; it means charity; it means kindness; it means forgiveness to a man whose life has been covered with slime and filth. If he has got religion, it ought to be kindness and charity and forgiveness to other men whose lives are like his. Would you have any confidence in religion if it didn't mean that? Would you have any confidence in a man's religion if he was as cruel, as heartless, as he was before?

Take Orchard. He was acquainted with Moyer, Haywood and Pettibone. He had worked himself into the confidence of Pettibone; had been invited to his house; had met his wife; had eaten at his table; had slept in his bed; was his friend. I ask you who watched him, who saw this monster on the witness stand, whether there was the least look of pity, the least sign of regret, the least feeling of sorrow, when he sought to hand over this man and his friends to execution? Did he look any different? Was there any different gleam in his eye or different cast in his countenance, or a single flutter of his iron nerve that wasn't there when he met a reeling, staggering, drunken man and shot him three times before he could raise his hand? If there is any pity in his soul, if there is any of the heavenly mercy, if there is any of the Christlike forgiveness there, it hasn't gone out to Pettibone.

The closing portion of Darrow's long and exhausting argument was a brilliant appeal for Haywood and for the workers whose cause Haywood espoused. Some of it may strike the reader as demagoguery, but Darrow believed every word of it. Delivered with all the native power and practiced talent of a great orator, it could not fail to stir the emotions and sway the judgments of the twelve men who sat in the jury box.

Gentlemen of the jury, this responsibility is upon you, and if I have done my part, I am glad to shift it upon your shoulders and be relieved of the load. I have known Haywood well and I believe in him. God knows it would be a sore day to me if he should ascend the scaffold. The sun would not shine and the birds would not sing on that day for me. I would think of him, I would think of his wife, of his mother; I would think of his babes; I would think of the great cause that he represents.

But, gentlemen, he and his mother and his wife and his children are not my chief concern in this case. If you should decree that he must die, ten thousand men will work down in the mines and send a portion of the proceeds of their labor to take care of that widow and those orphan children, and a million people throughout the length and breadth of the civilized world will send their messages of kindness and good cheer to comfort them in their bereavement.

It is not for them I plead. Other men have died in the same cause in which Haywood has risked his life. Men strong with devotion, men who love liberty, men who love their fellow man, have raised their voices in defense of the poor, in defense of justice, have made their good fight and have met death on the scaffold, in the wreck, in the flame; and they will meet it again until the world grows old and gray. Haywood is no better than the rest. He can die if need be. He can die if this jury decrees it.

But, oh, gentlemen, don't think for a minute that if you hang him you will crucify the labor movement of the world. Don't think that you will kill the hopes and the aspirations and the desires of the weak and the poor. You men, you people, who are anxious for his blood, are you so blind as to believe that liberty will die when he is dead? Do you think there are no other brave hearts and no other strong arms, no other devoted souls, who will risk their lives in that great cause which has demanded martyrs in every age of the world? There are others, and these others will come to take his place. They will come to carry the banner where he could not carry it.

Gentlemen, it is not for him alone that I speak. I speak for the poor, for the weak, for the weary, for men who, in darkness and despair, have done the labors of the human race. The eyes of the world are upon you—upon you twelve men of Idaho—tonight. Wherever the English language is spoken, wherever any foreign tongue known to the civilized world is spoken, men are talking and wondering and dreaming about the verdict of these twelve men that I see before me now.

If you kill him, your act will be applauded by many; if you should decree Haywood's death, in the great railroad offices of our great cities men will sing your praises. If you decree his death, among the spiders of Wall Street will go up paeans of praise for those twelve good men and true who killed Bill Haywood.

In almost every bank in the world, where men wish to get rid of agitators and disturbers, where men put in prison one who fights for the poor and against the accursed system upon which they live and grow fat, from all these you will receive blessings and praise that you have killed him.

But if you free him, there are still those who will reverently bow their heads and thank these twelve men for the character they have saved. Out on our broad prairies, where men toil with their hands; out on the broad ocean, where men are sailing the ships; through our mills and factories; down deep under the earth, thousands of men, of women, of children, men who labor, men who suffer, women and children weary with care and toil, these men and these women and these children will kneel tonight and ask their God to guide your judgment. These men and these women and these little children, the poor and the weak and the suffering of the world, will stretch out their hands to this jury and implore you to save Haywood's life.

In his last words, the exhausted Darrow, speaking in a voice scarcely above a whisper, returned to his central theme: No one should, and no one could, convict a man on the testimony of Orchard.

Gentlemen, there are many things that I would like to say, but I have not the strength and voice to say them. Perhaps it is lucky for you that I have not, and that I must leave the case here. Under the laws of Idaho the State has the last word, and when my voice is silent, and when Moyer and Haywood cannot speak, their accusers can be heard pleading against them. I know the ability of the eminent gentleman who will close this case. I know the appeal he will make to this jury. I know that he will talk of law and order and the flag which the mine owners have described time and again. I know the suspicious circumstances which will be woven into that appeal and handled by a tactful tongue and a skillful brain, and I must sit still and listen to it without chance to reply.

I can only ask you, gentlemen of the jury, to weigh with care and consideration every word that is uttered, to answer when I cannot answer, if there are any facts and any circumstances which will justify an answer. I ask you to remember that you are to explain every fact and circumstance in this case consistent with this man's innocence, if you can. I shall ask you to try, and if you try it will not be difficult, for there is nothing in this case but Orchard. Orchard, an unspeakable scoundrel; Orchard, a perjured villain; Orchard, the biggest coward on record; Orchard, shifting the burden of his sins upon these men to save his life.

If you men can kill my client on his testimony, then peace be with you.

Senator Borah followed Darrow with the closing argument for the prosecution. In striking contrast to Hawley's unorganized and vindictive tirade, it was a carefully thought-out, well-arranged, logical and scholarly analysis of the evidence and reply to the telling points Darrow had scored in his argument. Borah was a great orator. His presentation was brilliant and forceful. Reading his argument today in opposition to Darrow's, one is at a loss to suggest how anyone could have followed Darrow and done better.

Judge Wood's charge to the jury was comprehensive and impartial. The law of Idaho permits the judge to instruct the jury as to the law only, and the instructions must be in writing. In practice, the instructions are prepared by the attorneys and handed to the judge as suggestions, which the judge either includes in his charge or refuses.

At the instance of the defense, the Court instructed the jury that the defendant was clothed with the presumption of innocence which could be overcome only by proof of his guilt beyond a reasonable doubt. The law, said the Court, viewed with distrust the testimony of an accomplice on account of the motive he might have to secure immunity for his own participation in the crime charged. If the jury believed Orchard was influenced to become a witness and to testify in the case by any promises of immunity from prosecution or punishment, it should take that into consideration in determining the weight to be given to his testimony. Also, charged the Court, such testimony should be received with caution and scrutinized with great care; and even if the jury believed Orchard's testimony was true, it could not convict on that testimony unless it found that it was corroborated by other and independent evidence. Of very definite aid to the defense was the instruction—an eminently proper one—that such corroboration had to connect Haywood with the crime charged against him, and not with other crimes not alleged in the indictment.

The case was finished on Saturday July 28 in a night session. The jury retired at ten o'clock. After it had been out about seven hours, a rumor spread that it stood eleven to one for conviction. Two hours later, counsel were notified that the jury had agreed. Judge Wood arrived in court at eight o'clock to receive the verdict. Crowds of people jammed the courtroom, the corridors and the courthouse yard.

The usual formula was gone through. "Gentlemen of the jury," solemnly inquired Judge Wood, "have you agreed upon a verdict?" The foreman answered, "We have, Your Honor." "The clerk will read the verdict," rejoined the Court. And the clerk read in a loud, clear voice that resounded throughout the hushed courtroom: "We, the jury, find the defendant, William D. Haywood, not guilty." There was no cheering. The crowd had hoped for and had expected a verdict of conviction. The prosecution was stunned.

The defenders believed that, with the State beaten in its best case, the charges against Moyer and Pettibone would be dropped. They were doomed to disappointment. Within a fortnight counsel for Steve Adams were notified that the State would call up his case for retrial, this time in Rathdrum, Idaho, a small town in the extreme northern part of the state of which the prosecution had obtained a change of venue.

Darrow, although exhausted by his efforts in the Haywood trial and suffering grievously from an acute mastoid infection, carried the burden of Adams' defense. Richardson had withdrawn from the further defense of Adams, Moyer and Pettibone, because, it is said, of Darrow's refusal otherwise to continue in the cases. Again the jury disagreed. This time a posttrial canvass of the jurors showed they had stood ten to two for acquittal.

Pettibone was immediately put on trial in Boise. Darrow was now a very ill man. He went from a hospital bed direct to the courtroom to be present at the commencement of the trial. His associates, under his direction, picked the jury. The State's evidence was substantially the same as in the Haywood trial. Orchard's testimony followed largely its earlier pattern. According to his confession and testimony, Orchard talked over the contemplated assassination with Pettibone, and Pettibone supplied him with information concerning Caldwell and its surrounding geography, and Steunenberg's habits and associates.

Orchard was the last witness called by the State. Darrow conducted his cross-examination, and it was a masterpiece. In contrast to Richardson's noisy, belligerent and browbeating manner in the Haywood trial, Darrow was gentle and persuasive. He avoided Richardson's mistake in going over Orchard's testimony line by line and giving him the opportunity to repeat, emphasize and amplify it. As Darrow said in his autobiography, he had read it once, heard it twice and knew it by heart. He correctly decided that Pettibone's case would not be advantaged by having the jury hear it twice. Instead, he picked out, without reference to

the order in which Orchard had stated them, the most revolting of the many crimes—other than the murder of
Steunenberg—to which he had confessed and had him elab-
orate them in detail.

Darrow's cross-examination was directed to probing the
mind of Orchard and disclosing to the jury its quality—a
mind that could conceive and plan the obliteration of thirteen lives by the dynamite blast at Independence, a mind
that could in the dark of night stalk a reeling drunkard and
shoot him in the back, a mind that could calmly envisage
the possible death of an entire family through the poison-
ing of a bottle of milk with strychnine, a mind that could
betray host and friend by plotting the kidnaping of his
children. When Darrow finished the thin veneer of
sanctity with which the prosecution had covered Orchard
by playing up his repentance and conversion had fallen
away, and Orchard stood revealed to the jurors as a ruthless, callous, unregenerate criminal—an evil and repulsive thing—rather than a witness on whose credit they could
blot out the life of another human being.

The cross-examination had exhausted the last dram of
Darrow's strength. He begged for and secured a continu-
ance until the following day. The next morning he was
brought into the courtroom in a wheel chair. He told the
Court he was unable to proceed. Pettibone reluctantly
consented to his withdrawal from the case, and Darrow was
hurried to a Los Angeles hospital where for days he hov-
ered between life and death.

But the victory had been won. Irving Stone, in his fascinating biography of Darrow,[9] says that when he had
finished his cross-examination the jury "turned from Orchard as from the carcass of a dead animal." The situation
was indeed so favorable that Darrow's associates made a

---

9 *Clarence Darrow for the Defense* (Garden City, New York: Doubleday,
Doran & Company, Inc., 1941).

bold decision—a manifestation of the highest trial strategy if it succeeds, a tragic blunder if it fails. They announced to the Court that they would put on no evidence and would waive argument. With a repetition of the instructions given in the Haywood trial, the case went to the jury. In much less time than was spent in deliberating on the Haywood case, the jury returned a verdict of not guilty.

Was Orchard telling the truth? There is no doubt but that he planned and set the trap which killed Steunenberg. Was he telling the truth when he confessed that he was hired to do it by Haywood and Moyer? There is much in the record which would justify the conclusion that he was. On the other hand, the record does not exclude a reasonable doubt. Steunenberg was out of office and out of politics. His "offense" against the federation was six years old. What could it profit the cause of the miners to wreak a delayed vengeance upon him?

There was a suggestion—it can hardly be given a greater dignity—that Orchard might have done the killing to satisfy a personal grievance. During the 1899 Coeur d'Alene strike, Orchard, with other union agitators, had been compelled to flee the state. Before doing so he sacrificed a substantial interest which he then had in the unproved Hercules Mine. That mine later was developed into one of the richest in the area. Orchard's share, had he held it, would have been worth half a million dollars.

Had Orchard all these years nursed a grudge against Steunenberg as the author of his loss and waited until this late day to satisfy it? The jury was not called on to answer these questions, but to answer another: Had the State proved Haywood and Pettibone guilty of the murder of Steunenberg beyond a reasonable doubt? To that question the jury returned negative answers.

Aftermath

The acquittals of Haywood and Pettibone and the two unsuccessful attempts to convict Adams satisfied the State that the prosecution of Moyer would be futile. The case against him was dismissed. The prosecution of Adams continued. Abandoning hope of convicting him of the Tyler murder, the State, with the connivance of the governor of Colorado, extradited him to that state for a crime he was alleged to have committed there many years before. After a trial and an acquittal on that charge, he was finally set at liberty. Orchard got off with a sentence of life imprisonment.

Haywood, his radicalism unabated, continued his course. In 1917 he was caught up by the government with a number of other I.W.W. agitators and tried and convicted of systematic sabotage in vital war industries. He was sentenced to twenty years imprisonment, but released on bail pending his appeal. He forfeited his bond and escaped to Russia. Here he enjoyed the complete confidence of the Bolsheviks and, on his death in 1928, was accorded a state funeral and buried in the Kremlin, not far from the tomb of Lenin.

As this is written, all of the principal actors have passed to their last rewards with the exception of Judge Koelsche, one of the assistant prosecutors, and Orchard. Orchard, a privileged trusty, with his own shack on the state penitentiary grounds, and hale and hearty at eighty-five, divides his time between the prison garden and prayer. Perhaps his conversion, induced by the detective, McParland, was sincere. At any rate he has, through the years, continued, rather ostentatiously, his religious professions and devotions.

II

The Trial of

NICOLA SACCO
and
BARTOLOMEO VANZETTI

for the Murder of

ALESSANDRO BERARDELLI
and
FREDERICK A. PARMENTER
(1921)

2

The Sacco-Vanzetti Case

THERE *was nothing about the crime, the victims, or the ac-*
cused to give the Sacco-Vanzetti case a priority of interest
or importance over dozens of payroll holdups and accom-
panying murders which occur every year in the United
States. Its significance, as the most celebrated case in
America in the last fifty years, lies in the fact that the ac-
cused were radicals, possibly anarchists, and that many
people—not only radicals but conservatives—came to be-
lieve that the murder charges against the two men were
baseless; but that in an atmosphere of prejudice and hys-
teria against an imagined Red menace the accused had
been convicted and executed because of their real or sup-
posed anarchistic opinions and activities.

On the other hand, there are many, who followed the
evidence and the subsequent procedures in the trial and
the various appeals, who are equally sincere in the belief
that the men were justly convicted of murder, and that the
agitation in their behalf was inspired and kept alive by the
enemies of established government both here and abroad.

In this conflict of opinions, by no means resolved even
at this late date, it is fortunate, indeed, that a group of dis-
tinguished and farsighted American lawyers, aided by an
equally distinguished publishing house, provided and dis-
tributed to the libraries of America, without profit to
themselves, thousands of copies of the complete verbatim
record of this trial and the unprecedented proceedings in

the six years which intervened between the verdict and its execution.[1] The account of the case which follows is based upon that record.

BRAINTREE, MASSACHUSETTS, in 1920 was not unlike a score of other towns within a radius of twenty-five miles from Boston. Like many of these it had its treasured associations—the birthplace and early home of John Adams, one of the centers of prerevolutionary agitation against Great Britain and the site from which had emanated the stirring and provocative Braintree Resolutions. In the course of the century and a half after the independence it had followed the general pattern of industrial development in Massachusetts—iron molding, granite quarrying, textile milling and boot-and-shoe manufacturing. The last was its dominant industry in 1920.

South Braintree, which might be termed a suburb of Braintree, lay on the line of the New York, New Haven & Hartford Railroad about a mile and a half to the south of Braintree. East Braintree was a little farther to the east. The combined population of the three Braintrees, something less than 15,000, was heterogeneous—American-born descendants of the early English and Scotch settlers, native and American-born second and third-generation Irish, native Italians, Greeks and Spaniards. In the so-called foreign element the Italians predominated. Most of them were not citizens. Many of them were notorious radicals.

The towns round about the Braintrees—Weymouth, Plymouth, Stoughton, Brockton, Quincy, Bridgewater and West Bridgewater—were quite the same as the Braintrees in population make-up. These were not lawless communities. Prior to December 1919 there was no more crime in them than might be found in many towns of mixed pop-

---

[1] *Transcript of the Record of the Trial of Nicola Sacco and Bartolomeo Vanzetti in the Courts of Massachusetts and Subsequent Proceedings, 1920-27* (New York: Henry Holt & Company, 1929).

ulation in America which were in or adjacent to a large metropolitan manufacturing and industrial center.

Two crimes not of the mine-run did occur, however, on December 24, 1919, and April 15, 1920. In the broad daylight on December 24, a guarded truck of the paymaster of one of the large shoe manufactories in Bridgewater, en route from the local bank to the factory with a $33,000 payroll, was fired on by two men described as "Italians." The fire was promptly returned by the truck's guards, and the attempted robbery was frustrated. On April 15 following, and again in the broad light of day, Parmenter, paymaster of the Slater & Morrill shoe factory in South Braintree, and a guard named Berardelli, while walking from the company's office to its factory with the weekly payroll of $15,000, were attacked by two men who seized the boxes containing the payroll, shot and killed Parmenter and Berardelli and made their escape with the money in a planted automobile which probably held three accomplices.

As already stated, these crimes, although shocking, were not in themselves extraordinary. The victims were obscure individuals, and the men accused of the crime were two hitherto unknown Italian laborers. There was nothing unusual about the trial itself. The evidence as to identity was conflicting but no more so than in many cases where convictions have resulted. A jury was selected in accordance with approved procedure. Prosecution and defense alike were given full opportunity to present evidence. There was no curtailment of the right of summation. The Court's charge was unobjectionable. The jury found a verdict of guilty of first-degree murder, and the defendants were sentenced to death—the only punishment possible under that verdict.

In ordinary course that sentence, if affirmed on appeal and not altered by executive clemency, would have been promptly carried out and the case forgotten. Not so with the Sacco-Vanzetti case. Through an amazing campaign in their behalf which commenced when they were indicted and continued long after they were dead, the shots which were fired at South Braintree on April 15, 1920, and which killed Parmenter and Berardelli, like the shots fired 145 years before on the common at near-by Lexington, were "heard round the world," and the Sacco-Vanzetti case became the most celebrated case in American judicial history.

Except for the identity of the slayers and their accomplices, there was no dispute as to the circumstances of the killing of Parmenter and Berardelli. Slater & Morrill's offices and part of their manufacturing operations were located on the second and third floors of a four-story frame building called Hampton House. This building fronted on a north-and-south roadway known as Railroad Avenue which was a short distance north of Pearl Street, an east-and-west main thoroughfare. Railroad Avenue extended south from the New York, New Haven & Hartford Railroad depot for some 400 or 500 feet to, but not across, Pearl Street. Pearl Street extended east from Braintree Square—the convergence of Pearl, Hancock, and Washington streets in the center of town—out into the country. East of Railroad Avenue were six north-and-south railroad tracks which crossed Pearl Street and, adjoining them, six additional switch tracks which terminated at the north side of Pearl Street.

Just southwest of the railroad right of way at its intersection with Pearl Street was a small shanty from which a gatetender operated protective crossing gates. Immediately beyond a dirt driveway which was alongside the most easterly of the railroad tracks and on the north side of Pearl Street, an excavation was being dug for a new building (referred to in this narrative as the restaurant excavation). Almost directly across from this excavation and set back a few feet from the south sidewalk line of Pearl Street was the five-story brick shoe factory of Rice & Hutchins.

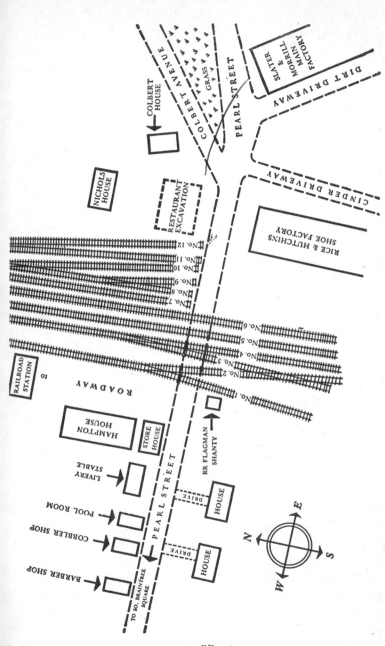

MAP OF THE AREA IN WHICH THE CRIME WAS COMMITTED.

North and east of the excavation were the Colbert and Nichols houses which figured in the later testimony. Some 200 feet farther east and also on the south side of Pearl Street was Slater & Morrill's main factory, a four-story frame building which came almost to the south sidewalk line. There was a pronounced downgrade in Pearl Street from the railroad crossing to the east.

About 3:00 P.M. on Thursday, April 15, 1920, Frederick A. Parmenter, paymaster for Slater & Morrill, and Alessandro Berardelli, a guard, left the offices of the company in Hampton House to go to the main factory to pay the help. Thursday was the company's regular payday. Each carried a box which was about two and a half feet long, one and a half feet deep and a foot wide and which contained the individual employees' pay envelopes. They left the entrance to Hampton House on Railroad Avenue, walked south to Pearl Street, turned east on the north side of that street, passed over all of the railroad tracks and reached a point opposite the Rice & Hutchins factory. There they were suddenly attacked by two armed men. One of these grappled with Berardelli and fired four shots into his body. Parmenter started across the street toward the restaurant excavation and was shot as he ran. Two bullets entered his body. Berardelli was almost instantly killed. Parmenter died the following day.

Coincident with the shooting an automobile drove west up Pearl Street and stopped just east of the railroad tracks. Either with or without assistance from the occupants of the car, the two gunmen hoisted the payroll boxes into the rear of the car and then got into the car, which proceeded westward as rapidly as the upgrade of the street would permit. On the way, a number of other shots were fired by one or more of the occupants at persons in the street. The car gathered speed and proceeded up Pearl Street to Braintree Square and from thence in the general direction of Brockton and Bridgewater.

Led by what they considered a set of suspicious circumstances, the police on May 5, 1920, arrested Nicola Sacco and Bartolomeo Vanzetti while they were riding on a streetcar bound for Brockton. On the car and later at the police station at Brockton they were searched. Sacco had a ten-shot, thirty-two-caliber Colt automatic revolver, fully loaded, underneath his vest and tucked inside the front waistband of his trousers, and there were twenty-one extra shells in his pants pockets. Vanzetti carried a fully loaded five-shot Harrington & Richardson revolver. He had no extra cartridges for it, but he had in his pocket four twelve-gauge shotgun shells loaded with buckshot.

When questioned by the police, the two men told unconvincing stories of their previous movements, intentions and reasons for the weapons and ammunition they were carrying. Many persons were brought to the jail to view them. A number of people identified Sacco as the man who had shot and killed Berardelli. Others identified Vanzetti as having been an occupant of the bandit car which had been engaged in the South Braintree robbery and murders and as the man who had fired the shotgun in the previously attempted payroll holdup at Bridgewater.

On June 11, 1920, two separate indictments were returned by a grand jury of Plymouth County against Vanzetti, one charging him with assault with intent to rob and the other with assault with intent to murder. On September 11, 1920, two separate indictments were returned by a grand jury of Norfolk County against Vanzetti and Sacco, charging them with the murders of Parmenter and Berardelli.

Vanzetti was thirty-three years old and unmarried. He had been in the United States thirteen years. He had worked at various laboring jobs and, intermittently, at buying and peddling fish in Plymouth and near-by towns. He had no criminal record antedating his arrest and indictment for the attempted Bridgewater robbery. In July of

1920 he was tried on that charge and convicted.[2] On August 16 he was sentenced to the penitentiary for a term of not less than twelve nor more than fifteen years.

Sacco was thirty years old, married and had one child. His first jobs in the United States were common laboring work; but he paid for an apprenticeship and learned the shoe-trimmer's trade, and at the time of his arrest he was earning, by piecework, anywhere from thirty to seventy dollars a week. He had been employed steadily for a number of years and had had no previous criminal record.

From the first, both Sacco and Vanzetti stoutly denied any knowledge of or complicity in the Braintree robbery and murders.

The case of the Commonwealth of Massachusetts against Nicola Sacco and Bartolomeo Vanzetti for the murder of Frederick A. Parmenter and Alessandro Berardelli came on for trial before the Honorable Webster Thayer and a jury in the Superior Court of Norfolk County at Dedham, Massachusetts, on May 31, 1921.

Appearing for the Commonwealth were Frederick G. Katzmann, district attorney, and Harold P. Williams, William F. Kane and George E. Adams, assistant district attorneys. Appearing for the defendant Sacco were Fred H. Moore and William J. Callahan; for the defendant Vanzetti were Jeremiah J. McAnarney and Thomas F. McAnarney.

Judge Thayer was sixty-four years old. He had served as a judge of the superior court since 1917. He possessed a splendid background of general and legal education and was acknowledged to be an unusually able lawyer.

---

2 Vanzetti was positively identified by several witnesses as a participant in the attempted holdup in which a dark Buick car, identified as the same which figured later in the South Braintree murders, was used. Vanzetti's sole defense was an alibi, testified to by a number of witnesses. He did not take the stand in his own defense. Exceptions taken to the judgment of conviction were not perfected in view of Vanzetti's almost immediately following trial and conviction for murder.

Katzmann had served as district attorney of Norfolk County for eleven years and was an able and experienced prosecutor. His principal assistant, Williams, who presented the evidence for the Commonwealth, was a painstaking, able lawyer.

Moore was a California attorney of radical views who had previously successfully defended two Massachusetts radicals for a murder which was committed during a strike at Lawrence. He was permitted by the Court and the district attorney, through customary comity, to appear for and represent Sacco. Callahan, who assisted him, was a competent local attorney.

Jeremiah J. McAnarney, who carried the burden for Vanzetti,[3] was an able, experienced and eloquent trial lawyer. Thomas F. McAnarney had served a term as judge of one of the local courts.

The trial got under way in an atmosphere of tension and apprehension. Whether justified or not, there had for three years been a Red scare in the United States, during which thousands of arrests and hundreds of deportations had been made. It was a period of industrial unrest. Strikes had been rampant, and many of them had been attended with serious violence. Riotous meetings of radicals in New York and Boston had frequently necessitated the calling out of the police. It was the prevailing belief in Plymouth and Norfolk counties that the Bridgewater and South Braintree robberies had been the work of "radicals." Vanzetti was known to be an active radical. Sacco was suspected. Crowds, far beyond the capacity of the Dedham courtroom, sought admission. Wild rumors were afloat of plans to break up the trial and forcibly take the defendants away from their custodians. Extra guards were placed in the

---

3 It developed in the course of the proceedings taken after the verdict that Moore had been placed in charge of the defense of both Sacco and Vanzetti, that he engaged Callahan and the McAnarneys to associate with him, and that the assignment of the McAnarneys to the representation of Vanzetti was merely a trial maneuver.

courtroom and around the courthouse. Strangers entering the courtroom were searched for concealed weapons. This extraordinary surveillance continued throughout the trial.

A regular panel of 500 veniremen was summoned. They were examined by the Court as to their qualifications with unusual care. Through challenges for cause and peremptories, only seven were passed by both sides as acceptable. Two hundred talesmen—bystanders—were then summoned. From these five more were finally agreed upon by both sides. The twelve men of the panel were from the neighboring towns of Avon, Weymouth, Quincy, Stoughton, Norwood, Brookline, Millis and Milton. They were representatives of the district: two real-estate men, one salesman, one stockroom clerk, one retail grocer, two machinists, one brick mason, one photographer, one farmer, one mill operative, and one shoe worker.

Before any evidence was heard, the jurors, on motion of the Commonwealth, with no objection from the defendants, were taken by automobile for a view of the scene of the crime, the territory traversed by the bandit car and the place where it later was found.

After the jury returned, Assistant District Attorney Williams made a long and detailed opening statement of what the Commonwealth expected to prove. The defendants reserved their openings. There was an order for the exclusion from the courtroom of all witnesses save the one undergoing examination, and the taking of testimony began.

The first witnesses called by the Commonwealth were a surveyor and photographer. They identified plats and photographs they had prepared which illustrated and represented the scene of the crime and the various streets, tracks, buildings and objects referred to in the later testimony. Several physicians were then called who had either viewed the bodies of Parmenter and Berardelli immediately after death or had participated in the autopsies. They accurately located and described the bullet wounds and the courses the bullets took after entering the victims' bodies. The four bullets extracted from Berardelli's body and the two taken from Parmenter's body were identified, marked and offered in evidence.[4]

The additional testimony—sixty-one witnesses—produced by the Commonwealth was directed to proving by direct and circumstantial evidence that the defendants were two of five men who planned and executed the robbery and participated in the murders of Berardelli and Parmenter, and that the actions and behavior of Sacco and Vanzetti when and after they were arrested indicated a consciousness of guilt of that crime.

The testimony produced on behalf of the two defendants—a total of 107 witnesses—was directed to an impeachment of the witnesses called by the prosecution, and to affirmative testimony that Sacco and Vanzetti had nothing to do with the robbery and killings, but at the time of the occurrence were miles away from the scene. Also, this testimony was directed to establishing that the actions of Sacco and Vanzetti when and after they were arrested were not induced by a consciousness of guilt of the Braintree robbery and murders but by fear of prosecution or personal harm because of their secret activities as radicals and because they had illegally evaded the military draft in 1917.

The record is voluminous—more than 2,100 printed pages. In order that the conflicts in the evidence may be more pointedly presented, the sequence in which the witnesses were called has been disregarded and the testimony—for the prosecution, for the defense and in rebuttal—congregated on the principal questions at issue.

The Commonwealth produced twenty-one witnesses who were at or near the scene of the shooting or saw the bandit

---

[4] These were officially numbered Commonwealth's exhibits 18 to 21, inclusive, and 24 and 25. They were also marked and more often referred to in the later testimony as "bullets numbers 1, 2, 3, 4, 5, and 6."

car and its occupants at different locations along the route traveled before and after the fatal shots were fired. The defense called twenty-eight such witnesses.[5]

There was substantial agreement on some points. There was virtual unanimity in the prosecution's and defense's description of the bandit car, a large five or seven-passenger, dark-colored touring car—many said a Buick—with adjustable top, side curtains closing it in back of the front or driver's seat, one or more curtains loose on the sides and flapping and a window broken out of in the rear end.[6] Three witnesses for the Commonwealth[7] testified that as they saw the bandit car going over the railroad crossing they noticed a long-barreled shotgun sticking about two feet out of an opening in the rear curtain of the car.

The overwhelming weight of the evidence showed that the driver of the car was pale, sickly-looking, light-complexioned and light-haired. This did not fit a description

[5] Because of the many misrepresentations which have appeared as to the weakness of the Commonwealth's case to identify Sacco or Vanzetti as participants in the crime and the strength of the defendants' case to the contrary, it is deemed essential, as a basis for an intelligent opinion on this vital question, that the evidence be carefully reviewed. Reference is omitted to witnesses whose testimony consisted solely of a description of the car.

[6] On April 17 an abandoned 1920 seven-passenger, dark-blue, Model K Buick, without number plates, was found by two horseback riders in an infrequently used country road approximately 500 or 600 feet from a main highway in Bridgewater and about eighteen miles from the scene of the crime. The top was up, but some of the side curtains had been torn loose and the window glass in the rear curtain was out. The police were notified and they examined the car. In the tonneau they found the rear light of glass and the strips of felt which had held it in place. Under the back edge of the front seat they found coins totaling sixty-two cents. These coins had undoubtedly dropped out of one of the envelopes when it was torn open by the robbers. (No trace was ever found of the balance of the money.) The factory number had been chipped off the frame of the car, and there was a hole in the right rear door which had been made by a bullet which passed from the inside of the car outward. Witnesses were called who proved that this car—positively identified by its engine number, which had not been erased, and other recognizable peculiarities—had been stolen from its owner in Natick, Massachusetts, on November 23, 1919; also, that 1920 license plates number 49783 had shortly thereafter been stolen from a Ford automobile in Needham, Massachusetts. The abandoned Buick was brought to Dedham at the time of the trial and identified by many of the witnesses as the car which had figured in the South Braintree robbery and murders.

[7] McGlone, a teamster working in the restaurant excavation, and Langlois and Behrsin, employees of Rice and Hutchins.

of either Sacco or Vanzetti,[8] and the Commonwealth, through its attorneys in both their opening statement and final argument, declared that the driver of the car was neither Sacco nor Vanzetti.

To connect Sacco with the holdup and murders the Commonwealth produced eleven witnesses. Six of these[9] swore that as the car passed over the railroad crossing and proceeded west on Pearl Street they saw a man either on the running board or "leaning out" from the car. Five of them testified he had a revolver which he waved menacingly and several times discharged at persons on the street who were near to or in the path of the moving car. There was substantial uniformity in the description of the man who, witnesses stated, was somewhere between twenty-five and thirty-five years of age, of medium height, weighing 140 or 145 pounds, dark-complexioned, with sharp features and black hair. One of the witnesses added: "a foreigner who looked like an Italian." Three of these witnesses, with varying degrees of certainty—as it will appear—identified Sacco as the man they saw.

The Commonwealth relied heavily upon the testimony of Mary Splaine, a bookkeeper employed by Slater & Morrill in their offices in Hampton House. She testified she saw Parmenter and Berardelli leave the building and followed their movements until they were about opposite the entrance to the Rice & Hutchins factory. A minute or two afterward she heard seven or eight shots in rapid succession. She went immediately to the window on the south side of the building and looked out. She saw a large, seven-passenger, dark-colored automobile coming up Pearl Street.

8 Both Sacco and Vanzetti were dark-complexioned and dark-haired. Sacco was smooth-faced, with clear-cut features. Vanzetti had high cheekbones and a dark, heavy mustache. Sacco was heavy-shouldered and weighed about 145 pounds. Vanzetti was not quite so strongly built but weighed about the same. Sacco was of medium height; Vanzetti, somewhat taller.

9 Misses Splaine, Devlin and Carrigan, employees of Slater & Morrill; De-Berardinis, who had a cobbler shop on Pearl Street near Railroad Avenue; Goodridge, a salesman; and Langlois, previously referred to.

When it was about halfway between the railroad crossing and Railroad Avenue she saw a man leaning out from the right side of the auto between the front and rear seat. The man, she said, was muscular, weighed about 140 pounds, had a clear-cut, narrow face, high forehead, hair brushed back, dark eyebrows and a peculiar greenish complexion.[10] She was positive the man was Sacco.

Miss Splaine was subjected to an exhaustive cross-examination. She admitted the car was fifty or sixty feet away from her[11] and she only had it within her view while it was traveling a distance of thirty or thirty-five feet. She also admitted she might have said at the preliminary hearing that Sacco "bore a striking resemblance" to the man she saw leaning out of the automobile, but said she might be mistaken and would not want to swear positively; that she did not think her opportunity for observation afforded her the right to say positively that Sacco was the man.[12] On redirect examination she reiterated her statement that she was now positive in her identification; that, while she had to admit a possibility of error, she was sure she was making no mistake.

Miss Splaine was corroborated by her fellow worker, Frances J. Devlin. On direct examination Miss Devlin positively identified Sacco as the man she had seen leaning out of the car and shooting at the crowd. Under cross-examination, however, she admitted she had stated at the preliminary hearing that she could not positively say Sacco was the man; but she had said, "He looks very much like the man who stood up in the back seat shooting." She said she testified that way at the preliminary hearing because at that time she did not want definitely to commit herself.

Louis Pelser, a shoe cutter employed by Rice & Hut-

---

10 An accurate description of Sacco.

11 A later witness for the defense showed that the actual distance, according to measurement, was 117 feet.

12 A shorthand transcript of the preliminary hearing proceedings, introduced later by the defense, showed that Miss Splaine had made these answers.

chins, gave important testimony. He said he was working on the first floor of the factory when he heard some shots. He opened the window opposite him, looked out and saw a man shooting at Berardelli, the guard, who lay on the ground not more than three feet away from him. He said the man doing the shooting was wearing a pair of dark-green pants and a tucked-in army shirt and was dark, wiry and had black, wavy hair. Pelser pointed to Sacco and said, "I wouldn't say it was him, but he's the dead image of him." He further testified that afterward he saw the automobile come up, and that one of the bandits flashed a gun in his direction and fired two shots which hit a little above the window where he was standing. He also testified that he saw the license plate on the rear of the car and caught the number—49783, 1920[13]—and wrote it down on a piece of board.

Pelser was subjected by both Moore and Jeremiah McAnarney to a grueling cross-examination. He admitted he had not told a representative of the defense who had talked to him the story he now told on the witness stand. His explanation was that he had wanted to avoid being a witness in the case. On redirect examination he testified he had not previously told the district attorney all that he had testified to in his direct examination, and for the same reason: He had not wanted to be a witness in the case. He repeated he would not identify Sacco as the man, but that Sacco was "the dead image of the man who shot Berardelli."[14]

A witness for the Commonwealth, who was destined to play an important role in the case even after the verdict

---

[13] This was the number plate stolen from a Ford automobile in Needham, Massachusetts. See previous footnote.

[14] The defense made a strong effort to impeach Pelser. Three witnesses, employees of Rice & Hutchins, testified they worked in the same room with Pelser and that they did not see him at the window when the shooting started; that when the shots were fired, one of the men, McCullum, opened the window and, seeing the bandits right in front of him, quickly closed it. As he did so he told his fellow employees to "duck," and all of them, Pelser included, dived under a table and did not come out to look again until they heard someone say the automobile was crossing the tracks. Then

was returned, was Lola L. Andrews. This was her testimony: With an elderly lady, Julia Campbell, she was in South Braintree on April 15 looking for employment. She first applied to Slater & Morrill's main factory. As she went into the building, sometime around eleven-thirty in the morning, she noticed an automobile standing about thirty feet east of the entrance. She saw two men working on the car but at that time did not stop to talk to them. She was unsuccessful in getting work at Slater & Morrill's, and she came out of the building about fifteen minutes after she had entered it. The automobile was still standing there, and a man was lying underneath it. She tapped him on the shoulder and asked him if he would direct her to the employees' entrance of Rice & Hutchins' factory. The man, she said, got out from under the car and pointed to the place she should go. She described him as being of medium height, smooth face, dark complexion and wearing dark clothes. She said she had a good look at the man, and she was positive he was Sacco.

Mrs. Andrews was subjected to a long and searching cross-examination by Moore. She admitted she had talked to Moore before the trial, but she denied any recollection of having made any of the many statements he attributed to her. After Moore had finished, Jeremiah McAnarney took over. His cross-examination was even more vigorous than Moore's and continued for hours. After she had been on the stand for practically an entire day she collapsed and further examination had to be postponed. In spite of her grilling Mrs. Andrews stuck to her story: She was positive the man she had talked to was Sacco.[15]

---

the window was again opened, according to the three witnesses, and Pelser got the number of the car. None of these witnesses was very effective. Under cross-examination they were not at all certain of either their own or Pelser's movements.

15 The defense brought Julia Campbell from Stockton Springs, Maine. She corroborated Mrs. Andrews' story that she was with her in South Braintree on April 15; but she swore that Mrs. Andrews did not talk to the man under the car, that the man never looked up, and that Mrs. Andrews could

A real-estate dealer named Tracy, who owned the building which housed the drugstore at the corner of Pearl and Hancock streets on Braintree Square, testified he was standing in front of his building on April 15 at approximately 11:40 A.M. and noticed two strangers looking into the drugstore window. Both of them were dark-complexioned, smoothly shaved, and they had dark hair. He said that, while he could not be positive, he felt sure one of the men was Sacco.

William J. Heron, a railroad private-police officer, testified that on April 15 at about 12:27 P.M. he saw two strange men—Italians—in the South Braintree railroad station near the gentlemen's toilet. One of them was about five feet six inches in height and weighed about 145 pounds. The other man was perhaps five inches taller and weighed about 160 pounds. Both of them, he said, were talking in Italian and appeared to be very nervous. He testified that he recognized one of the men five or six weeks later in the court at Quincy. It was Sacco. He was sure of that. The witness admitted on cross-examination that he had refused to talk to a representative of the defense but said he considered that his privilege. He continued strong in his identification.

The last witness to put the finger on Sacco was a Carlos E. Goodridge. He gave his occupation as a salesman. He testified that on April 15, at the time of the shooting, he was in Maguzu's poolroom on Pearl Street, a short distance west of Railroad Avenue, playing pool with Maguzu.

---

not have seen his face. Three witnesses testified for the defense as to having had conversations with Mrs. Andrews shortly after the shooting in which she told them she did not see the faces of any of the men at South Braintree and would not recognize them if she saw them. Another defense witness—a rooming-house keeper of a home where Mrs. Andrews had lived for a short time—testified that Mrs. Andrews' reputation for truth and veracity was bad. The Commonwealth in rebuttal brought in a Mrs. Gaines from Quincy who testified she knew Mrs. Andrews and Mrs. Campbell; that the three of them talked together of the Braintree murders within a week following the occurrence; and that Mrs. Andrews, in Mrs. Campbell's presence, told the same story she told on the witness stand. She said that Mrs. Campbell sat mute throughout the entire conversation.

When he heard the shots, he said, he went to the door and looked out but saw nothing and then went back to his game. He further testified that a few seconds later he heard some more shots and again went to the door. He looked toward the east and saw a large seven-passenger Buick automobile coming toward him. As the car went by him, he said, a man in the front seat or just back of it pointed a revolver at him; then he turned and hurried back into the poolroom. He described the man with the gun as being dark-complexioned and with a pointed face and dark hair which was blowing in the wind. He positively identified Sacco as the man whom he had seen.[16]

There was no evidence that Vanzetti participated in the actual shooting of Parmenter or Berardelli. It was the Commonwealth's contention that Vanzetti was present with Sacco in South Braintree, aiding and abetting him and others in the commission of the robbery and, therefore, as responsible in law for the consequential murders as the men who shot and killed the paymaster and the guard. The testimony of four of the Commonwealth's witnesses was specifically directed against Vanzetti.

A man named Faulkner, a patternmaker from Cohasset, gave this testimony:

On April 15, between 9:20 and 9:30 A.M., he was a passenger on a train traveling between Cohasset and Boston. He was riding in the front end of a car which he described as a combination baggage car and smoker. As the train approached East Weymouth a man who was sitting in a double seat opposite him said, "The man behind me wants

---

[16] The defense called three witnesses to impeach Goodridge. One of them swore that Goodridge told him he had not seen anyone in the automobile. Another testified that Goodridge's reputation for truth and veracity was bad, and that Goodridge had told him right after the shooting he could not possibly remember the faces of the men in the machine. Maguzu, the poolroom proprietor, confirmed Goodridge's story that they had been playing pool together, and that Goodridge told him one of the men had pointed a gun at him; but that when he—Maguzu—had asked him how the men looked Goodridge had said the man was young and light-complexioned, and that "this job wasn't pulled by foreign people."

to know if this is East Braintree." Faulkner looked at the man designated and saw a dark-complexioned foreigner with high cheekbones and a dark mustache. When the train got to East Braintree, he turned to the man and said, "This is East Braintree." The man got up and left the car. The witness was positive the man was Vanzetti. Faulkner was vigorously cross-examined, but he held tenaciously to his story. He said his eyesight and memory were both good, and he could not be mistaken.[17]

Harry E. Dolbeare, a piano repairman, was a telling witness against Vanzetti.[18] He testified that on April 15 some time between 10:00 A.M. and 12:00 noon he saw a large, seven-passenger, dark-colored automobile at Braintree Square, and that there were five men in the car—two on the front seat and three in the rear. He said that he particularly noticed one man in the rear of the car. This man leaned forward and talked to the men on the front seat. Dolbeare described the man as being dark-complexioned, foreign-looking and wearing a heavy, dark mustache. He was positive that the man was Vanzetti. The witness's testimony was unshaken by McAnarney's vigorous cross-examination.

Probably the most effective testimony against Vanzetti was given by a shoe worker and former railroad-crossing man for the New York, New Haven & Hartford Railroad named Reed. On April 15 this witness was stationed at the railroad's Mattfield Crossing, a short distance out of Brock-

17 The defense later made an attempt to impeach this witness through the testimony of the ticket agents of the railroad at stations between Plymouth and East Weymouth. These men stated that no ticket was sold, and that there was no record of a cash fare on April 15 for a ride between any of the intermediate stations and East Braintree. Other railroad employees testified that there was a full-length smoking car and no combination baggage and smoking car on the train Faulkner claimed to have been on. Pictures of Vanzetti were shown to the ticket agents, and Vanzetti was pointed out to them in the courtroom. All were certain they had never seen the man before.

18 It was developed during the examination of this witness that he had been summoned as one of the original panel of jurors but had been excused because he admitted to a knowledge of material facts in the case. The district attorney made much of this circumstance in his later argument.

ton. This was his testimony: About 4:15 P.M. he saw a large, dark-colored Buick automobile approaching the crossing at an unusually high rate of speed. A train was approaching, and he ran to the center of the street with his stop sign in his hand to flag the automobile. As the car came to a grinding stop, one of the men leaned out of the car, pointed his finger at Reed and hollered, "What in hell did you hold us up for?" The train passed over the crossing, and Reed waved the car to come ahead. As the car passed him the same man again leaned out and repeated, "What in hell did you hold us up for?" The witness further testified that the man who had twice spoken to him had a dark complexion, hollow cheeks, high cheekbones, bushy black hair and a stubby mustache. Three weeks later, Reed said, he saw the same man at the Brockton police station. He was Vanzetti. Reed was positive of it.

The witness's story was not weakened by cross-examination. He said he went to the police station voluntarily because he heard they had some Italian suspects there, and because he knew the men he had seen in the automobile three weeks before were Italians.

One of the Commonwealth's witnesses caused the district attorney no little embarrassment. He was Levangie, the railroad gatetender at the Pearl Street crossing. He testified he was in his gatehouse cleaning the windows when he heard twelve or fifteen blasts which sounded like shots; that almost immediately afterward the automatic bell which warned of oncoming trains rang, and he ran out to lower the gates for an approaching train from Brockton. He said he just about had the gates down when he noticed a big automobile coming up the hill toward the crossing. When it neared the crossing he saw a man behind the driver with a shiny revolver in his hand. The man pointed the revolver at him and motioned him to put up the gates. He said he was scared and did what he was told to do. He raised the gates and allowed the automobile to pass over the crossing ahead of the train. He could give no description of the man who pointed the revolver at him, but insisted that he saw the driver plainly. The driver, Levangie said, was dark-complexioned, had high cheekbones, black hair and a brown mustache. He was sure the man was Vanzetti.[19]

The foregoing constituted all of the Commonwealth's direct evidence on the identification of Sacco and Vanzetti.

Before any witnesses were called for the defense, Callahan, one of the attorneys for Sacco, made an opening statement. It was brief and very general. Witnesses, he said, would be produced who would tell where Sacco and Vanzetti were in the morning and afternoon of April 15, 1920. Neither of them, he declared, was in South Braintree. Other witnesses at the scene of the shooting would tell who and what they saw there.

Of the twenty-eight defense witnesses who testified to having seen the bandit car or the men who participated in the shooting, twelve were Italians.[20] None of the witnesses for the defense contradicted the Commonwealth's testimony as to the circumstances of the robbery and murders. Seven of them[21] testified that they saw the automobile as it went over the railroad crossing and west on Pearl Street, and that they saw one of its occupants climb from the rear

---

19 This witness was conclusively impeached. One witness testified Levangie told him the driver was a light-complexioned man; another, that Levangie told him it was hard to identify the men; another that he would not know any of the men if he saw them again. Levangie's description of the driver was at variance with all of the evidence in the case. In later argument the district attorney admitted the witness was mistaken and disclaimed his testimony.

20 This is noted because of the recognition by defense counsel of the existence of a local prejudice against Italians, and the emphasis they gave in their summations to the fact that the testimony of Sacco and Vanzetti—that they were not at the scene of the robbery and murders—was corroborated by fourteen witnesses who were not of their nationality.

21 Burke, an itinerant carnival performer; Pierce and Ferguson, shoe workers employed by Slater & Morrill; Celluci, a railroad track laborer; O'Neill, a college student; Olsen, a shoemaker; and Damato, who ran a barber shop on Pearl Street not far from Railroad Avenue.

to the front seat. All but one of these said the man had a gun in his hand, and three of them said he pointed or fired it at people in the street. Four of them were positive that neither the man with the gun nor any other occupant of the car which they could see was Sacco or Vanzetti.

One of the witnesses—Pierce—testified on cross-examination that he could "not honestly say that Sacco was not one of the men" he saw. Another—Ferguson—in answer to a question on direct examination as to whether he could say that the man with the gun he saw in the automobile was either Sacco or Vanzetti, answered, "not positively, but I don't believe it was." On cross-examination he qualified that answer by saying that the man he saw "might or might not" have been one of the defendants. Another of the witnesses—Olsen—testified positively that Vanzetti was not one of the men he saw in the automobile, but he could not tell about the other man—Sacco.

One of the first witnesses called was a Quincy fruit dealer named Frantello. He testified he had occasion to walk past Rice & Hutchins' factory about 2:55 or 3:00 P.M. on April 15 and saw two strangers leaning against a railing alongside the sidewalk. The one nearest him, he said, was dark-complexioned, wore dark clothes and had no overcoat. The other man he described as slimmer, light-complexioned, pale, with light hair and apparently about twenty years of age. He said as he passed them he heard them talking and they were speaking English. He was certain neither of these men was Sacco or Vanzetti.

District Attorney Katzmann resorted to a cross-examination which completely discredited this witness. After pinning Frantello down to the length of time he had these men under observation, he asked the witness to step down from the witness box and in front of the jury and glance for exactly the same length of time at the two middle jurors in the front row. The witness did so. He was then made to return to the stand, turn his back to the jurors and describe the two jurors he had observed. He said they had their hats off—which caused a titter in the courtroom—both wore blue suits, one had a mustache and the other a watch chain. These were the only things he had noticed. He was then asked to look again at the two jurors. He admitted he could see no watch chain on either of them and that neither had a mustache. The witness admitted he had been interviewed by one of the officers from the district attorney's office and might have told him that one of the men he saw looked to him like a "wop."

Four of the laborers who were working in the restaurant excavation were called as witnesses for the defense. All testified they heard the start of the shooting and looked up in time to see two men shooting at Parmenter and Berardelli. They gave conflicting descriptions of the men, but were positive neither was Sacco nor Vanzetti. All of them suffered from Katzmann's sharp cross-examinations. None of them seemed to have any knowledge or remembrance of anything beyond a description of the killers, and that the killers did not resemble the defendants. Their testimony was further weakened by the fact that two witnesses,[22] who at the time of the shooting were in their homes just north of the excavation, had previously testified for the Commonwealth that with the sound of the first shot all of the workmen in the excavation turned their backs on the scene of the tragedy and rushed wildly in the opposite direction.

Mrs. Barbara Liscomb, an employee of Rice & Hutchins, proved to be one of the best witnesses for the defendants. This was her testimony: Her place of work was on the second floor near the windows which fronted on Pearl Street. Her attention was arrested by some one "hollering" that a man had been shot, and she hurried to the nearest open window and looked out. She was confronted with the sight of two men lying on the ground and a short, dark-com-

---

[22] Horace Galbert and Mrs. Annie Nichols.

plexioned man facing her and holding a revolver. "I will always remember his face," she said earnestly. "I am positively sure," she continued, "that neither of the men in the dock is the man I saw with the gun." On cross-examination she added details to her description of the man which fitted Sacco, but she continued her insistence that Sacco was not the man.

Jennie Novelli, a nurse, testified that about 2:50 P.M. on April 15 she saw a large, dark-colored automobile going east on Pearl Street. When it got down as far as Slater & Morrill's main factory it turned around and faced west. She said that as the machine passed her she looked at both of the men in the front seat and particularly at the man beside the driver because she thought he was some one she knew. She gave a detailed description of both men and swore positively that neither of them was Sacco or Vanzetti.[23]

There was some railroad construction work going on near the New York, New Haven & Hartford Railroad freight house, some 350 or more feet away from the most westerly track of the Pearl Street railroad crossing. The work was being done by a gang of some twenty-five or thirty Italians under an Italian foreman named Ricci. Eight of these were called as witnesses for the defense. With slight variations, they all testified they heard the shooting and ran to the crossing to see what was happening. Six of them testified they saw nothing of the early shooting but saw the automobile as it was crossing the railroad tracks.

All of them described the driver as pale, light-complexioned, and sickly-looking. Those who claimed to have seen the man next to him in the front seat said he was dark and

23 A Pinkerton detective in the employ of the Commonwealth testified that on May 8, 1920, he interviewed Mrs. Novelli and showed her a photograph of Sacco which she said resembled one of the men she had seen in the bandit car. He also testified that the description she then gave of the men in the car was considerably at variance with that which she gave on the witness stand.

heavy-set, with no mustache. Four of them testified they saw a man who was standing up in the car back of the driver and who shot at them or other persons in the street. They described him as light-complexioned and with no mustache. All six testified positively that neither of the men they saw was Sacco or Vanzetti. Evidently confident that the jurors were giving little heed to these parrotlike recitals, the district attorney wasted little time in cross-examination.

One of the eight—Gatti—had known Sacco for seven years and testified this made him doubly sure he did not see Sacco that day. Another of the eight—Cellucci, who was then an enlisted sailor stationed at Hampton Roads—testified he heard the shots, dropped his tools and started, with some of the other laborers, in the direction of the crossing, about 350 feet away. He said that when he passed the railroad shanty the boss, Ricci, shouted to the men to stay where they were, and Cellucci thought all of them stopped except him; that he dodged behind a pile of dirt and "got away." He said when he reached the railroad crossing the bandit car passed within five feet of him, and he could plainly see five men in the car. One of them was in between the front and rear seats "sort of kneeling down" and had a Colt automatic revolver in his hand. He declared he knew it was a Colt and not a Bayard because of his previous experience with firearms.[24] He testified further that the man with the gun pointed it directly at him, and he had a good opportunity to see his face. He described him as being young, smooth-faced, but with what appeared to be a two or three-day growth of beard. The man on the front seat beside the driver he described as young, dark-complexioned and smooth-faced. He said he did not get a good enough look at the driver to describe him, but he was positive that neither of the two men he did describe was Sacco or Vanzetti. The witness's testimony was in no

---

[24] The significance of this will become apparent later in the narrative.

way impeached by Katzmann's vigorous cross-examination.[25]

Three defense witnesses[26] testified they saw the bandit car at various points on the route it took after leaving the scene of the crime. All agreed that the machine was being driven at a high and reckless rate of speed. They gave varying descriptions of the driver and the man beside him on the front seat, but all were positive that neither of them was Sacco or Vanzetti. One of these witnesses—Chase—admitted on cross-examination that the Bridgeport chief of police had shown him a photograph of Sacco, and he had told the chief that the kind of haircut in the picture made him think of the man he had seen in the front seat of the car beside the driver. Another—Dorr—was impeached by a Stoughton police officer who testified in rebuttal that he had previously talked to Dorr, and Dorr had told him he could not recognize any of the men in the car because of its terrific speed when it passed him.

Daniel Joseph O'Neill, a nineteen-year-old college student (see footnote 21), testified that just as he got off the train at South Braintree at about three o'clock on the afternoon of April 15 he heard six or seven shots. They seemed to come from Pearl Street, and he ran in that direction to see what the trouble was. He said there was an automobile coming over the railroad crossing when he reached Pearl Street, and he saw a man in the rear seat open the rear door of the car, get on the running board and walk toward the front seat.[27] His further testimony

---

25 The Commonwealth in rebuttal called Angelo Ricci, the railroad gang's foreman, who testified that when he heard the shooting the men began to run toward the railroad crossing. He ordered them to stop, and he thought all of them did stop; one or two of them might have slipped around the dirt pile, but he did not think so. He said it was his business to keep his men on the job and "his conscience told him they were all there."

26 Chase, a truck driver; Dorr, a public-road laborer; and Desmond, a tobacco salesman.

27 At the request of the district attorney, the jury was asked to look at the Buick automobile in the courthouse yard, which had been identified as the bandit car. On the basis of this view and what the jurors could see for them-

was that the man had a gun in his hand which he pointed
at another man on the sidewalk. He described the man
with the gun as broad-shouldered, light-complexioned,
clean-shaved and with dark, combed-back hair. He was
positive that neither Sacco nor Vanzetti was that man.

The last eye witness to the shooting called by the defense was William Gibson, a chauffeur for the contractor
who was doing the excavating job for the new restaurant
building. This was his testimony: About three o'clock on
the afternoon of April 15 he saw a dark-green Buick automobile start up from a point a short distance east of the
railroad crossing. It proceeded slowly—about eight miles
an hour—until it reached a point opposite the excavation.
He saw two men in the car, one in the driver's seat and one
in the rear. He described the driver as a young man weighing between 140 and 145 pounds, with a sallow, sickly complexion, a short mustache and wearing eyeglasses. The only
description he could give of the man in the rear seat was
that he had a "pea cap" on and might have weighed 135
pounds. He was positive neither of the men he saw was
Sacco or Vanzetti. The cross-examination of the district
attorney confused the witness and developed considerable
additional information. He further testified that immediately before he saw the automobile he heard some shots
and saw one man fall on the sidewalk and another run and
fall in the street. At the same time he saw two other men
opposite the restaurant excavation, each with a gun, grab
hold of a large black box and throw it into the back of the
car. In his ultimate confusion he admitted that all he had
intended to swear to in his direct examination was that
the driver of the car was neither Sacco nor Vanzetti.

This testimony, together with Sacco and Vanzetti's de-
nials that they were in or near South Braintree on April 15,

---

selves, it was later argued that the witness was either lying or mistaken; that
it would have been physically impossible for a man on the inside of the
moving automobile to open the rear door, get out of the car, close the door
and walk on the running board.

constituted the direct evidence of the defense that Sacco and Vanzetti were not two of the men who participated in the murders of Parmenter and Berardelli.

In rebuttal the Commonwealth called a witness who added a piece of circumstantial evidence linking Vanzetti to the crime. He was Frank W. Hawley, a Brockton salesman. He testified that on April 1, 1920, while driving his own auto in downtown Brockton, he turned his car in such a way as to block the course of a large, dark-colored, seven-passenger Buick, which was curtained in the back and had one side curtain flapping. There were five men in the car —two on the front seat and three in the rear. He said he had a clear view of the driver and the man sitting beside him. The driver, he said, stuck his head out of the car and inquired the way to Whitney. The witness described the man who made the inquiry and was positive he was Vanzetti. His testimony was strengthened rather than weakened by a long reiterative cross-examination.

The most important circumstantial evidence to link Sacco and Vanzetti with the Braintree murders was the testimony concerning the guns and ammunition which were found on their persons when they were arrested on May 5.

For the Commonwealth the arresting officers testified that when they took the defendants into custody Vanzetti had in his hip pocket a fully loaded, five-chamber Harrington & Richardson thirty-eight-caliber revolver and in one of his side coat pockets four twelve-gauge shotgun shells which were loaded with buckshot. Sacco, the officers testified, had, underneath his vest and tucked down between the front of his shirt and his trousers waistband, a fully loaded, ten-chamber, thirty-two-caliber automatic Colt revolver and, in one of his side pants pockets, twenty-two additional loaded thirty-two-caliber cartridges.

Mrs. Berardelli, the murdered guard's widow, testified

her husband had a revolver which had been given to him by Parmenter. Berardelli had showed it to her at some time in the early part of 1920. He called her attention to the fact that a spring in it needed repairing, and about three weeks before the robbery she had gone with him to the Iver-Johnson Sporting Goods Store in Boston to have it repaired. She said she saw her husband point out the defective spring to the store attendant. She did not know for certain whether he got the gun back from the store or not, but she did know that in the meantime Parmenter had supplied him with another. Margaret Mahoney, a pay-mistress for Slater & Morrill, testified that Berardelli owned a revolver. She did not know what kind.

Bostock, a Slater & Morrill employee who witnessed the shooting, testified he knew Berardelli always carried a revolver; that Berardelli had frequently shown him his revolver, the last time being the Saturday before the shooting; that it looked exactly like the Harrington & Richardson thirty-eight-caliber revolver in evidence. He also testified that right after the shooting he picked up four empty shells in the street and gave them to Trayer, the superintendent for Slater & Morrill. Trayer testified that Bostock gave him the shells, and that he turned them over to Captain Proctor of the state police. Another witness—Wade—swore that he saw Berardelli reach toward his hip pocket as he lay on the ground just before he was shot to death.

Three employees of the Iver-Johnson Sporting Goods Store in Boston testified from recollection and the company's records that on March 20, 1920, a Mr. Berardelli brought in a thirty-eight-caliber Harrington & Richardson revolver for repair which looked like the Harrington & Richardson revolver in evidence. There was a record entry "new hammer and repairs" indicating that a new hammer had been put in. One of the witnesses testified the gun must have been redelivered to its owner because it was the company's practice to have periodical sales of all uncalled-for, repaired merchandise, and the record kept of such sales showed the name of the defaulting owner and the type of gun sold. There was no record of such a sale of a Harrington & Richardson revolver subsequent to March 20. There was further testimony that a careful search had been made of the Iver-Johnson store's stock, and there was no used Harrington & Richardson thirty-eight-caliber revolver in the store.

Vanzetti's testimony concerning the shotgun shells was that on the Sunday before his arrest he was at Sacco's home. Mrs. Sacco was clearing out their belongings and packing up for an expected trip to Italy. There were three shotgun shells on the kitchen shelf, and she gave them to him. He told her he would take them to some friend of his in Plymouth who would know where to hunt in the wintertime. As to the Harrington & Richardson revolver, he said he bought it two or three months before from one Falzini for five dollars, because it was a pretty bad time and he was afraid of holdups. He said when he peddled fish he frequently was out late and might be carrying anywhere from eighty-five to one hundred and twenty dollars on his person. This story was pretty badly riddled by the district attorney's cross-examination. Under sharp and persistent questioning, Vanzetti professed he was unable to remember whether it was Sacco or his wife who gave him the shotgun shells or whether there were three or four. He admitted telling the police at the Brockton station that he could not tell in what month or what year he had got the gun, but he had bought it in Boston and had had it for a long time. He admitted that story was false. He testified he did not remember saying that he paid eighteen or nineteen dollars for the revolver, but, if he did say so, that also was false. He admitted that in an earlier statement he made to the district attorney he went into details concerning the alleged purchase of the gun which were false. He testified he did not remember telling Katzmann that he bought the cartridges at the same place he bought the revolver or that he bought a whole box and, when he had fired all but six of them, had put those six in the revolver and thrown away the box. He said that if he had said those things, they were false. He testified he did not know that the revolver had only five chambers.

By three witnesses, counsel for Vanzetti attempted to prove an entirely different story from that which he had told the police and the district attorney as to how he came into possession of the Harrington & Richardson revolver. Eldridge A. Atwater of Dexter, Maine, was shown the revolver and testified that from some worn places on it he recognized it as a gun which had once belonged to his mother-in-law. He said he had fired the gun seventy-five or a hundred times and was thoroughly familiar with it. Katzmann's cross-examination demonstrated that the witness knew little or nothing about revolvers, but his story otherwise was unshaken.

Rexford Slater also of Dexter, Maine, gave similar testimony. He recognized the Harrington & Richardson revolver in evidence as one which had been in the possession of his mother-in-law, who was also the witness Atwater's mother-in-law. He testified he had fired it a number of times and, in the fall of 1919, had sold it for four dollars to an Italian named Orciani. His story was considerably weakened on cross-examination. He declared he could not be positive it was the same gun; that he had never seen any distinguishing marks on it except a place where some nickel had been knocked off the end of the barrel.

Luigi Falzini of Framingham, Massachusetts, testified he bought the Harrington & Richardson revolver in evidence from Orciani in October 1919 and sold it to Vanzetti for five dollars in February 1920. On cross-examination he testified he did not know the number of the revolver, had never discharged it, had never taken it apart, had sold no cartridges with it and never knew whether it was loaded or not, but he thought it was. He further admitted he had seen Orciani, the man from whom he said he bought the gun, on the street outside the courthouse during the week before he testified.[28]

The defense also called Aldeah Florence who testified that she was acquainted with Mrs. Berardelli and had talked to her on two occasions about Berardelli and his revolver—once before and once after the shooting. She said in the first conversation Mrs. Berardelli told her that Berardelli never carried a revolver; that he had one which was broken, and she was going to have it fixed in Boston. At the conversation after the shooting, she testified, Mrs. Berardelli said, "Oh, dear, if he [Berardelli] had taken my advice and taken the revolver out of the shop he would not be in the condition he is today." Evidently the district attorney considered that this testimony suggested its own implausibility. He led her on cross-examination to give quite contradictory versions of both conversations, but he did not trouble Mrs. Berardelli to take the stand in rebuttal to deny them.

Two witnesses who qualified as ballistics experts testified for the defense that the Harrington & Richardson thirty-eight-caliber revolver shown them—the one taken from Vanzetti—was fifteen or sixteen years old, and that the hammer was no newer than any other part of the gun.

As to the Colt automatic thirty-two-caliber revolver and the twenty-two extra cartridges taken from Sacco, the Commonwealth produced evidence that at the Brockton police station Sacco, when asked why he carried the revolver, said, "For protection—lots of bad men." Asked why he had so many extra cartridges, he replied that he and a friend of Vanzetti's were going to shoot them off in the woods. Asked where he bought the revolver, he said in a store in Han-

---

28 The Commonwealth made a telling point in argument that in spite of this and other evidence which linked Orciani with the defendants he was not called as a defense witness.

over Street in Boston from a man whose name he did not know.

George T. Kelley, superintendent of the shoe factory in Stoughton where Sacco had worked before his arrest, testified that for a period of six months in 1919 Sacco had acted as night watchman; that he knew Sacco had a gun, but he had never seen it.

Cellucci, who claimed to have witnessed some of the shooting, testified that as the automobile passed him he saw a man kneeling between the front and rear seats with a Colt revolver in his hand.[29]

The two ballistics experts called by the Commonwealth testified that the four empty shells picked up by Bostock were of different makes. They said the thirty-two cartridges found in Sacco's possession were of varying makes—Remington, Peters, Winchester and of U. S. Cartridge Company manufacture; and that the cartridges taken from the Harrington & Richardson thirty-eight-caliber revolver found on Vanzetti were likewise of different makes. From an examination of the six bullets taken from the bodies of Berardelli and Parmenter, both experts were of the opinion that all had been fired from a Savage automatic, with the exception of Commonwealth's exhibit eighteen—bullet number three—which had been fired from a thirty-two-caliber Colt automatic. They testified that bullet number three in evidence was of a practically obsolete type, very difficult to obtain on the market, but that several of the extra cartridges found in Sacco's possession at the time of his arrest were of this identical type. They testified also to numerous tests they had made by firing cartridges of various manufactures from different guns, including the thirty-two-caliber Colt automatic found on Sacco, into a mass of sawdust and recovering the bullets for an examination and comparison of significant markings on the bullets. From these tests one of the experts, Cap-

---

29 As previously stated, he testified the man was not Sacco.

tain Procter of the state police, testified that every mark he saw on bullet number three was consistent with his opinion that it had been fired from the Colt automatic found in Sacco's possession. The other expert gave the more definite opinion that it had been fired from the Sacco revolver.

In his defense Sacco testified he bought the revolver and bullets in a "public store" in Milford sometime in 1917 and paid sixteen dollars for it; that on the afternoon of May 5, 1920, he and his wife were packing and getting ready to go to Italy. He said his wife in cleaning out a bureau drawer found the pistol and bullets. She asked him what he was going to do with them, and he told her he and Vanzetti were going to the woods and shoot them off, and then he put the revolver and the bullets in his pockets. He said about 4:30 P.M. Orciani and Boda came to his house and an argument started; that he forgot all about the revolver and the bullets, and therefore when he was arrested he still had them. He further testified that he had never seen the Harrington & Richardson revolver before the night of May 5, when he and Vanzetti were arrested. He denied knowing or ever having heard of Berardelli until after the Braintree shooting. He declared emphatically he had not taken a revolver away from Berardelli on April 15.

On cross-examination, Sacco testified he had never done any shooting. He admitted the possession of the loaded thirty-two-caliber Colt automatic and the twenty-two extra shells when he was arrested. He said he had bought the cartridges in one box and did not know that sixteen of them were Peters manufacture; three, Remington; seven, United States; and six, Winchester. He admitted he lied to the district attorney or had "forgotten" when he told him he had bought the gun in Hanover Street in Boston two years before and had given a false name. He also admitted he had been asked where he bought the cartridges and had not told the truth when he said he did not know, but that he had bought a brand-new box. He testified that on May 5 he carried the gun in his trousers waistband and did so because a person would not find it as readily there as if it was in his pocket; that he had heard one could get a year in jail for carrying a gun. He admitted that the revolver and cartridges were quite heavy, but he stuck to his story that when he left the house with Boda, Orciani and Vanzetti he had forgotten all about them.

With reference to the shotgun shells which were found on Vanzetti and which Vanzetti testified had been given to him by Sacco's wife, Sacco testified that a man—unidentified—came to his house in 1918 or 1919. He said the man had a shotgun and some shells and went out into the woods and used up all of the shells except these three (the police said they found four); that the man had left these in Sacco's house and everyone had forgotten about them until his wife found them when she was cleaning the house, preparatory for their trip to Italy. Vanzetti asked her what she was going to do with them, and then she gave them to Vanzetti, who said he would give them to some friend of his in Plymouth and "make fifty cents for the benefit of the prisoner and other things." Sacco's wife corroborated this testimony.

The two ballistics experts called by the defense testified that bullet number three, taken from Berardelli's body, could have been fired from a Colt or a Bayard revolver. One of them said that from the way the bullet was "deformed" it was probably fired from a Colt. Both, however, gave it as their opinion, based on their comparisons of the test bullets fired from the Colt in evidence and from other Colt revolvers, that bullet number three had not been fired from the Colt revolver taken from Sacco. They said there were definitely different markings on the test bullets fired from Sacco's revolver and the number three bullet in evidence. Photographs of the bullets and a cast of the Sacco gun were identified and offered in evidence which was directed to proving that these differences existed. This latter testimony was sharply challenged in the extensive and intelligent cross-examination of the district attorney, who denied there were any of the differences indicated by the witnesses or the photographs between bullet number three and the test bullets which had been fired from the Colt taken from Sacco.

All of the bullets and shells—the six bullets taken from the bodies of Berardelli and Parmenter, the empty shells picked up by the witness Bostock and the test bullets and their shells—were submitted to the jurors for examination during the questioning of the experts and, together with the photographs and the cast, were taken by them on their retirement to the jury room. It was claimed and later argued by both sides that all the claimed distinguishing marks of similarity or dissimilarity between bullet number three and the Colt test bullets which had been pointed out by the respective experts were discernible to the layman either by the naked eye or by the photographs or through the enlargements of a magnifying glass.

Another piece of circumstantial evidence linking Sacco to the murder of Berardelli was the testimony of Fred Loring, a shoe worker for Slater & Morrill, that he found a worn man's cap beside the body of Berardelli immediately after the shooting. It was the contention of the Commonwealth that this was Sacco's cap which had fallen from his head during his struggle with Berardelli.

While the evidence was conflicting, the weight of it was that the man on the street near the restaurant excavation who shot Berardelli wore a cap, but that the man who shot from the automobile after he left the railroad crossing, and who was identified by several of the witnesses as the same man who had shot Berardelli, was bareheaded. Mrs. Berardelli testified that the cap had not belonged to her husband.

George T. Kelly, superintendent of the 3 K Shoe Factory in Stoughton where Sacco had worked up to May 1, 1920, testified that he knew Sacco well and that he sometimes wore a dark cap "similar in color" to the cap produced by the witness Loring. On the basis of this testimony, the cap was admitted in evidence and marked as an exhibit. Kelly was recalled by the defense. He was shown another cap—admittedly Sacco's—and when asked if that did not look more like Sacco's cap than the one produced by the Commonwealth he said it did.

On cross-examination, Kelly made a significant and damaging admission. Asked if his testimony was influenced by fear, he said, "No." Asked if immediately after Sacco's arrest he had not been asked by the police to describe the cap Sacco usually wore, he replied, "Well, I described it pretty well, didn't I?" He then admitted that when first shown the cap found beside Berardelli he might have said to the police, "I have my opinion about the cap, but I don't want to get a bomb up my ass."

Sacco denied that the cap found near Berardelli's body was his; that it was a smaller head size than he wore. He admitted ownership of the other cap and attempted to demonstrate to the jury by putting on and taking off the two caps that the cap found on the street by Berardelli's body was too small for him.

In his opening statement, Williams, for the Commonwealth, had declared that the prosecution would prove that a man named Boda, who owned an Overland automobile, had been seen driving a 1920 Buick early in April with four dark-complexioned men in it. Boda, he said, kept his Overland in a shed in the rear of a building designated as the Coacci house. After the Braintree shooting the police visited the shed and found pieces of curtains nailed to the windows of the shed, traces of a hole dug in the floor and tire marks indicating there had been two automobiles in the shed. The Coacci house and shed were only a short distance—less than two miles—from where the abandoned Buick bandit car was found on April 17. The implication was that Boda had also kept the bandit car in the shed before April 15 and sought to conceal it, and that two of the four dark-complexioned men seen riding with him were Sacco and Vanzetti. Boda, said Williams, had delivered the Overland to a West Bridgewater garageman named Johnson for some repairs. The police, who were searching for Boda, had arranged with Johnson and his wife to be notified when Boda came for his car.

Most of this evidence when offered was excluded by the Court on defendants' motion. The rest of it, with other evidence, was admitted on the theory that it was for the jury to determine whether certain actions of the defendants showed a consciousness of guilt of the Braintree murders.

Ruth C. Johnson, wife of the garageman, testified as follows: On the night of May 5, about 9:00 P.M., she heard a noise outside her house. Her husband was in bed, and she went to the front door. She saw a man standing near a bridge a short distance away. As he came toward her she recognized him as Boda. He asked her if her husband was home. She called to her husband, and then she told Boda her husband would see him in a few minutes. She then came out and walked a hundred feet or more to the Bartlett house next door, intending to telephone the police. As she stepped out of her door she saw a brightly lighted motorcycle and three men standing beside it. They followed her to the Bartlett house and, when she had finished telephoning, followed her back to her own house. She could plainly see their faces. One of them she positively identified as Sacco. Later at the police station she identified one of the others as Orciani. She further testified that when she got back to her doorway her husband was there talking to Boda.

Simeon E. Johnson corroborated his wife's testimony.

He testified that when he had dressed and got to the door he met Boda, whom he had known since the previous December. He described him as being about five feet six inches tall and weighing about 125 pounds, and that while Boda usually dressed very well, on this night he wore shabby clothes and a slouch hat. Johnson said that on April 19, 1920, he had gone to Boda's house and picked up an Overland car to repair it. When Boda called at his house on the evening of May 5 to get his car, he told him it had no 1920 license plates, and he would advise him not to take out the car without them. Boda then told him he would get some plates and be back the next day. He testified Boda did not call for the car the next day, and he had never seen him since.[30] He further testified that when he came out of his house he saw three other men standing near a lighted motorcycle with a sidecar. When he had finished talking with Boda one of the men got on the motorcycle, Boda got into the sidecar and they rode away. The other two men started walking in the direction of Elm Street Square.[31]

Austin C. Cole, who was a streetcar conductor working on a run between East Bridgewater and Brockton on the night of May 5, testified that on his 9:30-10:15 trip two men, whom he identified as Sacco and Vanzetti, got on his car about a mile and a half from Elm Street and paid their fares to Brockton. At 10:05 some police officers boarded the car and arrested them. He saw the officers search them and saw one of the officers with a gun in his hand. Later a police patrol car drove up alongside his car, and the men were taken from it and put in the police car. He further

---

[30] Boda disappeared and up to the time of the trial had not been apprehended by the police.

[31] Both Mr. and Mrs. Johnson were searchingly cross-examined, the clear implication being that defense counsel disbelieved their testimony. Sacco and Vanzetti when they took the stand several days later gave practically identical testimony. The district attorney was to argue later that this shift in plan indicated that the supplemental testimony concerning the collection and secreting of radical literature was improvised for the reason, among others, of neutralizing this evidence.

testified that either on the previous April 14 or 15 he had seen Sacco and Vanzetti on his car at the same place where they had boarded it on May 5.

Michael J. Connolly, a Brockton police officer, told of the arrest of Sacco and Vanzetti. He testified that while they were still on the streetcar Vanzetti made a movement toward his hip pocket and he (Connolly) told him to keep his hands in his lap or he would be sorry.[32] Vanzetti was searched. The loaded Harrington & Richardson revolver was found in his hip pocket and the four twelve-gauge shotgun shells in one of the side pockets of his coat. Sacco, said Connolly, was given a "slight going over" in the car, but no weapon was then found. When Sacco and Vanzetti were taken from the car and put in the police patrol car, Connolly said he noticed that Sacco kept reaching underneath his overcoat, and he told him to keep his hands outside. He said he asked Sacco if he had a gun and Sacco answered, "I ain't got no gun." At the station Sacco was thoroughly searched and the loaded thirty-two-caliber Colt automatic found beneath his vest, tucked down between the front of his trousers and his trousers waistband. The twenty-two loose thirty-two-caliber shells were also found in one of his pants pockets.

Officer Spear, one of the policemen who helped take Sacco and Vanzetti off the streetcar and put them in the police car, corroborated Connolly's statement that Sacco reached under his overcoat; that Connolly told him to keep his hands outside; and that Sacco told Connolly he had no gun. He also corroborated Connolly's testimony as to the search of Sacco at the police station and the finding of the Colt revolver and the twenty-two extra cartridges.

Chief Stewart of the Bridgewater police force testified to his questioning of Sacco and Vanzetti after their arrest. He said he first talked to Vanzetti. Vanzetti told him that

---

[32] At this point in the testimony Vanzetti shouted at the witness, "You are a liar!"

when he and Sacco were arrested they were on their way to Bridgewater to see a man named Pappi, whom he (Vanzetti) had known for a long time and once worked with in Plymouth. He denied knowing Boda or having seen him or a motorcycle on the night of May 5. The witness testified that in response to his questions Sacco told him that Vanzetti was his friend and had asked him to go with him to see Pappi; that he had never been in Bridgewater before; that he did not know Boda or Orciani, and that he had seen no motorcycle that night or at any time within the previous week.

Vanzetti on his direct examination testified he was at Sacco's house on May 5. About 4:30 P.M. Orciani and Boda drove up in Orciani's motorcycle. At 7:00 P.M. they all left for Bridgewater. Orciani and Boda went in the motorcycle and he and Sacco took the streetcar to Brockton. At Brockton they went into a lunchroom for some cigars and coffee, and while they were there he drafted a notice calling for a public meeting of radicals at Boston on the following Sunday. Later they got on the street car for Bridgewater. While on the car he redrafted the notice and gave it to Sacco to fill in the name of the hall—which he had left blank—and arrange for its printing and distribution.[33]

Vanzetti further testified they got off at Elm Square, expecting to meet Boda and Orciani there and go with them to get Boda's automobile. When they did not see Boda and Orciani they walked toward Brockton, and in front of a house they had never seen before they saw the motorcycle and Boda and Orciani. Boda went to the door of the house and talked to a man he later learned was Johnson. Then Boda came back to where he and Sacco were standing and told them that Johnson had said the car could not be taken out because it did not have new license

---

[33] This is the first suggestion in the record of the so-called radical activities of Vanzetti and Sacco. The subject was introduced by the defendants themselves.

numbers. Boda then said he and Orciani would take the motorcycle and Sacco and he (Vanzetti) should take the streetcar and go home. Boda said he would get some new license plates, and when he was ready he would let them know.

They had intended to use Boda's automobile, Vanzetti said, to call at the houses of a number of their friends in five or six neighboring towns. These friends had radical literature, and they intended to get it and take it away and secrete it in some "proper place" where policemen could not find it. At that time, said Vanzetti, police were searching the homes of many men who were active in the radical, Socialist and labor movements and those who had been caught with radical literature in their possession had been arrested, misused in jail and deported. Vanzetti had learned this from reading the newspapers and while he was in New York on April 27 as the representative of a committee of Boston radicals, who were interested in the defense of Salsedo and Elia whom he termed "political prisoners."

Vanzetti further testified that after Boda and Orciani left them, he and Sacco walked about a mile to a streetcar and got on the car to go to Brockton. He had never been on that car before. After a few minutes some police officers got on the car. One of them pointed a revolver at him and said, "Don't move, you dirty thing." Shortly after that the car stopped; and three or four policemen took them off the car, put them in a police patrol car and took them to the Brockton police station. When they got there he was put in a cell and Chief Stewart and the other policemen started to question him. When he answered one of them called him a liar, another "acted like he was going to take a punch" at him, another threatened him with a revolver and another said that in the morning they would put him in a line between chairs and shoot him.

Vanzetti denied that after his arrest he reached toward

his hip pocket and that any police officer told him to keep his hands in his lap or he would be sorry. He said he repeatedly asked the police what he had been arrested for, and they would not tell him. He admitted he had lied to the police officers and the district attorney. He said he had not told the truth about his movements on May 5, and about not knowing Boda and Orciani, and about the motorcycle. He admitted that the story he had told them about where he had got the Richardson & Harrington revolver was false; as was also his statement that he and Sacco were on their way to see Pappi when they were arrested. He admitted he did not tell the police anything about the radical literature or the plan to collect and secrete it. He did this, he said, because "feeling was high against the Socialist element" and he feared deportation, and that if he gave the names of any of his friends they, too, would be arrested and mistreated. Vanzetti also testified on his direct examination that he and Sacco left Plymouth in 1917 and went to Mexico to evade the draft; and when the police and the district attorney questioned him he was also in fear that he might be arrested and punished for that offense. That, he said, was another reason why he had given false answers to their questions.

On cross-examination Vanzetti admitted he lied when he was asked how long he had known Sacco and had answered a year and a half; that he had actually known him three or four years. He said he lied because he and Sacco had been draft dodgers together in 1917. He reluctantly admitted that the lie he told the district attorney about when and where he had got the revolver which was found on him at the time of his arrest had no relationship to his fears of punishment because of his radical activities or because he had been a draft dodger.

On redirect examination Vanzetti testified that when he was in New York in the latter part of April, he was told there would be many arrests of radicals after May 1;

and he was "set wise" that if he or any of his friends had radical literature they should put it in some place where it could not be found by the police. He said he had learned on May 4 that Salsedo had committed suicide by jumping from an upper-story window in the Department of Justice Building in New York to escape police brutality, and these things had made him apprehensive. When he was asked by the police on May 5 if he was a Socialist, an I.W.W., a radical, a Communist or a Blackhander, he thought his arrest was for a "political matter," and that was why he had lied to the police and the district attorney.

Sacco, in his direct examination, testified he had known Orciani for seven years and Boda for three. The purpose of the trip to Johnson's house was to get Boda's car and then to call on various friends who had radical literature, to collect it and find a safe place in which to secrete it. Among others, he said he intended to see Mike Colombo and Rocco Delasandro. Orciani had suggested Boda because Boda was an active Socialist. On May 2, at a meeting in Boston, Vanzetti—who had been in New York to find out who was getting the money for the defense of the two Socialists, Salsedo and Elia—reported that a spy had found out about the activities of the radicals in Boston; and he (Vanzetti) had been advised by people in New York to hide all radical literature where it could not be found by the police. Sacco told of his arrest on the streetcar. He denied that he had ever ridden on that car before. He also denied that while in the police patrol car he had reached for his revolver.

Sacco further testified as follows: When the police got him to the station he was asked by Chief of Police Stewart and others why he was in Bridgewater and if he was a Socialist. He told them he was a Socialist and was going with Vanzetti to see Vanzetti's friend Pappi. He admitted that in a later conversation with the district attorney he did not answer truthfully all of the questions put to him and did not give the names of any of his friends, because the police would not tell him what he was charged with. He thought this was because he was a radical and that they were treating him as they were treating radicals in New York. Many of his friends were radicals and slackers like himself and to have told their names might have resulted in their arrest or deportation. He had known several persons—Fruzetti, Papetti, Coacci and Mondanari—who had been deported because they were radicals.

Sacco testified on cross-examination that after returning from Mexico, where he had gone with Vanzetti to evade the draft, he assumed the name of Masmacotelli and worked under that name at various places in Massachusetts, including Rice & Hutchins' factory in South Braintree. He had worked there for seven or eight days. Under some provoking questions from the district attorney, Sacco launched into a long harangue in which he stated his creed: He did not believe in war and killing his fellow men. He had been disillusioned by his life in America. In Italy the working man was better off, because he had better food and did not have to work so hard. The best men in America—Debs, for example—were in prison because they were Socialists. Men were sent to die in prison because of their opinions. The capitalistic class—men like Rockefeller and Morgan—did not want the mass of the people educated; they wanted to keep the masses in slavery. It was the capitalists who wanted wars, and they started them for their own profit.

Sacco also testified he subscribed to and read socialistic and anarchistic literature and had some in his home on the evening of May 5. He said he was afraid when he was arrested that it was because he was a radical; that he might be deported like Fruzetti who—Sacco said—was an anarchist; and that "anarchistic was not criminal." He admitted he had repeatedly lied to the district attorney. He had lied about his movements on May 5 when he said he and Vanzetti were intending to call on Pappi. He had lied when he told about when and where he had got the Colt revolver and the cartridges. He had lied when he denied that he had ever worked for Rice & Hutchins at South Braintree. He had lied when he denied knowing where Orciani lived and said that he had never been to his house. He had lied when he said that Vanzetti did not know Orciani. He had lied when he said he had only known Vanzetti for a short time. He had lied when he told the judge at the preliminary hearing that he did not know he had to have a permit for carrying a gun. All these lies, he said, he told because he assumed he was being arrested for his radical activities or because he was a draft dodger, and he did not want to give any information against himself which might subject him to punishment or deportation or which would implicate his friends.

In corroboration, the defendants offered the testimony of a New York attorney, Walter Nelles, that in April 1920 he had been retained to defend Salsedo, and shortly before Salsedo's death on May 3 he had talked with Luigi Quintilino, a representative of the Italian Defense Committee and advised him to dispose of any radical literature he might have. Quintilino took the stand to corroborate Nelles. He testified he had seen Vanzetti in New York on April 27 and had repeated to him what Nelles had said.

Rocco Delasandro, Michael Colombo and Pardo Montagano testified they knew Sacco, and that they had talked to him and among themselves of collecting radical literature which was in the hands of their friends and secreting it where it could not be found by the police. Frank Lopez, a member of the Italian Defense Committee, testified he saw both Sacco and Vanzetti in a meeting in Boston on April 20 and talked to Vanzetti about his contemplated trip to New York in behalf of Salsedo and about securing all outstanding radical literature and putting it in a safe place. George T. Kelly, of the 3 K Shoe Factory in Stoughton, testified he told Sacco several months before April

1920 that his activities in the radical movement were being investigated.

Stewart, the chief of the Bridgewater Police Department, recalled by the Commonwealth in rebuttal, denied Vanzetti's testimony that during his interrogation on May 5 anyone had called Vanzetti a liar, or acted as though he were going to strike him, or had threatened him with a revolver, or told him that he would be put in a line between chairs and shot. He also testified he had asked Vanzetti if he were an anarchist, and Vanzetti had answered, "Well, I don't know what you call it. I like things a little different." Stewart also testified Vanzetti told him that he sometimes read anarchistic papers which a man gave him. Sacco, Chief Stewart testified, in answer to the same question, said, "Some things in the United States government I like a little different."

When Sacco was searched at the Brockton police station, the police found in one of his pockets the draft of a circular calling for a radical meeting in Boston. It was translated from the Italian, the translation was agreed to as correct by both sides and, on the offer of the Commonwealth, it was received in evidence. It read as follows:

Fellow War Workers: You have fought all the wars. You have worked for all the capitalists. You have wandered over all countries. Have you harvested the fruits of your labors, the price of your victories? Does the past comfort you? Does the future smile on you? Does the future promise you anything? Have you found a piece of land where you can live like a human being and die like a human being? On these questions, on these arguments, on this theme—the struggle for existence—Bartolomeo Vanzetti will speak at the hour,_____ day_____, Hall_____. Admission free. Freedom of discussion to all. Bring the ladies with you.

The above was all of the evidence admitted on the theory that the actions of the defendants at the time of and immediately after their arrest indicated a consciousness of guilt. The issue, as is apparent, was whether the evidence indicated a consciousness of guilt of the Braintree robbery and murders, or a consciousness of guilt as possessors and secreters of anarchistic literature or as draft evaders. The Commonwealth contended for the first. The defendants contended for the latter alternative. The Court left the determination of the issue to the jury.

Both Sacco and Vanzetti offered their own and supporting testimony to establish alibis.

Sacco testified in substance as follows: His mother had died on March 7, 1920. He heard of her death by letter during the last part of March or the first part of April. He and his wife had for some time been talking of going back to Italy. His mother's death and the added news that his aged father was not well determined them to leave for Italy immediately and reside there permanently. He said that he had arranged with his employer, George Kelly, to be off from work April 15 in order that he might visit the Italian consulate in Boston and arrange for passports for himself and family. He took a Boston-bound train at Stoughton at 8:56 on the morning of April 15 and arrived in Boston at 9:35.

He described his subsequent movements: He met a friend—one Monello—and went "shopping" with him. Around noon he went to Boni's Restaurant and there met a Professor Guadenagi and later one Williams and one Bosco. He stayed in the restaurant until about 1:30 P.M. and then went to the office of the Italian consulate. There he saw an official who told him the photographs he had brought for his passports were too large, and it would be necessary for him to have some smaller ones made. He was in the consul's office about ten minutes. After leaving the consul's office he went out and bought some groceries, met a man named Affe, to whom he paid a bill, and sometime around three went into an Italian coffee shop, where he again met Guadenagi who was in the company of a man named Dentamore. He spent about twenty-five or thirty minutes with them and at 4:12 P.M. took a train for Stoughton and arrived at his home around six o'clock.

Sacco testified that a few days before he took the stand he had pointed out to Jeremiah McAnarney a man in the courtroom—later identified as James M. Hayes—who looked very much like a man he saw on the train on April 15 when he was returning from Boston to Stoughton. He denied specifically that he had been in South Braintree or near there at any time on April 15, or that he saw Vanzetti anywhere on that day.

On cross-examination Sacco testified he had gone to the Italian consulate in Boston three times in all—once in the first part of March, once on April 15 and once at a later date. He said that the pictures which he took to the consul's office on April 15 had been made in February before his mother died, and that no one in the consul's office had told him, on his first visit, the kind and size of photographs which would be required for his passport. He admitted that when he arranged with Kelly to be absent from work on April 15 he told him he would hurry and try to get back in the afternoon; but he had wasted the entire morning by wandering around in Boston and had made no attempt to see anyone in the consulate. When he saw Kelly the following day he told him that there was such a crowd in the consul's office that he missed the noon train. He admitted this was a lie and could give no reason for telling it. He also admitted that when on May 6 the district attorney asked him if he had worked on the day before he read in the papers of the Braintree murders (which was April 16) he had answered first, "I think I did," and later, "Sure." This, he said, was also untrue, but at the time he was questioned—twenty days after the event—he did not remember. Later, he said, he considered it carefully and knew April 15 was the date he went into Boston to get his passport.

Sacco called as witnesses to substantiate his alibi Monello, Guadenago, Williams, Bosco, Affe and Dentamore. By association with other events, to which they attached special significance, these men declared positively that they saw Sacco in Boston on April 15 at various times between ten o'clock in the morning and four o'clock in the afternoon. All were more or less shaken by searching cross-examinations of the district attorney which were calculated to raise considerable doubt as to whether their meetings with Sacco had actually occurred on April 15.

Dominick Ricci, a carpenter of Needham, Massachusetts, testified he had known Sacco for about two years, and that he saw him on the railroad station platform at Stoughton between 7:15 and 7:40 on the morning of April 15 and talked to Sacco about his passport. Ricci said he fixed the date by the fact that he saw Sacco the next day, April 16, and they talked about the Braintree holdup which had taken place the day before.

In his deposition taken in Rome, Italy, Guiseppi Andrower deposed that on April 15, 1920, he was a clerk in the office of the Italian consulate in Boston and was one of the clerks who handled passport applications; that he handled between 150 and 200 such applications daily. Andrower, in his deposition, made the following statements: Sacco came into the office on April 15 and showed him some photographs which were too large for passport purposes, and he told Sacco that he would have to get others. He had not known Sacco before, and Sacco was only in the office for six or seven minutes. He was sure of the date.

There was no testimony as to how Andrower fixed the date. He gave an accurate description of Sacco: well-built, medium-sized, dark-complexioned and clean-shaved.

James M. Hayes, whom Sacco had pointed out in the courtroom, gave his business as a mason-contractor and testified he was on a train going from Boston to Stoughton between five and six o'clock on April 15. He did not know that Sacco was on that train. The district attorney brought out what apparently seemed to him suspicious circumstances with respect to this witness: He had been in the courtroom during the drawing of the jury. He said he had come to Dedham to see a man named Woodbury, who was connected with the defense and with whom he had some unrelated business. He said he had become interested and had returned later to listen to the trial.

Sacco's wife corroborated his story that they had talked for some time about going back to Italy, and that their plans were hastened by the death of Sacco's mother and Sacco's expressed wish to see his father before he died. She also produced a savings bankbook which showed a balance of something over $1,500. The aggregate was made up of regular weekly deposits which commenced early in 1918.

In rebuttal the Commonwealth offered in evidence a portion of the stenographic transcript of the interview between Sacco and the district attorney on May 6. It showed that at that time Sacco said he had never taken more than one full day off from his work to go to Boston to see about his passport, and he thought that that day was in the beginning of the month of April; also, that he had said he read of the Braintree murders on April 16 and felt sure he had been working at Stoughton the day before.

Vanzetti's alibi was less plausible and less well supported than Sacco's. This was Vanzetti's story: He peddled fish in Plymouth and the surrounding neighborhood on April 13, 14 and 15. On the fifteenth, as he was pushing his cart along one of the streets of North Plymouth, he met a cloth peddler whom he knew and bought a piece of woolen suiting from him. Before he closed the purchase he took the cloth to the house of a Mrs. Brini, so that she might examine it. She approved it, and he completed the purchase. It was then about one o'clock. After that he went out and sold the rest of his fish, and then called at the house of a man named Corl on the seashore. Corl was painting a boat.

During the ensuing hour in which he talked with him, two other men—one Jesse and one Holmes—came by. Later he took his fish cart and went to his boarding place in Plymouth, changed his clothes and stayed there all night. He denied he was in South Braintree at any time on April 15 or had ever been there, or that he and Sacco had been anywhere together on that day. He also denied that he was in a Buick driven over the Mattfield Crossing near West Bridgewater on April 15 at about 4:15 P.M., as testified by Commonwealth's witness Reed.

Vanzetti gave a more or less detailed description of his movements for every day after April 15 until he was arrested on May 5. Apparently he was unemployed during this period. He attended a number of radical meetings in Boston and from April 25 to 27 was in New York as representative of one of these groups interested in the defense of Salsedo and Elia. On cross-examination he admitted that the members of the Brini family were close friends of his, and that he had once boarded with them. He also admitted that shortly after his arrest he told the district attorney he could not remember where he was on the Thursday before Patriots' Day (April 19) but figured it out afterward.

Vanzetti called twelve witnesses to substantiate his alibi. Only five of these were at all definite in their recollection of having seen Vanzetti in North Plymouth or Plymouth on April 15. The principal witness was Joseph Rosen, an itinerant peddler of woolens, who supported Vanzetti's testimony as to the purchase of a piece of suiting from him on April 15. Rosen testified he fixed the date by a poll-tax receipt which he remembered he paid on the same day. He produced the receipt, which bore a date stamp of April 15, 1920. The district attorney cross-examined on collateral details and happenings on other days. There were a great many "I don't remembers," but the witness held stoutly to his story that he had read of Vanzetti's arrest shortly after it happened and that the tax receipt and the fact that he had rented a room in Plymouth and slept there that night fixed in his mind the date on which he had sold the cloth to Vanzetti.

Mrs. Alphonsine Brini testified Vanzetti came to her house between eleven and twelve o'clock on April 15 and showed her a piece of cloth he was thinking of buying from a peddler who was with him; that the man looked like Rosen. She said she remembered the date was the fifteenth, because she had been home from the hospital only a week, again became sick on the fourteenth and called for a doctor who visited her on the fifteenth.

La Favre Brini, daughter of Mrs. Alphonsine Brini, testified she saw Vanzetti in Plymouth at her house between 10:00 and 10:30 on the morning of April 15 and bought some fish from him. She said she remembered the date because her mother was sick; that she had called the doctor the day before; and her father had called for a nurse on the fifteenth, and the nurse came on that day. On cross-examination the district attorney developed that the witness regarded Vanzetti almost in the light of a relative. He subjected her to an examination on collateral details and other dates, which showed she had a very poor memory for anything that had happened in April outside of her mother's illness and the purchase of fish from Vanzetti on the fifteenth. Mary Matthews, a nurse, testified she called on Mrs. Brini some time between the fifteenth and twentieth of April. She could not be any more certain than that about the date.

Melvin Corl, a Plymouth fisherman, testified he knew Vanzetti and had sold him fish. He said that on the afternoon of April 15 Vanzetti came to where he was painting a boat. He remembered that Jesse came by, and he heard Jesse and Vanzetti talking together about an automobile. On cross-examination it was developed that the only way the witness fixed the date was by the fact that he had put his boat in the water a week before. Corl learned of Vanzetti's arrest on May 6 and figured the days back. On a collateral examination on details and events on other days, the witness showed a complete lack of memory.

Angel Guidobone, a laborer in a rug factory at Plymouth, testified he had known Vanzetti for five or six years, and he saw him in Plymouth on April 15 selling fish. He said he remembered the date because Vanzetti put a codfish in his hand at thirteen or fourteen minutes past twelve; also, that he had had a surgical operation on April 19. On cross-examination he insisted that the fact of his operation on the nineteenth enabled him to fix the fifteenth as the date on which he had seen Vanzetti and Vanzetti had put the fish in his hand. He also declared it must have been Thursday, because he always bought fish on Thursday to eat on Friday.

The foregoing summarizes all of the vital evidence received upon the trial. One additional item deserves mention. Each of the defendants before he took the stand called several witnesses who testified that his reputation as a peaceful and law-abiding citizen was good. In the cross-examination of Mrs. Brini—one of Vanzetti's alibi witnesses—the district attorney asked her if she had not testified on Vanzetti's behalf in a previous case. The defendants objected to the question, and a conference, out of the presence of the jury, resulted in which both parties and the Court expressed a desire to keep from the jury any information respecting the Bridgewater trial in which Vanzetti had been convicted.

It was recognized that it would have been proper to ask Vanzetti's good-reputation witnesses on cross-examination if they had ever heard this offense discussed in connection with his reputation. Counsel for the defendants, therefore, asked that all the good-reputation testimony be stricken and the jury instructed to disregard it. This was agreed to by the district attorney, and the Court so charged the jury. It was also stipulated that the record might show that Mrs. Brini had testified for Vanzetti on another trial. It was further stipulated between counsel—but not made a matter of record—that no further reference should be made to Vanzetti's former trial and conviction.

All of the evidence was concluded on July 11, and on July 13 the attorneys commenced their summations. There was no opening for the Commonwealth. Moore, on behalf of Sacco, made the initial argument. His promised dispassionate review of the Commonwealth's evidence was a selection and discussion of the witnesses who had made no positive identification of Sacco, or of those who had identified him but had—Moore asserted—been so completely impeached as to be unworthy of belief. Of Dolbeare, Tracy and Heron, who did not fall into these categories, he said little or nothing. Bostock and Behrsin, who had made no identification of Sacco, were characterized as "high-grade," "clean-cut," "fine" and "honest" men. Faulkner, Mrs. Andrews, Pelser, and Goodridge, he said, had been completely eliminated by impeaching testimony. Miss Splaine and Miss Devlin, he claimed, had been too far away to render their descriptions and identifications of any value; moreover, both had been impeached by contradictory statements they had made before the trial and Miss Splaine "was one of your positive type of women who knows everything." Moore declared, "You could not take away a human life on such testimony as that."

Moore discussed briefly the witnesses called by the defense. Sensing an atmosphere of prejudice against the Italian witnesses, he first referred to Burke, Pierce, Ferguson, Miss Liscomb, O'Neill, Chase, Olsen, Gibson, Dorr and Desmond. "I have not," he said, "mentioned a foreign name yet; I have only mentioned English stock and Anglo-American stock, but there are also the DiBonas, Falcone,

Miss Novelli, Cellucci, Magnerelli, Antonello and Frabizio, and all say none of the bandits was Sacco."

Moore declared there was not a scintilla of evidence to connect Boda with the Buick. He admitted that Sacco had lied to the police and the district attorney, but he said Sacco did it out of fear and apprehension of punishment for matters entirely unrelated to the Braintree murders. Vanzetti, Moore said, had been told to have his friends get rid of their radical literature; Sacco had got this information from Vanzetti. Sacco had a quantity of such literature. He had read of Salsedo's fate—his dead body found crushed on a New York sidewalk in front of the Department of Justice Building window. Kelly had told him he was being investigated for his radical activities. Sacco knew that he and Vanzetti had fled to Mexico in 1917 to evade the draft and were liable to prosecution for it. These, Moore said, were the things Sacco had in his mind on May 5; that is why he lied to the police and Katzmann. Those facts, he declared, "justified all of Sacco's lies."

Moore reviewed briefly the alibi testimony and concluded:

Why, gentlemen, what have you got to do in this case in order to return a verdict? You have got to say that the whole Kelly family lied. You have got to say that some twenty-odd witnesses called in connection with various movements of the defendants are all liars—unequivocal, unmitigated and unfaltering liars—and on top of that you have got to say that the counsel have aided, abetted, advised and encouraged their perjury. . . . Bosco, Dentamore, Williams, Affe, Kelly, Hayes and the consul's deposition have all told you about Sacco's movements on April 15. You have got to say that all these men committed perjury. . . . You have got to say that these men who knew Sacco, these men who have talked with Sacco, that these men— some Americans and some Italians—have stooped to the commission of perjury, and the dragging of justice in the mire, in order to save these men. You have got to say that Mary Splaine, Lola Andrews and this fellow Goodridge, and all of these people who never saw the defendant before—and when they did see him only saw him for a matter of seconds—that they are right and that the defendant and Dentamore and all the others are wrong.

Jeremiah McAnarney, counsel for Vanzetti, followed Moore. His argument was as much one for Sacco as for his own client. Early in his presentation he paid high tribute to Judge Thayer: "one of the most learned judges we have, one whose ability is acknowledged by the bar, by the judges of the Supreme and superior courts, and every court in this land."

McAnarney faced frankly what he conceived to be the real difficulty of the defense.

At the start we may say, "What case is this?" There was a shooting over in Braintree on the fifteenth of April; one Berardelli and one Parmenter were shot. We have drifted miles away from that case, miles away. We had almost forgotten that those men had been shot; and we have drifted, we have drifted with the tide, and we have drifted just exactly where this case belongs. We have drifted right to the issue. We have drifted to the reason these men were arrested. We have drifted to the fact that these men are radicals; and that they were apprehended because they were radicals, as every bit of this evidence—when it is weighed—absolutely proves. You cannot kick a ball around five or six weeks but what it will get its level. You cannot play with this case as a case of murder at Braintree for five or six weeks and conceal the true issue in this case. This case cannot be won on the facts of that shooting or that identification at Braintree. You would not kill a dog on that identification at Braintree.

McAnarney then proceeded to discuss the uncertainties and impeachments of the testimony of the Commonwealth's witnesses: Miss Splaine, Miss Devlin, Mrs. Andrews, Levangie and Goodridge. He stressed the testimony of the Commonwealth's witnesses Bostock and McGlone and the defense's witnesses Mrs. Novello, Miss Liscomb and Chase. All of these were either unable to identify Sacco or Vanzetti or, along with a score of others, swore positively that none of the bandits they saw was either of the defendants.

He referred to and argued fully and intelligently the testimony of the various ballistics experts which he termed "highly conflicting opinion testimony at best" and certainly "not the kind of evidence upon which to send a fellow human being to death." McAnarney argued the absurdity of the Commonwealth's contention that Sacco, who had worked at Rice & Hutchins factory and was known to some of its employees there, would chance a robbery in broad daylight and put himself in the central spot of observation. He reviewed Sacco's record as a hard-working man; that he certainly was not a man of the "bandit type."

He met the implications the jurors were apt to draw from the frequent references in the testimony to the activities of the Sacco-Vanzetti Defense Committee. It was natural and commendable for Sacco's friends to rally to his defense when they were certain he had been unjustly accused. McAnarney recognized frankly the natural resentment of the jurors toward the defendants as radicals and draft dodgers, but he asked them to remember that the word *radicalism* was indefinite and relative, that the "legislation of today is the radicalism of fifty years ago," and throughout the history of the world there have been men who sincerely believed and were willing to die for their belief that it was wrong to kill one's fellow beings even in war; that a man they might despise as a slacker might possess high moral courage.

"No more popular thing was ever given to a district attorney to play a note to a jury on than this case," declared McAnarney. "He can stand up to this rail and say to you, 'Gentlemen, what have we been here for six weeks for? For two men who did not think enough of their country but what they would go to Mexico—murderers, slackers, anarchists.' Ring the changes on that, gentlemen, and you can play any tune you want to on it. And you have got to be very careful that you don't vibrate in unison with those words. They are fearful, they are potent, they are laden to the limit. But these men are not to be punished because they are radicals or because they were slackers. . . . They are entitled to be condemned for that as hard as you want to condemn them . . . but does that prove, gentlemen, that they killed over in South Braintree?"

McAnarney's argument was direct, courageous and challenging. The issues as they might have been formed in the jurors' minds had to be faced. If argument could have won the case, his was the type of argument best calculated to the purpose.

The nature of the case would have led many elected prosecutors to seize the opportunity offered for a display of extravagant and sensational rhetoric. The summation of District Attorney Katzmann was quite otherwise. It was fair advocacy—responsible, restrained, dignified. He began with a fine tribute to the presiding judge whom he said was "a learned justice" with "a kindly heart and an inherent sense of justice that cannot be swerved from the impartial performance of duty to both parties to a case." He stated, without reservation, the obligation of the Commonwealth to prove the defendants guilty beyond a reasonable doubt and to a degree of moral certainty which excluded any reasonable hypothesis of innocence.

The Commonwealth's claim, said the district attorney, was that Sacco fired from a Colt thirty-two-caliber automatic revolver one of the bullets which killed Berardelli; that some other person—not apprehended—fired from a Savage automatic the shots which killed Parmenter; that there was no evidence Vanzetti fired any firearm that killed either Berardelli or Parmenter, but that "he was there, aiding and abetting, ready to aid and in law equally as guilty as Sacco who pulled the trigger of the gun that shot and killed Berardelli."

Katzmann took up in order and discussed the testimony of the defendants' witnesses who had sworn to having seen either the shooting or the escaping automobile. The men who were in the restaurant excavation, he said, were in hopeless disagreement, and the fact, as he believed it, was to be had from the testimony of Horace Colbert and Mrs. Nichols: that as soon as the shooting started every man in the excavation turned his back and ran as fast as he could toward the Nichols' house and a place of safety. Similarly, as to the eighteen or twenty railroad-track laborers of whom the defense had produced eight or ten, the believable testimony was that of Ricci, their foreman, which was corroborated by the sailor Cellucci: that none of them, except possibly Cellucci, dropped his work and, against the foreman's shouted protest, ran deliberately 350 feet or more into the "shooting zone."

Frantello's evidence, Katzmann said, was a joke. He contrasted the "magnificent description" Frantello gave of the two strangers who were beside the fence with the "pitiful exhibition" he made when he attempted to describe accurately two of the jurors. Burke, the glass blower, Katzmann said, had disagreed with every other witness in his description of the man who sat on the right-hand side of the driver. Chase, when shown a picture of Sacco, had told Chief of Police Stewart that the hair of the man he saw resembled that of Sacco, and that was all he could tell. It was impossible, stated the district attorney, for Dorr to have formed an impression sufficient for him to give a detailed description of the four men in the escaping automobile when he admitted it went by him at a speed of fifty miles an hour. Miss Novelli had been impeached by Hillyer, the Pinkerton detective, who testified he showed her a picture of Sacco and she said it resembled very much the man she had seen in the automobile. The testimony of the defense's witness O'Neill, said Katzmann—that he saw a man on the rear seat of the automobile open the door while he was inside the car, get out, close the door and then walk on the running board toward the front seat—was utterly incredible. The jurors had looked at the automobile immediately after that testimony had been given and had seen for themselves that the story was impossible.

Katzmann put the Commonwealth's case on identification directly against the witnesses produced by the defense. Levangie, he said, was obviously mistaken in his identification of Vanzetti as the driver of the automobile. But, he said, there was the convincing testimony of Pelser, Heron, Miss Splaine, Miss Devlin, Tracy, Lola Andrews and Goodridge that one of the bandits was Sacco. Neither Heron nor Tracy, he said, had been impeached in any way; and Miss Splaine and Miss Devlin were "fine women" with no possible interest in the case except to tell the truth. He characterized Mrs. Andrews as "one of the most convincing witnesses I have ever seen" and defended her and Pelser and Goodridge against the alleged impeachment of their testimony by defense witnesses.

Faulkner, Dolbeare, and Reed, Katzmann declared, had been positive in their identification of Vanzetti; and all were fine respectable citizens, without interest in the case, and none of them had in any way been impeached. Dolbeare, he added, had been summoned originally as one of the jury panel and excused because of his personal knowledge of material evidence in the case; he was the same "type of man" as the jurors themselves.

The district attorney next discussed the weapons and ammunition found on the defendants at the time of their arrest. Of some facts, he said, there could be no question. These facts were: A fully loaded thirty-two-caliber Colt automatic revolver and twenty-two extra cartridges had been found on Sacco. A fully loaded Harrington & Richardson revolver and four twelve-gauge shotgun shells had been found on Vanzetti. Berardelli had owned and carried a thirty-eight-caliber Harrington & Richardson revolver. Berardelli had been killed with a bullet discharged from a Colt automatic thirty-two-caliber revolver. A shotgun had been seen sticking out of the rear window opening of the escaping bandit car.

Katzmann ridiculed Vanzetti's contention that he had bought the Harrington & Richardson revolver from Falzini who bought it from the "elusive Orciani." The identity of the gun, the district attorney stated, had been conclusively established by the three disinterested witnesses from the Iver-Johnson Sporting Goods Store in Boston who testified that a thirty-eight-caliber Harrington & Richardson revolver had been brought in for repair. It most certainly had been redelivered to Berardelli. The store did not have it now and there was no record that it had been sold as uncalled-for repaired merchandise. Moreover, said the district attorney, Bostock, a witness to whom the defense had given a certificate of honesty, had testified that Berardelli showed him a Harrington & Richardson revolver, which looked just like the gun in evidence, on the Saturday before the shooting and told him he always carried it. He dismissed the testimony of defense witness Aldeah Florence as an obvious fabrication.

District Attorney Katzmann went into the testimony of the ballistics experts in great detail, contrasting the "evasive testimony" of the defense witness with the "positive testimony" of the Commonwealth's experts and—after his own demonstrations—invited the jurors when they retired to their jury room to examine and compare the scorings and pit marks on bullet number three, which had been taken from Berardelli's body, with the "test bullets" and decide for themselves whether or not the fatal bullet had been fired from Sacco's Colt revolver.

The cap found near Berardelli's body had its significance, said the district attorney. Whose cap was it, he in-

quired, if it were not Sacco's? Kelly, Sacco's friend, had
said it looked like Sacco's cap. While Sacco had made a
great show on the witness stand of trying on the cap and
saying it was too small, the best test was for any juror with
a seven-and-one-eighth head size to try on all three caps in
evidence—two of which were admittedly Sacco's; he would
find all three caps fitted equally well.

Katzmann next discussed the defendants' alibis. They
were, he said, afterthoughts, the frantic effort of friendly and interested witnesses to aid the defendants; but the
circumstances alleged and relied on to fix upon April 15 as
the date on which they had seen either Sacco or Vanzetti
were unconvincing. He ridiculed the deposition of the
consular clerk: Out of an average of 150 or 200 applications a day for passports he had pretended to remember the
case of one man whom he had never seen before and then
had seen for only six or seven minutes. That the clerk had
remembered him because the photographs he brought with
his application were too large was absurd, said the district
attorney. How many uninstructed applicants did the jury
think brought in unsuitable photographs? How could that
undoubtedly common incident fix in anyone's mind a date
for a routine transaction? Strange, too, declared the advocate, that no opening statement had been made on behalf
of Vanzetti, that no intimation had been given of his alibi
until after he commenced his testimony, and that his attorney had not seen fit to mention it in his argument.

Katzmann devoted much of his time to a discussion of
the evidence of the actions of the defendants just preceding, during and after their arrest which showed a consciousness of guilt of the Braintree murders. The following is the evidence cited by Katzmann: Their visit, they
being fully armed, to the Johnson house and their furtive
actions there on the night of May 5 were suspicious. When
arrested each of the defendants had reached for his weapon
and was probably restrained from using it only because

Officer Connolly "had the drop" on him. When they got to the station and were questioned, they lied about almost everything that was asked them.

The district attorney declared the defense offered for this mass of lies—that Sacco and Vanzetti told them because they had a consciousness of guilt as the possessors and se-creters of radical literature—"was born after the defense opened." Why, otherwise, inquired he, did the defense counsel cross-examine the Johnsons for hours on the de-tails of what they now conceded was truthful testimony?

He followed this with other questions and answers: Would a consciousness only of guilt of handling anarchistic literature and of draft evasion have led them to reach for their revolvers when they were arrested? Why should Sacco fear deportation? He was going to Italy anyway; and he had a one-way passport in his pocket and had no intention of returning. Orciani had figured prominently in Sacco's and Vanzetti's testimony. It was he who suggested getting Boda and his automobile. It was he who was going to help assemble and hide the radical literature. It was he, with his motorcycle, who was at the Johnson house with Sacco and Vanzetti and who, with them, followed Mrs. Johnson when she went to and from the Bartlett house. It was he who was supposed to have sold the Harrington & Richardson re-volver to Falzini which Falzini testified he sold to Vanzetti. Why had not the defense called Orciani? He was available since he was in Dedham, and he had been seen in the court-house yard while defense testimony was being given. The answer was plain: The defendants had not called him be-cause they were afraid his testimony would harm them. Their failure to call him was a circumstance the jury might properly consider.

Katzmann's peroration was eloquent:

If the Commonwealth has satisfied you beyond a reason-able doubt that they are guilty, the Commonwealth expects you to say so like men of honor and men of courage. And the Commonwealth expects you to say they are not guilty if it has failed to satisfy you in accordance with the requirements of the law. Make a decision, gentlemen. This case can never be more ably tried in the interests of these defendants than it has been in this trial. They have both had their day in court, and the Commonwealth has had its day in court. Both parties desire a final decision on this accusation. . . .

The question is one of fact, gentlemen, to be arrived at under the rules of law. It has been said to you that your decision will take away the lives of two men if it be that of guilty. Well, gentlemen, that is not so in one sense. You are not taking away the lives of the defendants by finding them guilty of a murder of which they are guilty. The law takes their lives away, not you. It is for you to say they are guilty, and you are done. You pronounce no sentence of death. . . . You are the consultants here, gentlemen, the twelve of you, and the parties come to you and ask you to find what the truth is on the two issues of guilt or innocence. Gentlemen of the jury, do your duty. Do it like men. Stand together, you men of Norfolk.

Judge Thayer's charge to the jury was a complete statement of the law applicable to the case, with such references to the evidence as are permissible under Massachusetts law. At the outset, he cautioned the jury against permitting prejudice against the defendants because of their race or opinions to influence its verdict.

"Under our law," Judge Thayer declared, "all classes of society, the poor and the rich, the learned and the ignorant, the most powerful as well as the most humble, the believer as well as the unbeliever, the radical as well as the conservative, the foreign-born as well as the native-born, are entitled to and should receive in all trials . . . the same rights, privileges and consideration as the logic of the law, reason, sound judgment and common sense demand. I, therefore, beseech you not to allow the fact that the defendants are Italians to influence or prejudice you in the least degree. They are entitled, under the law, to the same rights and consideration as though their ancestors came over in the *Mayflower*."

The Court's instructions on the law as to consciousness of guilt were definite and incapable of misunderstanding. The jurors were told that if the evidence did not establish facts from which guilt might be reasonably inferred, they should eliminate from their consideration all evidence directed to establishing a consciousness of guilt on the part of the defendants; that the question was: Did the actions, speech and conduct of the defendants on the night of May 5 indicate that their (the defendants') minds were then conscious of having committed some crime.

That consciousness, the judge declared, had to be directed to the charge of murder; if directed only to the consciousness of being slackers or being liable to be deported "that is immaterial, because they are being tried for murder and for nothing else. The law requires that there must be a causal connection or some probative relationship between the evidence tending to prove a consciousness of guilt and the crime charged in the indictments." The Court concluded: "The determination of that, and all other questions of fact, is for you."

At the close of his charge Judge Thayer called all counsel to the bench and asked if they had any suggestions for corrections or additions to his charge. Moore raised some points of minor inaccuracies in the statements of the evidence. These the judge corrected, and at the same time told the jury it was not for the Court to state what the evidence was, nor for counsel to state it; that the jurors were to be guided by their recollections and thus determine for themselves what the evidence was. After he amended the charge Judge Thayer again asked if either side had any additional suggestions or objections. There was none, and at one o'clock on the afternoon of July 14 the jurors retired to their jury room in charge of a sworn custodian.

They had been out only a short time when they sent for a magnifying glass. Without objection from either party, it was furnished them.

At seven-thirty in the evening the jurors made known to the officer who had them in charge that they had reached a verdict. Slowly the twelve men filed into the court-room. There, in the presence of Judge Thayer, the several counsel and the defendants, the jury's determinations were formally announced—verdicts under both indictments which found the defendants guilty of first-degree murder.

The silence which followed the solemn pronouncement was broken by the shrill voice of Sacco: "They kill an innocent man! They kill two innocent men!"

Aftermath

A student of crime and criminal procedure will seek vainly for a parallel to the succession of amazing events which followed the conviction of Sacco and Vanzetti. Into the period between July 14, 1921, when the verdict was returned, and August 23, 1927, when the sentence of death was executed, were crowded and intermingled the extraordinary but entirely lawful efforts of their counsel and other well-meaning persons to obtain a new trial and the diverse efforts, lawful and unlawful, of Sacco's and Vanzetti's associates all over the world so to terrorize and intimidate the constituted authorities of Massachusetts and at Washington that they would be compelled to interfere to prevent the verdict from being given effect.

Some confusion must necessarily result from the lack of related continuity incident to the intermingling of these diverse events. In no other way, however, can the atmosphere of continuous agitation, uncertainty and tension which persisted through six long years be reproduced.

The Massachusetts associates of Sacco and Vanzetti rushed to their aid immediately after their arrest. The Sacco-Vanzetti Defense Committee was organized and began its operations May 7, 1920. The effectiveness of it can best be judged by the fact that between that date and July 31, 1925, it collected and disbursed more than $282,000.[34]

Immediately following the verdict counsel for Sacco and Vanzetti filed the customary motion for a new trial, urging as error every adverse ruling made by Judge Thayer during the trial and claiming that the verdict was contrary to the manifest weight of the evidence. There was apparently no disposition on anyone's part to hasten a decision on the motion, and it was not disposed of until the following December.

Meanwhile unexpected outbreaks and protests against the conviction emanated from surprising sources.[35] In Italy, during the month of October, speakers harangued street audiences in Milan, and the Milan and Rome press urged "American authorities" to grant a new trial. In France on October 19 American Ambassador Herrick's house in Paris was bombed, and he received messages threatening personal violence unless favorable action was taken promptly in behalf of Sacco and Vanzetti.

In Brest on October 21 Reds stormed the American consulate. On October 22 in a Red protest meeting in Paris a grenade was exploded, and twenty persons were injured. On the twenty-third another protest bomb was exploded in Marseilles. On the twenty-fourth four Communist members of the French Chamber of Deputies petitioned

---

[34] From an item in the New York *Times* of October 4, 1925, stating that the committee, through its secretary-treasurer, Felicano, had printed and released 10,000 copies of its financial statement for the period named. Among the larger items of disbursements listed are: $40,000 for "legal fees," $20,000 for "legal fees and expenses since the trial," $42,000 for "investigations before and after trial," $34,000 for "Fred H. Moore's personal expenses," $31,000 for "publicity and printing," and $16,000 for "salaries."

[35] The incidents which follow are taken from contemporary newspaper accounts which appeared chiefly in the New York *Times* and the Boston *Transcript*.

President Harding for Sacco's and Vanzetti's release. In Switzerland on October 23 and 29 there were protest meetings of the Reds in Basle, and demonstrators in front of the American embassy were dispersed by the police. In England a demonstration, planned to take place before the American embassy in London on October 22, was frustrated by the prompt action of the authorities.

In Argentina a protest meeting was held in Buenos Aires on October 29, which was followed by street rioting which lasted until November 1. In Uruguay on the same day the Montevideo Workmen's Federation called a general strike in protest, and the American consulate was menaced. In Havana on November 1 terrorists exploded a bomb near the headquarters of United States Representative Major General Crowder. In Mexico on November 8 and 27 the American consul at Tampico received warnings threatening him with death if Sacco and Vanzetti were executed. In Lisbon, Rotterdam, Brussels, Stockholm, Sofia, Prague, Athens, Morocco, Sydney and Lima there were protest meetings and rioting.

Strangely enough, the disturbances in the United States were not so widespread. Ever since the verdict Judge Thayer had been receiving threatening letters, and on October 22 his house was placed under guard, and the police detail around the courthouse was reinforced. On October 31 the police raided and dispersed a riotous protest meeting in Philadelphia. On November 22 in Chicago a protest meeting sponsored by the Friends of Soviet Russia was broken up by the police. Later in the month a protest mass meeting, made up chiefly of Italians, was held in New York City. A heavy detachment of police was on hand to prevent rioting, and there was none. These scattered and abortive efforts prompted the Workers' Defense Council, an organization active in the defendants' behalf, to publish in its official organ that "the United States campaign was altogether disappointing."

On December 24, 1921, after extensive oral and written arguments, Judge Thayer overruled the defendants' motion for a new trial. Immediately after the verdict was returned, Moore, aided by a staff of assistants and detectives and apparently unlimited funds provided by the Sacco-Vanzetti Defense Committee, commenced a search to discover new evidence and an investigation of the jurors and of the Commonwealth's witnesses to develop facts which could form the basis of supplemental motions for a new trial. The results of these efforts and the means used to obtain them appear in the five supplemental motions which were filed between November 8, 1921, and November 5, 1923, and the decisions of Judge Thayer thereon.

The first of these motions, usually referred to as the Ripley Motion, alleged prejudicial misconduct on the part of Walter H. Ripley, foreman of the jury, who died shortly after the trial. It was charged that Ripley owned a Harrington & Richardson revolver and, during the trial of the case and during the jury's deliberations, had three loaded thirty-eight-caliber shells[36] in his pockets which he compared with the shells in evidence and tried to fit into the muzzle of the Harrington & Richardson revolver in evidence and which he later discussed with his fellow jurors in the jury room. The motion was accompanied by the affidavits of three of the jurors who said they either had seen the shells in Ripley's possession or had heard him discuss them with members of the jury. The remaining eight jurors gave affidavits that they did not know that Ripley had any shells and at no time heard any discussion of them.

The defendants' second supplemental motion for a new trial was based on affidavits that one Roy E. Gould, a carnival performer and friend of the defense witness Burke, had witnessed the shooting and had given his name to the

---

36 These had been obtained by defense representatives from Ripley's widow.

police; that he had not been called by the Commonwealth and at the time of the trial was unknown to the defense; that on a new trial he would testify that he saw the escaping automobile from a vantage point not occupied by any other witness; and that the man who was shooting from behind the front seat was neither Sacco nor Vanzetti.

The defendants' third supplemental motion for a new trial, sometimes called the Goodridge Motion, was based on affidavits that Commonwealth's witness Goodridge had perjured himself on the witness stand; that his name was not Goodridge, but Whitney, and under the name of Whitney he had been indicted and convicted of larceny and had served a penitentiary sentence. It was charged he had told several persons, whose affidavits were presented, that he had given the testimony he had against the defendants not because it was true, but because he hated all Italians.

The Commonwealth opposed this motion with the affidavit of Goodridge in which he admitted his real name was Whitney and that he had been convicted and had served time in prison, but in which he denied that his testimony on the trial had been motivated by a hatred for Italians or that he had ever said so. It further averred that Moore, Sacco's lawyer, having failed to induce Goodridge to repudiate his testimony, had turned him over to the police as a fugitive or parole violator; and that except that his real name was Whitney and not Goodridge all of the testimony the witness had given on the trial at Dedham was the truth.

The defendants' fourth supplemental motion for a new trial, usually referred to as the Andrews Motion, was based on affidavits—one of them by Mrs. Andrews—that the testimony she had given on the trial was false; that the statement she had previously given to Defense Attorney Moore was true, and that she could not identify Sacco as the man she saw on April 15, 1920. Other affidavits offered by the defense showed that this repudiation of her testimony had been brought about by her son, from whom she had long been estranged, and that he had been prompted to that action by the representations and persuasions of two men connected with the Massachusetts branch of the American Federation of Labor.

The Commonwealth countered the motion with a sworn shorthand interview with Mrs. Andrews by District Attorney Katzmann from which it appeared that Mrs. Andrews had been put in a state of terror by the representations of her son and the two union representatives; that her son's future would be ruined by the disclosures about to be made of discreditable things in her past life; that her son had said the labor men had thirteen or fourteen statements detailing such misconduct, but they would not be used against her if she would be sure she had not recognized Sacco. Mrs. Andrews declared the labor representatives had also told her that she and all the other witnesses who had testified against Sacco and Vanzetti would be punished, and these representations and threats so upset her that her will was overcome, she "was in a trance," and made any statement and signed any papers that Moore or anyone else put in front of her. She further declared she did not consciously and voluntarily make the statements which the defense affidavits attributed to her; and she was not repudiating the testimony she had given on the trial; that it was all true.

The fifth supplemental motion for a new trial, sometimes referred to as the Hamilton-Proctor Motion, was based on affidavits which charged that one of the Commonwealth's ballistics experts had, in effect, repudiated his testimony and on "newly discovered evidence" that new tests made by two experts—Hamilton and Gill, of alleged higher qualifications than any who had previously testified— showed that the hammer of the Harrington & Richardson thirty-eight-caliber revolver found in Vanzetti's possession was not new and that bullet number three found in Berardelli's body could not have been fired from the thirty-two-caliber automatic revolver taken from Sacco.

The alleged repudiation concerned Commonwealth's witness Police Captain Proctor, who made affidavit that when he was asked whether in his opinion bullet number three was fired from Sacco's Colt and had answered: "My opinion is that it is consistent with having been fired from that pistol"; he had not intended to imply that he had found any evidence that the bullet had passed through Sacco's gun; and if he had been asked directly whether he found any such affirmative evidence, he would have given a negative answer; that Katzmann and Williams both knew his state of mind and framed the question to him accordingly.

Both Katzmann and Williams filed affidavits, unequivocally denying Proctor's allegations.[37] They also filed the affidavits of Van Amburgh, who had previously testified as an expert for the Commonwealth, and of another ballistics expert named Robinson. Both contradicted Hamilton and Gill and swore they were "absolutely convinced" that bullet number three had been fired from the thirty-two-caliber Colt automatic found in Sacco's possession when he was arrested.

No determination of these motions was made until nearly a year and a half after the first one was filed. Meanwhile there was mounting criticism of Judge Thayer from certain sections of the Massachusetts public for his failure to compel completion of the appeal or to see that the verdict of the jury was carried out. Defense counsel met this with a public statement absolving the judge of all responsibility for the delay and declaring it had been necessary

---

[37] It later appeared that Captain Proctor and Katzmann had fallen out after the verdict, when the district attorney refused to approve the policeman's bill against the county for $500 for his expert services.

and was justified by a succession of proper legal procedures taken for the protection of their clients' rights.

From other elements came resentment of a different sort. On April 17, 1923, a bomb was exploded in Wall Street, killing and injuring a number of people. Without any direct proof, it was believed by many to have been the act of anarchists and linked to the Sacco-Vanzetti case.

On October 1, 1924, Judge Thayer handed down long written opinions denying all of the pending motions for a new trial. He reviewed the evidence received on the trial and declared it fully justified the jury's verdict of guilty.

The first motion, or Ripley Motion, he said, might be decided on the well-known rule of law that to protect the sanctity of a jury's deliberations, it is against public policy to consider after a verdict evidence from whatever source of what took place in the jury room.

But, passing this technical defense, the judge held that the bullets and revolvers in evidence had been in the custody of the sheriff at all times during the trial and until the jury retired; that there was no possibility that any use of the Ripley bullets could have been made during the trial; and that the great preponderance of the evidence—as contained in the affidavits and counter affidavits—showed that the Ripley bullets were neither exhibited nor discussed in the jury room.

The second motion, or Gould Motion, Judge Thayer ruled, did not justify a new trial; the alleged "newly discovered evidence" was merely cumulative—an addition of one to the forty or more witnesses who had already testified to the identity or nonidentity of the defendants—and had it been heard by the jury would not in his opinion have affected the result.

The third motion, or Goodridge Motion, he likewise disposed of on the ground that the alleged newly discovered evidence was merely cumulative testimonial impeachment which would not have affected the result. In his opinion disposing of this motion, Judge Thayer took occasion to characterize Defense Attorney Moore's activities—using the discovered delinquencies in Goodridge's past life in an attempt to force him to repudiate his testimony and then, when he refused to do so, turning him over to the public authorities—as unprofessional conduct savoring of blackmail.

In the Court's opinion denying the fourth motion, or Andrews Motion, Attorney Moore came in for even severer castigation: The entire scheme to have Mrs. Andrews repudiate her testimony, said Judge Thayer, was a fraud "in which her son had been used as bait." The attorney's conduct, added the judge, was highly unprofessional.

The contention respecting Captain Proctor's testimony made in the fifth motion, or Hamilton-Proctor Motion, the Court held, was absurd in that it was utterly inconsistent with his testimony on the trial to which he still adhered. The alleged newly discovered ballistics testimony of the two additional experts, he said, was merely cumulative, could have been obtained and used upon the trial and was denied in the Commonwealth's counter affidavits.

As to all the motions, the Court stressed that the trial of the defendants had taken six weeks; that every opportunity had been afforded the defendants to present and argue their defenses; that the Commonwealth also had rights one of which was not to be compelled to expend the time and incur the expense incident to a retrial, unless there had been error in the trial proceedings or some other and compelling reason; and that he had found no error in the record, and the defendants had offered no such compelling reason.

Whether it was consequential or mere coincidence, Judge Thayer's action was followed by the withdrawal of Moore as counsel for Sacco on November 9 and of the two

McAnarneys on December 11 as counsel for Vanzetti. Other counsel were substituted who carried on the subsequent proceedings.[38]

Shortly after Judge Thayer's decision on the motions there was an intervening event which must be noticed. The peculiar actions of Vanzetti during the last three or four months of 1924 prompted the penitentiary physicians to examine into his mental condition. As a result they determined he was not entirely normal and recommended that he be removed to the State Hospital for the Criminal Insane. Vanzetti entered the hospital January 3, 1925. His actions during the ensuing four months, when he was under the close observation of alienists, were determined to be entirely normal, and on April 25 he was returned to the Charlestown prison, where he thereafter remained. Vanzetti's counsel took advantage of this situation and made an added point in their appeal that the sentence against him could not be executed because he was insane.

The first appeal on the overruling of the initial motion and the Ripley, Gould, and Proctor-Hamilton supplemental motions for a new trial[39] was argued before the Supreme Judicial Court of Massachusetts from January 11—13, 1926. That Court handed down its unanimous decision on May 12 following.[40] It held that: (1) there had been no question of Vanzetti's sanity at the time he was tried; that after he had been returned from the State Hospital for the Criminal Insane as cured, no subsequent inquiry had been applied for in his behalf and his present sanity had to be presumed; (2) there had been no error in

---

[38] William G. Thompson, Herbert E. Ehrmann, Arthur D. Hill, Elias Field and Michael A. Musmanna, of the Massachusetts bar, later appeared for Sacco and Vanzetti. Shortly after the jury's verdict Katzmann was succeeded as district attorney by Williams, and the later proceedings were handled in behalf of the Commonwealth by either Katzmann, as special assistant district attorney, or by Dudley P. Ranney, first assistant district attorney.

[39] No appeal had been taken from Judge Thayer's denial of the Goodridge and Andrews motions.

[40] *Commonwealth* v. *Sacco, et al.*, 255 Mass. 369, 151 N.E. 839.

the summoning of the jurors or in the admission or rejection of evidence; (3) the district attorney in his summation had not transgressed the bounds of legitimate argument; and (4) the evidence as against both Sacco and Vanzetti warranted the jury in finding them guilty.

The Court dismissed the claim of error that radicalism rather than murder had been made the issue in the case, holding that the issue of radicalism had been introduced into the case by the defendants' counsel themselves in their direct examinations, and that the cross-examinations of the defendants on their radical activities and conceptions were the necessary and proper consequences of those direct examinations. It stressed particularly Judge Thayer's charge that the defendants were not being tried for their radical activities or opinions, but for murder, and were entitled to the same presumptions in their favor and the same consideration "as though their ancestors came over in the *Mayflower.*" The Court further held there was no error in the trial court's denial of the Ripley, Gould and Proctor-Hamilton supplemental motions for a new trial.

The reaction to the supreme court's decision was immediate and violent. On May 18 a bomb was exploded at the United States embassy in Buenos Aires. On the twenty-fourth, because of threats received, the American embassy at Havana was placed under guard. On June 2 the home of Ruth Johnson, one of the Commonwealth's witnesses, was bombed; the homes of other witnesses were immediately put under guard. On June 4 Communists in Paris staged a protest demonstration. On the fifth the United States embassy at Montevideo was bombed. On the seventh threats received by Governor Alvan T. Fuller of Massachusetts prompted security measures. On the twenty-second Reds in Mexico City paraded in protest.

On July 8 the German Reichstag sent a resolution to Governor Fuller protesting execution of the death sentence against Sacco and Vanzetti. On July 18, in consequence of threats, the American legation at Basle, Switzerland, was put under armed guard. On the twenty-seventh a similar action was taken in Paris to protect United States Ambassador Herrick. On the thirtieth the Labor party and the Trades-Union Congress of England passed resolutions urging the release of the prisoners. On August 8 in New York City twenty Italian societies joined in a mass demonstration of sympathy and protest. On October 7 there were demonstrations of the Chilean Communists in Santiago. On October 12 the American Federation of Labor demanded a congressional investigation into the trial of the two defendants. On the twenty-seventh there were huge Communist demonstrations in Paris and Berlin. On the thirty-first the Federation of French Labor and various French Communist organizations filed protests at the American embassy against the execution of Sacco and Vanzetti and Communist members of the French Chamber of Deputies dispatched another protest to Washington.

On November 7 thirty foreign-language and labor newspaper editors filed a joint petition with the governor, asking for the removal of Judge Thayer.[41] On the twenty-third trade-unionists in a mass demonstration in Madison Square Garden in New York City demanded a new trial for the defendants "in the sacred name of justice." The agitation for the year 1926 was rounded out by the introduction into the Congress of the United States by a representative from Illinois of a resolution asking an investigation of the charges being made by the protagonists of Sacco and Vanzetti against the Federal Department of Justice.

The year 1926 witnessed another sensational court procedure to obtain a new trial for Sacco and Vanzetti. This

---

41 The suggested ground for impeachment was that: "On the records of the case, Judge Thayer stands accused of being partly responsible for the verdict based upon prejudice rather than evidence, and that he should himself be the one to decide the question of a new trial is illogical and revolting to the most elementary sense of justice." (This petition was made after the Supreme Judicial Court of Massachusetts had handed down its opinion, affirming Judge Thayer's judgment.)

was a motion for a new trial addressed to the Superior
Court of Norfolk County, based on more "newly discovered evidence"; this time, that one Celestino Madeiros,
under sentence of death for another murder, had confessed
that a "Morelli gang," of Providence, Rhode Island, with
which he had associated, and not Sacco or Vanzetti, had
committed the Braintree murders. Although the confession had been obtained in November of 1925, presentation
of the motion for a new trial was delayed until May 26,
1926, because Madeiros was awaiting determination of his
own appeal from a conviction for murder; and if he secured a new trial, he did not want to be prejudiced by an
outstanding confession that he had participated in another
murder.

Madeiros' appeal was successful; but he had been retried,
again found guilty of first-degree murder, and was under
sentence of death when the seventh Sacco-Vanzetti motion
for a new trial was filed. The motion was supported by affidavits as to the confession made by Madeiros and certain
collateral acts of alleged confirmation. Unrelated to the
Madeiros confession, but included in the motion, were
other allegations—made as statements of fact—that there
had been a conspiracy between the Department of Justice
of the United States and the prosecutor's office for the
southeastern district of Massachusetts to secure either a
conviction of the defendants for murder or proof that they
were dangerous radicals subject to deportation and punishment under Federal laws.

The motion was argued at length before Judge Thayer
from September 13–17 and denied on the twenty-third of
October following. In his written opinion Judge Thayer
held that the lack of credibility of Madeiros—"a crook, a
thief, a robber, a rumrunner . . . a smuggler and a man
twice tried and twice convicted of murder"—the circumstances under which the confession had been made and the
many "inconsistencies, contradictions and falsehoods" con-

tained in it entitled it to little, if any, weight as against all of the other evidence which had been heard by the jury; and that it fell far short of raising a reasonable doubt as to the guilt of the defendants.[42] The charges in the motion of conspiracy between the Federal Department of Justice and the Massachusetts prosecuting officials he rejected and dismissed as wholly without supporting evidence.

An exception and appeal were taken from Judge Thayer's ruling on this latest motion to the Supreme Judicial Court of Massachusetts, and on the fifth of April following that Court handed down its opinion that the motion presented pure questions of fact which were for the determination of the lower Court; that in the absence of evidence of an abuse of judicial discretion, such a determination was final; and that there was no error of law or evidence of an abuse of discretion in the denial of the motion.[43]

On April 9, 1927, Sacco and Vanzetti were sentenced to die in the electric chair during the week of July 10 following.

There were occasional widely-scattered outbreaks and threats of violence in the first half of 1927 in Europe and in Central and South America; but, with hope for favorable action through the courts all but exhausted, the campaign now took a new direction: appeals and other pressures directed to the governor.

One type of appeal, initiated by the Sacco-Vanzetti Defense Committee, attracted many genuinely concerned and well-meaning people to its support. It was a plea that the governor appoint a special committee from among the state's most highly regarded citizens to "review the case" and advise him so that he might have the benefit of their

---

[42] The findings of Governor Fuller and his advisory committee, who later considered the confession, were put in even stronger language. They found it "unworthy of belief" and "entitled to no weight at all."

[43] *Commonwealth* v. *Sacco*, 259 Mass. 369, 156 N.E. 57.

dispassionate and disinterested views in making his official determination whether or not to interfere to prevent the execution. Governor Fuller's first reaction was against the suggestion: The responsibility was his and his alone; he could not delegate it.

The idea, however, gathered force. Organizations and individuals of quite a different type from those who had hitherto criticized the decisions of the courts and questioned the verdict reiterated the request—ministers and rabbis of important congregations, the deans of two Eastern law schools, members of the law and social science faculties of several universities, teachers' unions, civic societies and a score or more of prominent individuals who were above suspicion for any interest or motive except a desire to safeguard two human beings against the possibility of a miscarriage of justice.

Governor Fuller finally yielded and on July 1 announced the appointment of President Abbott Lawrence Lowell of Harvard, President Samuel W. Stratton of Massachusetts Institute of Technology and Robert Grant, a former judge of the Probate Court of Suffolk County,[44] as an advisory committee to review the case in its entirety and submit to him its report. That the committee might not be crowded for time, the governor granted the defendants a reprieve to August 10.

Despite this extraordinary action in the defendants' interests by the state's chief executive, the radicals and anarchists kept up their campaign of violence and terror. In July there was a protest parade in Philadelphia. There was a riotous meeting in Union Square in New York City. In Mexico City Communists marched upon the American consulate. A bomb was thrown into the garden of the American consulate in Nice, Italy; the Washington monu-

---

[44] Judge Grant was a Ph.D. and L.L.B. of Columbia University. He had served as judge of the Probate Court of Insolvency of Suffolk County from 1893 to 1923 and was a lawyer of recognized distinction.

ment in Buenos Aires was wrecked. There were Communist demonstrations in France, Switzerland and Belgium, and United States legations and consulates in those countries were placed under guard.

The governor's advisory committee did a conscientious job of investigation and inquiry. They had been asked to advise the governor on three questions: (1) Was the trial fairly conducted? (2) Was subsequently discovered evidence such that a new trial should have been granted? and (3) Were they or were they not convinced beyond a reasonable doubt that Sacco and Vanzetti were guilty of murder? The records of the Superior Court of Norfolk County and the Supreme Judicial Court of Massachusetts were carefully studied.

The eleven living jurors, Superior Court Judge Thayer, and Supreme Court Justice Hall appeared before the committee and were questioned. Because of the confidential nature of the inquiries directed to these men, no record was kept of the interrogation and defense counsel were not permitted to be present. During the examination, however, of the forty-one other witnesses who appeared before the committee, defendants' counsel were present and conducted direct or cross-examinations. These witnesses included District Attorney Katzmann, who voluntarily submitted himself to adversary cross-examination, persons who had testified on the trial and "newly discovered witnesses" produced by both the defendants and the Commonwealth.

The governor and the committee members interviewed Sacco, Vanzetti and Madeiros in prison. After counsel for the Commonwealth and the defendants announced they had no more witnesses to present, or whom they desired to have called, the committee heard extended arguments from both sides. There was no advance criticism from any quarter that the governor and the committee had not explored every avenue of information and afforded the defendants full opportunity to present their witnesses and arguments.

There was little presented that was new except the testimony of a number of newspaper reporters, who testified to Judge Thayer's conduct on the trial and out of court. The consensus of this testimony was that while Judge Thayer's statements for the record on the trial could not be criticized, his manner throughout the trial showed definite and unmistakable hostility to Defense Attorney Moore and prejudice against the defendants; and that in conversations with them outside of court he had declared many times, and often in intemperate language, that the defendants were guilty and ought to be convicted.

The committee completed its hearings and submitted its report to the governor on July 27. It found that the trial had been fairly conducted; that while Judge Thayer's statements of his personal opinions outside the courtroom constituted "a grave breach of judicial decorum" the record of the proceedings in court showed no criticizable statements or conduct, and the charge that the jury might have been prejudiced by Judge Thayer's attitude had been refuted by the jurors themselves. All eleven of them, so the report said, had told the committee they had perceived no evidence of bias or prejudice on the part of the judge at any time and, after his charge, could not tell whether he thought the defendants guilty or innocent.

Answering its other assignments, the committee found there was no merit in the numerous motions for a new trial based on alleged newly discovered evidence, and that the trial Court's action in denying them had been legal and proper; and that both Sacco and Vanzetti had been proved guilty beyond a reasonable doubt.

On August 3 the governor issued a formal statement reciting the conclusion of the advisory committee. He declared his complete agreement with it, based on his own investigations, and announced he would not interfere to prevent the execution of the death sentence.

The general reaction of the Massachusetts press to Gov-

ernor Fuller's action was one of satisfaction and relief. The
governor's statement, in which he announced his decision
and reasons for it, was haled as a "splendid document
worthy of the great Commonwealth for which he admin-
istered ably the high office entrusted to him." The press
said it was "convincing," "final," "a decision which vindi-
cates the courts, preserves untarnished the fair name of the
state, and ends forever a case that ought never have been
permitted to encumber the courts for seven years."

Press reaction outside of Massachusetts was mixed. The
St. Louis *Post-Dispatch* and the New York *Evening World*
declared they were far from satisfied that Sacco and Vanzetti had been proved beyond a reasonable doubt to be
guilty. Other papers found fault: the hearings of the
Lowell committee should have been thrown open to the
public, which "would have been nearer to the open trial
which the public had demanded." On the other hand, the
vast majority of the press took the view expressed by the
New York *Times,* "Human law can do no more," and by
the Philadelphia *Inquirer,* "No men, convicted by due
process of law, ever had greater consideration."

Despite the failure of what had been their fairest hope,
counsel for the defendants refused to give up. Immediately
after the announcement of the governor's decision an original petition for a writ of habeas corpus, a stay of execution and a writ of error was filed in the Supreme Judicial
Court of Massachusetts.

On August 6 an eighth motion for a new trial was filed
in the Superior Court of Norfolk County. This motion
was based on a claim of more newly discovered evidence
and allegations that throughout the trial and subsequent
proceedings before him, Judge Thayer was "so prejudiced
against the defendants and their counsel that they had not
had such a trial as that to which they are entitled under the
constitutions of the Commonwealth of Massachusetts and
of the United States of America." This motion, like the

preceding ones, by direction of the Supreme Judicial Court of Massachusetts, came on for hearing before Judge Thayer. It was fully argued on August 8, and then it was denied on the ground that since the sentence had been passed on the defendants the Court was without jurisdiction to entertain another motion for a new trial. An appeal was promptly taken to the supreme judicial court of the state.

The lawlessness of the Sacco-Vanzetti partisans continued. There were threats against President Coolidge and his secret-service detail was augmented. Governor Fuller and Judge Thayer were threatened, and their persons were strongly guarded. There were protest meetings, parades of radicals and rioting in Boston, New York City, Philadelphia and in a number of the European and South American capitals.

On August 8 the Supreme Judicial Court of Massachusetts denied the application made to it for a writ of habeas corpus, a stay of execution and a new trial. Because the appeal from Judge Thayer's order denying the eighth motion for a new trial was still pending, Governor Fuller again stayed the execution of the death sentence "through the twenty-second of August" to permit this "final judicial review."

The decision of the supreme court on the last appeal was not handed down until August 19. In the interim there were other developments. A Citizens' National Committee, headed by Robert M. Lovett, petitioned President Coolidge to intervene. The President refused. The district attorney released a report containing the opinion of Calvin H. Goddard—generally recognized as the foremost ballistics expert in America—that it was his definite opinion that the number three bullet which killed Berardelli had been fired from Sacco's pistol. Sacco's father petitioned Mussolini to intervene. No action seems to have been taken on this plea. The violence continued. There were protest meetings and strikes in London, in the European and South American capitals and in Boston and New York City. On August 17, the home of McHardy, one of the Norfolk County jurors, was bombed.

On August 10 the defendants presented a petition for a writ of habeas corpus to United States Circuit Court Judge Anderson and to United States Supreme Court Justice Holmes. Both judges refused the writ on the ground that the Federal courts were powerless to interfere with the regularly entered judgments of state courts.

On August 19 the Supreme Judicial Court of Massachusetts handed down its third written opinion and decision in the Sacco-Vanzetti case.[45] After reciting the previous history of the case on appeal and stating that there had already been "full and exhaustive" argument "covering every error claimed to have been committed either at the trial or in any of the subsequent proceedings," and that it had been "decided as a matter of law there was evidence which would warrant the jury in finding the defendants guilty," it affirmed the judgment of the lower Court.

On August 19 the defendants made their last efforts: a petition to United States District Court Judge James M. Morton for a writ of habeas corpus, which was promptly heard and denied, and a petition for a writ of certiorari (review) filed with the clerk of the Supreme Court of the United States. Successive applications under this petition for a stay of execution, pending its consideration and determination, were presented to United States Supreme Court Justices Holmes and Stone. Defendants' counsel were given a hearing on both applications and both were denied. The governor refused to grant a further reprieve and arrangements were made for the execution of the long-delayed sentence of death.

Extra precautions were taken to forestall any last-minute, forcible attempt to rescue Sacco and Vanzetti from the

---

45 261 Mass. 12, 158 N.E. 167.

authorities. On the night of August 23 the Charlestown prison was armed and garrisoned as if to withstand a siege. Machine guns, gas and tear bombs, riot guns and pistols constituted the armament and to man these weapons were 500 patrolmen, plain-clothes men and state constables, besides the usual prison guards. All of the streets leading to the sprawling collection of steel-barred brick and cement buildings were barricaded so that no one could get within blocks of the entrance to the prison.

Both condemned men refused religious consolation. Both protested their innocence to the last. Vanzetti, during the final preparations, was calm and resigned. He made a brief and poignant statement in which he forgave "some people for what they are now doing to me." Sacco, sullen and bitter, as the guards strapped him to the death chair shouted in Italian his last earthly defiance, "Long live anarchy!"

The reaction to the execution was not unexpected. All day August 23 and for forty-eight hours after the execution a milling, shouting crowd picketed the State House in Boston. To disperse them, it was finally necessary to call out the police. Over 150 were arrested, among them such distinguished liberals as the poetess Edna St. Vincent Millay, the author John Dos Passos, and the seventy-year-old Preceptress at Wellesley, Ellen Hayes.

There were renewed riots and protest strikes in the usual foreign quarters. Memorial services, attended by thousands, were held in New York City and Boston. The Communists in Moscow set aside a special day of mourning. Death masks were made of the "martyrs." Their bodies were cremated. The urns containing their ashes, on the way to Italy for burial, were held in Paris in order that they might be carried in a giant Communist parade.

The anarchy invoked by Sacco persisted after his death. On May 18, 1928, the home of R. G. Elliott, the prison official whose duty compelled him to throw the death switch, was bombed. August 23, the anniversary of the execution, was celebrated by radicals and Communists as a memorial-day holiday for at least seven years afterward in New York City, Boston, Mexico City, Tampico, Rio de Janeiro, Buenos Aires, Paris, Moscow and throughout Italy. In Buenos Aires in 1928 there was agitation by the radicals to change the names of New York and United States streets to Sacco and Vanzetti streets. In August of 1930 memorial meetings in memory of Sacco and Vanzetti held in far-off Indo-China ended in riots in which two persons were killed. In 1932 Judge Thayer's home was bombed and completely wrecked; and because of threats to their lives and property, guards were placed around the homes of Governor Fuller, Harvard University's President Lowell, and the Sacco-Vanzetti jurors and witnesses.

Sentiment on the Sacco-Vanzetti case has changed but little with the passage of the years. The idea, so industriously propagated by the radical press and the partisans of Sacco and Vanzetti during the six years of their imprisonment, that they had not had a fair trial, but were the martyrs of a high-level conspiracy to eliminate them because they were radicals or anarchists, has been kept alive through the efforts of intellectual revolutionists here and abroad and is held by many people. While the authentic record of the case may have gathered a lot of dust, it has served and will continue to serve to prevent that idea from becoming a legend.

To the bald charge, so frequently made, that Sacco and Vanzetti were convicted without evidence and unjustly, this record holds the facts that the Supreme Judicial Court of Massachusetts, one of the most respected judicial tribunals in America, after the consideration of three separate appeals found the evidence amply sufficient to justify the jury's verdict of conviction, and that a reviewing committee of three of the most intelligent and distinguished citizens of Massachusetts, appointed by an honest and fearless governor, concurred in that view.

To the contention made in some quarters that "the world-wide reaction against the verdict" was an "international protest" comparable to that which followed the condemnation of Dreyfuss the noted dean of the Northwestern University Law School, John H. Wigmore, offered an answer which no dispassionate reader of the long record of violence attending this case can ignore. The reason for the international interest which the case excited, said Professor Wigmore, was not the result of any honest feeling that justice had been outraged; but that the real reason was "the two accused appeared to be valued members of a powerful international fraternity or cabal or gang who have, since the trial and conviction, sought to give aid to their convicted associates by the most extensive system of international terrorism that the world has known for the century past. Ever since the trial started in 1921, this terrorism has been carried on. If it had succeeded, justice in the United States would be at its mercy."[46]

---

[46] Taken from an article published in the Boston *Evening Transcript* under the date of April 25, 1927.

III

The Trial of

RICHARD LOEB
and
NATHAN LEOPOLD

for the Murder of

ROBERT ("BOBBIE") FRANKS
(1924)

3

The Loeb-Leopold Case

THE SIGNIFICANCE *of this case as a* cause célèbre *is that, judged by ordinary concepts, it was a motiveless crime committed by two youthful perverts, the children of over-indulgent and careless parents who had given them every material advantage excessive wealth could provide. One of them, Leopold, was an intellectual prodigy. Both of them had been allowed to grow up with practically no religious or moral instruction.*

The challenge which the crime hurled at society was tersely summed up in an editorial of the Chicago Daily News: *"There are several warnings and object lessons in the astonishing affair. Here are . . . young men without religious or moral convictions, without respect for tradition and law; young men who are proud of their emancipation from all superstition and sneer at distinctions between good and evil and indulge all of their whims and caprices; young men who, with Nietzsche, talk of 'living dangerously,' seeking risk and adventure at any cost; young men who, if tempted, would not shrink even from murder, especially when saturated with ideas derived from the literature of Satanism, sadism and other perversities. Further developments in this extraordinary case need not be anticipated, but enough is already known or reasonably suspected to give psychologists, alienists and educators plenty of food for thought and for instructive contrasts and comparisons."*

The trial has an additional significance, because it pro-vided a forum for the presentation of the case against capi-

tal punishment by its most distinguished exponent, the counsel for the defense, Clarence Darrow.

As a study for lawyers, Darrow's argument exhibits a persuasive eloquence fit for a place alongside the most brilliant efforts of Brougham, Curran, Erskine, Rufus Choate and Webster.

CHICAGO has not merited its reputation as the "world's wickedest city." There are other American cities with an equal or better claim to that title. Despite this half defense the record compels the admission that Chicago in the last seventy-five years has had a crowded calendar of crime, solved and unsolved. While largely of the usual sordid sort—crimes of passion, murder, robbery and arson for gain, gangster killings and the mine-run of lesser felonies and misdemeanors—the big town has had at least its fair share of crimes which were sufficiently sensational and unusual to claim national and even international attention.

There was the Haymarket Riot and dynamiting, which claimed the lives of seven policemen and resulted in the prompt conviction, on highly controversial circumstantial evidence, of eight persons, four of whom were hanged. There was the murder of Dr. Cronin by the agents of an Irish secret society and the attempt to conceal the crime by dropping his body through a manhole in the city's sewer system. There was the killing by Luettgert, a sausage maker, of his wife and his attempt to dispose of the corpus delicti by disarticulating the body and incinerating the bones and flesh to oblivion in his sausage vats. There was the case of Johann Hoch, the Chicago "Bluebeard" for the murder of one wife, with evidentiary details strongly suggesting a similar removal of half a dozen of her predecessors.

All of these were sensational trials. They had their hour,

their meed of notoriety; but, save for the crime chronicler and those blessed or cursed with tenacious memories for the morbid, they have passed into the limbo of things forgotten.

There was nothing in the account of the murder of Bobbie Franks, as reported in an afternoon newspaper on May 22, 1924, which suggested an aftermath that would relegate these and other sensational crimes in Chicago's previous colorful history to a competition for second place. Moreover, the Franks murder, under its common reference, "The Loeb-Leopold Case," would not be so soon forgotten. A leaded two-inch headline stretched across the front page of a morning newspaper announced the crime: "Kidnapers Kill Boy As Wealthy Father Seeks To Pay $10,000."

On the day before, Robert (Bobbie) Franks, the thirteen-year-old son of Jacob Franks, a well-known and highly regarded Chicago capitalist, left the Harvard School for Boys in fashionable South Side Kenwood after his last class. It was about five o'clock in the afternoon. His home was less than four blocks away, and the boy usually arrived there well in advance of the six-thirty dinner hour. When he failed to appear Franks telephoned the school authorities and notified some of his neighborhood friends. Together they made a search of the school buildings and grounds and the neighboring streets. It proved fruitless, and about ten o'clock they gave it up.

Franks returned to his home and was just on the point of notifying the police when the telephone rang. The caller identified himself as "George Johnson." "You know by this time," said the voice, "that Robert has been kidnaped, but you needn't worry. He is safe and unharmed, but do not try to trace me. We need the money. We will let you know what we want. We are kidnapers, and we mean business. If you refuse or report to the police, we will kill the boy."

Franks called his attorney and, on his advice, did notify the police. They promised, however, to give the report no publicity pending the further moves of the kidnapers.

The family, with a relative and close friend, kept an all-night vigil. There were no further telephone calls, but at nine-thirty in the morning a post-office messenger arrived with a special-delivery letter. It bore a South Side post-mark and contained the following message type-written on a piece of plain, white paper:

Dear Sir:

As you no doubt know by this time your son has been kidnapped. Allow us to assure you that he is at present well and safe. You need fear no physical harm for him provided you live up carefully to the following instructions and such others as you will receive by further communications. Should you, however, disobey any of our instructions, even slightly, his death will be the penalty.

1. For obvious reasons make absolutely no attempt to communicate with the police authorities or any private agencies. Should you already have communicated with the police allow them to continue their investigation but do not mention this letter.

2. Secure before noon today $10,000. This amount must be composed entirely of old bills of the following denominations:

$2,000 in $20 bills
$8,000 in $50 bills

The money must be old. Any attempt to include new or marked bills will render the entire venture futile.

3. The money should be placed in a small cigar box or if this is impossible in a heavy cardboard box, securely closed and wrapped in a white paper. The wrapping paper should be sealed at all openings with sealing wax.

4. Have this money with you prepared as directed above and remain home after one o'clock P.M. See that the telephone is not in use. You will receive further instructions then instructing you as to your final course.

As a final word of warning, this is a strictly commercial proposition and we are prepared to put our threat into execution should we have reasonable grounds to believe that you have committed an infraction of the above instructions. However, should you carefully follow out our instructions, we can assure you that your son will be safely returned to you within six hours of receipt of the money.

The letter concluded "yours truly" and was subscribed with the name "George Johnson" well and clearly written in black ink.

The frantic father promptly procured the money in the specified denominations, put it in a cigar box, wrapped and sealed it, as directed, and sat at the telephone awaiting the kidnapers' promised call.

Shortly after noon the Franks were notified by the police that the naked, dead body of a young boy had been found in a swamp in the outskirts of the city, where it had been partly wedged into a concrete drain pipe. Franks, certain the kidnapers would not harm his son, at first refused to listen to the suggestion that some member of the family should visit the mortuary to which the discovered body had been removed; but as time went on and he did not hear from the kidnapers, he finally asked his brother-in-law to go out and look at it.

Still hopeful, however, Franks kept close to the telephone. At three o'clock it rang. It was Johnson calling. "I am sending a Yellow Cab for you," said a quick-speaking, excited voice. "Get into it and go to the drugstore at 1463 East 63rd Street. Have the money with you." Before Franks could ask for a verification of the number given, the connection was broken.

He was still puzzling over the address when the doorbell rang, and he was told that a Yellow Cab was waiting. He started for the door, but before he reached it the phone rang again. This time it was his brother-in-law calling. He had identified the body reported by the police as that of Bobbie Franks. The boy had been brutally murdered.

Goaded by the newspapers and spurred by the promise

of a substantial reward, the city's police force, the chief of detectives and the state's attorney[1] began the most intensive man hunt recorded in the criminal annals of Chicago. The Yellow Cab which had called for Franks was traced. The call had been made to a regular cabstand, and the driver was selected because he was next in line. He had received no instructions except to call at the Frankses' home. Police headquarters broadcasted a general appeal to the public to report to the department any unusual circumstances which might provide a working clue. People in the neighborhood of the Harvard School at about the time of the kidnaping reported having seen a gray Winton automobile being driven up and down the streets in a manner which had seemed suspicious. Others said they had seen a car of the same description later in the evening in the vicinity of 118th Street and the Pennsylvania tracks, where the body was found. There was a roundup and questioning of dozens of owners and drivers of gray Wintons.

The coroner's physician reported that an examination of the boy's body indicated that he might have been the victim of a sex pervert. Immediately word went out to bring in all known or suspected degenerates. Many persons were arrested and questioned, among them two hitherto highly regarded teachers at the Harvard School. They were held in custody, put in the "showup" to be viewed by persons who claimed to have seen the gray Winton and mercilessly grilled. Nothing was developed which suggested their connection with the crime, and after five days of such torture they were released on writs of habeas corpus.

A girl "mystic," living somewhere in Kansas and sup-

---

1 By a long-standing practice, the state's attorney of Cook County has a number of city police officers assigned to his office. The number has varied all the way from twenty to two hundred. While generally used to assist in the preparation of pending cases, they are frequently used to hunt down suspects and secure incriminating evidence as the basis for criminal indictments.

posed by her psychic powers to have assisted the police in many places in the identification and discovery of criminals, furnished the police with a "psychic description" of the kidnapers—two young men (with details as to age, height, weight, dress and habits) and a redheaded woman of about thirty-five years of age. Promptly the neighborhood of the Frankses' home was scoured for redheaded women. Several were arrested and were taken to the state's attorney's office for questioning.

Typewriting experts had given their opinions that the ransom notes had been written on a Corona typewriter. The Harvard School and the neighborhood were searched for such a machine. Someone reported to the police that three young men had been seen carrying a Corona typewriter from a North Side apartment building. The tip included a description of their car and the license number. By radio call every roving police car was alerted. The suspicious car was located and followed until it stopped at a typewriter repair shop. The proprietors were well-established typewriter mechanics. The machine belonged to a respectable merchant and had been picked up by car delivery in response to a telephone call. It was not a Corona.

As is not at all unusual in such widely publicized cases, there were many "crank" performances. One was a floral wreath sent to the boy's funeral with a card on which was written "George Johnson." The piece was traced to a South Side florist shop and the purchaser vaguely described as "a tall man about thirty-two years of age." Another was a letter confessing the crime and saying that the writer was about to commit suicide. There was an anonymous letter sent to the Franks, threatening other members of the family if they persisted in their efforts to apprehend the kidnapers. The Louisville police reported the arrest as a suspect of a South Side Chicago druggist. Investigation disclosed that the man had become temporarily deranged, because of his fancied likeness to one of the persons described by the Kansas psychic, and had taken poison in a suicide attempt. Further investigation demonstrated that he could not possibly have had any connection with the crime.

These were the unproductive clues and leads. There were others, however, which as the result of efficient police work yielded sensational results. The place where the body had been found was subjected to an inch by inch search. Auto tracks were traced in the adjacent road, but they were not sufficiently clear to disclose tire identities. One of the boy's stockings was found floating in a near-by pool of water. A number of pressed building bricks were picked up not far from where the body was found. Most important of all, a laborer employed in the vicinity found on the bank near the culvert a pair of horn-rimmed glasses which he turned over to the police.

A man who lived not far from the swamp where the attempt had been made to conceal the body told the police that on the day of the murder he had picked up a blood-stained taped chisel which he had seen thrown from a moving automobile which he described as a gray sedan. There were numerous cuts on the boy's head which might have been made by such an instrument.

The bricks taken from the scene of the crime were found to match those used in a building which was under construction near the Harvard School. A canvass was made of all the downtown and South Side optometrists in an effort to locate by their prescription records the purchaser of the horn-rimmed glasses. On May 30, eight days after the murder, this persistence was rewarded. The records of a well-known Loop optometrist revealed the names of two persons to whom horn-rimmed glasses of the prescription of those found at the place of the discovery of the body had been sold. One of these was Nathan Leopold, Jr. The address given was 4754 Greenwood Avenue, in the immediate neighborhood of the Harvard School and the Frankses' home.

The police found Leopold at his home, arrested him and rushed him to the state's attorney's office for questioning. Leopold, it developed, was nineteen years old, the son of a millionaire, a graduate with the degree of Bachelor of Philosophy from the University of Chicago, a Phi Beta Kappa and at the time of his arrest a student in the University of Chicago Law School. Asked as to his movements on the twenty-first of May, Leopold declared that he and Richard Loeb during the afternoon and evening had been driving around in the Leopold family car, a red Willys-Knight. The following day Loeb was taken into custody. Loeb, aged eighteen, was the son of a wealthy retired vice-president of one of the country's largest mail-order houses and a graduate—the youngest on record at that time—of the University of Michigan.

Both boys at first stoutly denied any knowledge of the crime. Leopold was the more assured of the two. He affected an ease of manner and answered questions promptly. He readily admitted ownership of the glasses, but he said he seldom wore them and must have left them at home. When faced with the fact that they had been picked up at the place where the Franks boy's body was found, Leopold said he was an amateur ornithologist, taught classes on the subject, and must have lost his glasses out of his pocket on one of his frequent excursions to outlying territory to study the habits of birds.

Asked if he knew Bobbie Franks, Leopold said: "Yes, he was a nice little boy. What motive did I have for killing him? I didn't need the money; my father is rich. Whenever I want money all I have to do is to ask him for it." He added: "I earn money myself. I teach classes in ornithology, and get paid for it." He smiled when shown the first ransom note, denied having written it, and pointed out that the word "kidnapped" was misspelled.

But the state's attorney and his police were not so easily put off. As soon as Leopold or Loeb made a factual statement, a detective was dispatched to check on it. The story of Leopold's interest in ornithology was verified, but the Leopold chauffeur shattered their alibi by declaring positively that the family car had not been out of the garage between one o'clock in the afternoon and ten o'clock at night on the twenty-first of May.

Loeb and Leopold were then questioned separately. Confronted with the chauffeur's testimony and pressed for details as to their movements during the afternoon and evening of May 21 they became hopelessly involved in contradictory stories. The gruelling went on relentlessly, hour after hour, day and night. Sunday morning June 1 Loeb broke down and confessed his participation in the kidnaping. He said the boy struggled with Leopold and Leopold hit him on the head with a chisel. Leopold, advised of Loeb's confession, admitted his participation, but he charged Loeb with the killing.

When finally released for publication, the full confessions of Leopold and Loeb agreed in all substantial particulars. They had commenced planning what they conceived as "the perfect crime" as early as the preceding November. The plan contemplated the kidnaping of "some rich boy," killing him and, before the killing was discovered, getting ransom money from his family.

In furtherance of the scheme they had, in April, opened separate bank accounts under assumed names—Leopold as Morton D. Ballard and Loeb as Louis Mason. Leopold identifying himself as Ballard and giving Mason (Loeb) as a reference established a credit with a Rent-A-Car agency, so they would have available when they came to execute their design an automobile which could not be traced to them. To give further credence to Ballard's existence, Loeb registered as Ballard at a Loop hotel, was assigned a room and had mail to Ballard directed there.

There had been a further extensive preliminary planning of details. While most of it was directed to avoiding discovery in the process of collecting the ransom, the youthful pair had considered and agreed on the means to be employed in the killing and had selected the place and determined the method of concealing the body. The plan for obtaining the ransom was ingenious. The necessary telephone calls would be made from drugstore pay stations so as not to be easily traceable.

Had Jacob Franks remembered the correct location of the drugstore, as telephoned to him just before he received word of his son's death, and gone there promptly, he would, upon his arrival, have received another telephone message telling him to board at a specified time a southbound Michigan Central train at 63rd Street, and go to a designated Pullman car in the train where he would find final instructions written on a piece of note paper in the time table rack. The last detail had been worked out by providing that Loeb, disguised by borrowed clothes and dark glasses, should take the Michigan Central train at a station north of 63rd Street, place the note in the rack of the identified car and alight at 63rd Street. The note to be left in the rack directed Franks to proceed immediately to the rear of the train, watch the east side of the track, have his package of ransom bills ready, look for a red-brick factory building with a large black water tower on top lettered with the word "Champion," wait until the train passed the south end of the building, and then throw the package as far to the east of the train as he could. One of the two would be waiting there to pick it up.

On May 20 Loeb and Leopold together composed the ransom note, and Leopold typed it on paper purchased especially for the purpose. The typewriter was an Underwood (not a Corona) which the boys had stolen in Ann Arbor some months before. Leopold also typed the letter of final instructions to be left on the train and the exact wording of each of the projected telephone calls.

They next proceeded to assemble their equipment. They

purchased a cold chisel and a length of rope from a hardware store on Cottage Grove Avenue, near 43rd Street. (The original plan had been to strangle their victim with a rope, each of the boys participating in the act so that the murder would be their joint responsibility.) From a drugstore in the same neighborhood they procured a bottle of hydrochloric acid. From the Leopold house and garage they obtained rags which were to be used as gags, a pair of hip boots and a lap robe.

They wrapped the chisel with adhesive tape and concealed it and their other paraphernalia until eleven o'clock the next morning, when they put it in Leopold's automobile and drove downtown. They parked the car at 16th Street and Michigan Avenue, not far from the Rent-A-Car station. From the rental station they procured a light-blue Willys-Knight, drove to where the Leopold car was parked and transferred their criminal instruments. One of the boys then drove the Leopold car back to the Leopold garage.

In the late afternoon the two boys, in the rented car, commenced a canvass of the neighborhood of the Harvard School in search of a victim. They stopped at a building which was in process of construction and picked up six or seven building bricks. These were intended to weight the body if they finally decided to throw it into Lake Michigan. Loeb got out of the car near the Harvard School and walked around the neighborhood; Leopold meanwhile ranged the streets a short distance away. Loeb met and talked to several people—his younger brother, a tutor at the school and a young boy pupil named Levinson. Leopold showed up and Loeb returned to the car. They set out to find the Levinson boy, but somehow they missed him. Leopold told of seeing a number of boys on Ellis Avenue, and they drove into that street.

The first boy they spotted was Bobbie Franks. He was not a predestined victim. As Loeb said, "He just hap-

pened along, and we got him." The boy knew them both
and quite readily accepted their invitation to show him a
new tennis racquet and drive him home. Almost immediately, according to the confessions, one of the two (probably Loeb) struck Bobbie several times on the head with
the chisel, stuffed a wadded cloth soaked with hydrochloric acid in his mouth and, after the boy became uncon-
scious, wrapped and covered him with the lap robe. He
bled profusely. The blood saturated the robe and some of
it escaped to the floor of the car.

The pair now made for the open country in the extreme
southeast portion of the city. They stopped in a country
lane and took off the boy's shoes and hid them in some
roadside bushes. They unbuckled his belt and took off his
pants and stockings. The latter they left in the car, but the
belt and belt buckle they threw out into the street. It was
now dark. They drove to a roadhouse restaurant, got out
of the car, went inside and ate some sandwiches. The car
with its gruesome load was parked in the street near by.
When they finished their meal, they set about to dispose of
the body.

The place they had predetermined on was a wide stretch
of marshland alongside the Pennsylvania Railroad tracks
between 118th and 123rd Streets. It was a sparsely settled
industrial neighborhood, usually completely deserted after
sundown. They drove the car as far as they could and then
carried the body a block and a half to a patch of water-
covered swampland, where there was a large concrete drain-
age culvert, one end of which was open.

There they stripped the boy naked. The boy was dead
and rigor mortis had already set in, but to make assurance
doubly sure they pushed his head under water and held
it there for several minutes. They then poured the rest
of the acid over the body and jammed it head first into the
culvert. Leopold put on the boots, waded out into the
swamp and endeavored to hide some of the boy's blood-

stained clothing in the mud. After washing the blood and dirt from his hands, he took off his boots, threw them into the car and put on his shoes. The pair then returned to the car and drove to the nearest drugstore where Leopold telephoned his home to say he would be late getting in. While there he looked up the Frankses' address and printed it on the envelope containing the ransom note.

It was nine o'clock when the pair began their return journey. On their way back they threw the blood-smeared, taped chisel out of the car. When they reached Loeb's home they lighted a fire in the basement and burned what remained of the boy's clothing. They tried, but without much success, to wash the bloodstains out of the lap robe and off the floor of the car. Next Leopold telephoned the Frankses, advising of the kidnaping and making the ransom demand. After that he mailed the ransom letter. The perfectly planned crime was thought to have been perfectly executed.

The boys drove the rented car to a quiet street not far from the Leopold home, parked it and walked into the Leopold home about ten-thirty. They drank and played cards until after midnight. Then Leopold drove Loeb home in the Leopold car. The next morning they picked up the rented car and drove it to the Leopold garage. There they made another attempt to eradicate the bloodstains from the floor. In the afternoon they drove the rented car to 18th Street and Wabash Avenue, where they parked it. Loeb proceeded to the Park Row Railroad Station to purchase his ticket and board the southbound Michigan Central train. Leopold repaired to a drugstore to make his final call to the Frankses.

Loeb carried out his part of the plot. He boarded the train, left the note in the designated timetable rack and got off the train at 63rd Street. Leopold made his call arranging for the taxicab, but, of course, was unsuccessful in establishing contact with Franks at the designated drug-

store. When Leopold left the drugstore his eyes met the
headlines in the afternoon papers announcing the finding
of the body. The ransom part of the perfect crime had mis-
carried.

Leopold immediately returned the rented car. When he
reached home the family chauffeur told him of the murder. The next morning (Saturday) Leopold, driving his
own car, picked up Loeb and together they drove to an un-
frequented road alongside the Jackson Park lagoon. Leopold had with him the Underwood typewriter on which he
had typed the ransom notes. With a pair of pliers they
twisted off the letter keys and threw them into the lagoon.
A short distance farther along the road they threw in the
typewriter. Then they returned to the Leopold garage,
saturated the lap robe with gasoline, took it to a vacant lot
in the outskirts of the city and burned it.

While the premature discovery of the body had defeated
their plan to collect ransom, both of the boys were su-
premely confident that by their perfect planning every clue
which might have connected them with the crime had been
destroyed. There was ground for their optimism, for it is
altogether likely that had Leopold not dropped his horn-
rimmed glasses on the bank near the culvert the murder of
Bobbie Franks would have gone down on the Chicago
police records as one more unsolved murder. Loeb, before his arrest, either because of this confidence or for an
additional thrill, actually volunteered his services to the
police and suggested and participated in a canvass of 63rd
Street drugstores to trace the kidnaper's telephone calls.

City and state's attorney's detectives set to work immediately to corroborate the confessions. From the details
furnished they soon confirmed the rental of the death car.
The identities of Ballard and Mason as Loeb and Leopold
were readily established by bank and hotel employees. The
hardware, drug and stationery stores from which the boys
had purchased the chisel, rope, hydrochloric acid and

paper used for typing the ransom demands, were located without difficulty and persons found who remembered the sales. A Michigan Central ticket agent identified Loeb as one to whom he had sold a ticket to Michigan City on May 22. A Michigan Central car employee found the final note of instructions to Franks in the timetable rack where Loeb confessed he had put it. The dead boy's shoes, some of his clothes and his belt, belt buckle and class pin were found at places where Loeb said they had been hidden or thrown from the death car. Leopold's battered typewriter was recovered from the Jackson Park lagoon. There could be no doubt of the truth of the confessions. The case against Loeb and Leopold was complete.

Events now moved rapidly. On June 6 a grand jury returned joint indictments of murder and kidnaping against Loeb and Leopold. They were arraigned on the eleventh, and, through their attorneys, entered pleas of not guilty. August 4 was fixed as the date of trial. On July 21 the plea of not guilty was withdrawn, a plea of guilty substituted and the case advanced for hearing before the court, without a jury, to July 23.

On July 23, 1924, the case against Leopold and Loeb for the murder of Bobbie Franks came on for trial. Appearing for the State were the State's Attorney Robert E. Crowe —a former judge of the Circuit Court of Cook County— and his principal assistants, Thomas Marshall, Joseph P. Savage, John A. Sbarbaro and Milton D. Smith. Clarence Darrow, Benjamin Bachrach and Walter Bachrach appeared for the defendants. Judge Crowe, an experienced trial lawyer—alert, resourceful, sharp-tongued and belligerent—presented the State's case and cross-examined most of the defendants' witnesses.

Darrow and his associates divided the work of the defense. The elder of the Bachrach brothers had had a rather extensive experience in the handling of trials and appeals in criminal cases. Darrow was unquestionably the fore-most criminal lawyer in America. The presiding judge was the Honorable John R. Caverly, chief justice of the Criminal Court of Cook County.[2]

The issue was clear from the start. Crowe, sustained by incessant newspaper clamor and aware of the opportunity offered to further an unlimited political ambition, was prepared for an all-out effort to hang the defendants—"defeat the effort of a million dollars to save the lives of two ruthless murderers." Darrow and his associates had but one hope—to save their clients from the gallows. It was to that end they had pleaded them guilty and obtained leave to offer evidence in mitigation of punishment.

Despite the fact that a very few witnesses would have sufficed to prove the corpus delicti—the confessions of the defendants and convincing corroboration of those confessions—the State elected to prove every incident of the crime with the same completeness and particularity as though there had been a plea of not guilty. There was an obvious purpose in this. The details of the cold-blooded crime would furnish the basis for the argument that (1) every step in its execution had been premeditated and shrewdly calculated to insure its success and to escape detection, and (2) the ruthlessness and remorselessness of the murderers excluded any justification for clemency.

In a meticulously prepared and skillfully arranged case, witnesses were called to prove every detail in the planning and execution of the crime which has been recited. In addition to these the State called as a witness a member of the faculty of the University of Chicago Law School—a professor of criminal law—who testified that the day after the

---

2 The judges of the Circuit and Superior courts of Cook County annually select one of their number to serve as chief justice of the criminal court. Judge Caverly had previously served many years as a judge of the Circuit Court of Cook County and the Municipal Court of Chicago. He had presided in many criminal trials and was known as a kindly man and a humane judge.

murder Leopold discussed with him a hypothetical case: what the crime would be if x forcibly seized a person with intent to kill him, or seized him to hold him for ransom, or seized him with intent to commit indecent liberties upon him and in connection therewith killed him.

Five young men, fellow students of Leopold at the University, produced and identified typewritten letters and memoranda which Leopold had at various times given them. Two eminent questioned-document examiners testified that the signature "George Johnson" on the first ransom note was in Leopold's handwriting, and that both the ransom note and the letter of instructions left in the Michigan Central Pullman car had been written on a typewriter of the same make and series as the one owned by Leopold and recovered in the lagoon. By enlarged photographs, they demonstrated that the specimens of typewriting given by Leopold to his fellow students and the ransom notes had all been written on the same machine. The prosecution's case in chief was concluded with proof and a reading of the confessions. There was no cross-examination of any of these witnesses.

The first witness called by the defense—a nationally known psychiatrist—precipitated a storm of argument. The State objected to any evidence of "insanity" on the ground that (1) such evidence was inconsistent with the defendants' pleas of guilty, and (2) under Illinois law such a defense had to be passed on by jury.

It is rare indeed that an argument on a legal objection to evidence reaches the heights of eloquence, but Darrow's reply to the State's contentions was one of those occasions:

We make no claim that the defendants were legally insane, but we do claim and we will show that there are many mental conditions which fall short of the legal definition of insanity, and would not avail us for a moment in the defense of this case. We know that men and women may be and are seriously ill mentally and yet may know the difference and be able to choose between right and wrong; but they are still mentally afflicted, and the Court will take account of their condition.

We have in this state a statute which says the Court may inquire into any facts mitigating punishment or modifying it. Is there a catalogue of mitigating circumstances? Is the state's attorney to tell you what mitigating circumstances are? There is only one person who can say whether circumstances are mitigating or not, and that is the Court, who is charged with the responsibility and the fate of the defendants who are before him.

We are not going to introduce evidence of insanity, but we do intend to show that our clients are mentally diseased. We intend to exhibit a condition of mind which does not fall within the legal definition of insanity which has to do with the recognition of right and wrong and the power to choose between them. The mental condition we will exhibit does not constitute a defense but it certainly constitutes evidence which should be heard in mitigation on a plea of guilty, just as testimony regarding youth or the circumstances surrounding the crime may be heard. Youth itself is only relevant because it affects the condition of the mind.

The state's attorney's reply to Darrow's argument was bitter and sarcastic—it was all nonsense; either the defendants were sane or they were insane; either they knew the difference between right and wrong or they didn't; the evidence offered by the State showed a deliberate, cruel and wanton murder without a single extenuating circumstance; justice and an outraged public demanded and he would insist upon the extreme penalty.

This afforded Darrow a rare opportunity of which he was quick to take advantage. "It seems to me," Darrow declared, with measured pauses and in a voice deep with emotion, "if I could ever bring my mind to ask for the death penalty, I would do it not boastfully and exultantly or in anger or hate, but I would do it with the deepest regret that it must be done, and I would do it with sympathy even for the ones whose lives were to be taken. That has not been done in this case. I have never seen a more deliberate effort to turn the human beings of a community into ravening wolves and take advantage of everything that was offered to create an unreasoned hatred against these two boys."

Darrow followed this emotional appeal with a telling practical one. He cited three cases tried in the Criminal Court of Cook County where identical evidence of mental condition was admitted under a plea of guilty, and he added that the state's attorney himself, while sitting as a judge in the criminal court, had presided in one of those cases.

Judge Caverly, after a recess for consideration, overruled the State's objection and announced that he would hear any evidence the defense desired to offer which would aid him in determining whether there were mitigating circumstances.

The defense had been built around the findings of four eminent medical specialists—alienists, psychiatrists and neurologists. The testimony of these witnesses was based on their numerous physical examinations of the defendants and many hours of questioning. The physical examination comprehended the vascular and nervous systems, and every organ, bone, gland and tissue of the body that could be explored by visual examination, microscopy, roentgenology or test. The questioning of the defendants covered their acts and thoughts from their earliest recollections to the hour of interrogation. The resulting opinions of these experts were drawn from such objective conditions as they found and their deductions from the information obtained from the defendants concerning their childhood, their care and development, their social, moral and religious supervision and training, their education and associations, their habits, traits and dispositions, their thoughts and philosophies of life, their ambitions, pleasures, dreams, fantasies, delusions and the presence or absence of normal emotional reactions.

The physical examination of Leopold revealed that there had been a premature involution of the thymus gland and a premature calcification of the pineal gland in the skull; that the pituitary gland was smaller than normal; that the thyroid gland was overactive; and that the adrenal glands did not function normally. One of the doctors gave it as his opinion that these abnormalities produced an early sex development and had a direct relationship to Leopold's extraordinary precocity and his mental condition.

The physical examination of Loeb disclosed conditions which the doctors said were equally serious. His blood pressure was subnormal, the blood carbon-dioxide content was markedly low, his basal metabolism was minus seventeen. These combined conditions definitely indicated a disorder of the endocrine glands; he was subject to fainting spells and suffered a nervous disorder which manifested itself in a periodic tremor and twitching of the facial tissues. Such abnormalities, said the physician, were definitely related to Loeb's mental condition.

The prolonged questioning of Leopold and Loeb by medical experts for the defense had developed a mass of startling information which, after such corroboration as could be made of it, they accepted as facts for the purposes of their opinions.

Loeb's early care and education had been turned over to nurses and governesses. He developed into a physically strong, good-looking, winsome and mild-mannered boy. His only apparent physical defects were a stuttering speech —which he had overcome—and a not-too-noticeable nervous tic in the muscles of his face.

When he was about eleven years old, he came under the care of a governess—a strong-minded, Canadian woman of middle age, who was a strict disciplinarian with orthodox ideas of punishment. She developed an inordinate fondness for the boy which exhibited itself in an intimate supervision not only of his routine studies but of everything he read, his movements and his associates. Breaches of her iron discipline were inevitably followed by small penalties —extra study hours or the deprivation of small privileges. Apparently there was little or nothing of religious or ethical training in her program. Loeb, for his part, both loved and feared her. To escape her displeasure and punishments, he deceived her, read books which she had forbidden to him, or of which he knew she would disapprove, and associated with boys, usually older than himself, whom she regarded as undesirable companions.

Loeb was far above the average boy of his age in intelligence and was an avid reader. His secret reading, however, was confined almost entirely to biographical and fictional accounts of bizarre and unusual crimes, of criminals and detectives. He began to have fantasies. Sometimes he imagined himself as an heroic frontiersman, killing Indians and cattle rustlers. Sometimes he saw himself as a master criminal, now avoiding capture and laughing at the police, at other times languishing in prison. Sometimes he was the master detective, ferreting out the truth of crimes which baffled the police. He took to shadowing people, just to see if he could do it. He would get off by himself and, as the imagined leader of a gang, or chief of a squad of detectives, give orders to imaginary subordinates.

When he began to attend school his advanced standing threw him with older boys, whom he attempted to ape. He commenced to drink immoderately before he was fifteen. In college, to make himself a "big shot" with his older companions, he invented tall stories of his athletic exploits and affairs with girls. His associates regarded him as "immature," "childish" and "queer." His fainting spells, which were frequent, rather set him apart from his fellows.

Loeb's fantasies and efforts to satisfy an inferiority complex became stronger and multiplied as time went on. His sense of inferiority and frustration induced spells of morbidity during which he seriously contemplated suicide. He began to play with the idea of testing his notion of the arch criminal by planning and executing the "perfect crime"— a murder, nothing less; one which would startle the country and confound the police. He even considered his younger brother as a possible victim. He became utterly unscrupulous—a liar, a thief and a mischief-maker. Conceptions of right and wrong troubled him not at all. Such were Loeb's personality and state of mind when his association with Leopold began.

Leopold, like Loeb, had been allowed to grow up under the care of nurses and governesses. From his babyhood on his parents indulged the boy's every whim; and, wittingly or unwittingly, his father fostered in him the notion that he was born to wealth which put him in a special position, superior to that of boys less fortunate.

By one of his governesses his development was influenced in a way quite different from the case of Loeb. She entered Leopold's life when he was just fourteen. The record is rather vague as to her antecedents but clear enough as to the fact that she was a pervert, who initiated Leopold into the practices of and submissions to various types of sexual perversion.

Leopold was not a prepossessing youth. He was undersized, round-shouldered and had rather bulging eyes—a condition of which he was extremely sensitive. On the other hand, from early boyhood he had displayed a remarkable precocity and at fourteen had mastered several languages, had read deeply in the sciences, and was possessed of an intellectual capacity out of all proportion to his years. His avidity for reading, wholly unsupervised, led him into the fields of religion and philosophy. He rejected all religion as superstition and, after his mother's death when he was sixteen, became an avowed atheist.

Philosophies with orthodox, ethical concepts he likewise rejected, accepting only the hedonistic philosophy that any action was justified if it gave the actor pleasure. The so-called philosophy of Nietzsche fascinated him. There were men and supermen. The conventions were for ordinary men. Supermen were above them. Supermen became such by the power of intellect and their imperviousness to human emotions. The superman was governed by no code; he could do no wrong. The only possibility he must reckon with was an error of intellectual judgment—a thing impossible to the true superman. Leopold would become a superman. So he crammed his mind not only with knowledge of every sort, but schooled himself to stifle all such common emotions as sympathy, pity or remorse.

In Leopold's philosophy deceit, thieving, perversion, rape, murder—all were justified. Even before his association with Loeb he admitted many petty thefts and other derelictions. Leopold, too, had his fantasies. He pictured himself as the slave to some superman, one whom he would love to the point of idolatry, one to whom he could submit himself in abject obedience. Such were the personality and state of mind of Leopold when he came to know Loeb.

When the association between them began Leopold was fifteen, Loeb a year younger. Leopold had found his superman. There can be little doubt of his infatuation. He told the doctors that he loved Loeb so much that he was jealous of the food he ate and the water he drank, because these "became a part of his being." Loeb needed an audience for the recitation of his criminal plans and a highly intelligent accomplice to aid him in carrying them out. According to the accounts of both boys, which was corroborated by other evidence, this mutuality of interests led to their entering into a most extraordinary "compact." By this weird arrangement—in the discreet language of one of the doctors—"Leopold acquiesced in Loeb's criminalistic endeavors and received in return opportunities for certain twisted biological satisfactions."[3]

While this relationship persisted until their apprehension as the perpetrators of the Franks crime, it was at times a stormy one. Loeb detested Leopold and his perversions. Leopold, while devoted to Loeb, was irked by what he considered Loeb's childishness, immaturity and mental inferiority. They quarreled frequently, sometimes going so far as to threaten each other's lives. Loeb's criminal propensities, however, found scope and assistance. "For the thrill of it" they devised a system for cheating at bridge, they threw bricks through plate-glass windows and automobile windshields, they turned in false fire alarms. In Ann Arbor they set fire to an abandoned building and looted one of the fraternity houses. In none of these derelictions was there a money motive. The boys were, at all times, liberally supplied with money.

They had considered other victims for what proved to be their final crime. They talked about a young boy named Rubel, but they rejected him because his "father was a tight-wad" and might not pay the ransom money demanded. Leopold suggested that if they were going to kill someone, why not a young girl whom they would first rape. Leopold said he got this idea from a story he had read of a young French girl who was raped and then murdered by a German soldier during the occupation.

Both boys discussed with the doctors their latest crime without the slightest indication of revulsion, remorse or grief for the stricken parents of Bobbie Franks. Loeb admitted the murder had been his long-cherished idea of the "perfect crime." Leopold declared it was Loeb's idea, and he had helped Loeb to carry it out because he was Loeb's slave and would do anything Loeb wanted him to do.

---

[3] The details of the compact, as well as of Leopold's unnatural relations with Loeb and with his governess, were heard in chambers.

On the basis of the foregoing, the defense experts gave it as their opinion that while intellectually Loeb was above normal and Leopold supernormal, the emotional development of each was far below normal; that their emotional age was not more than seven or eight years; that it is the emotions rather than the intellect which furnish the primary urge to actions; and that each of the boys "suffered from a profound discord between his intellectual and emotional life." Both were definitely paranoic. Speaking of Leopold, one of the psychiatrists testified: "I have never seen such a definite psychosis in one so young."

In varying language the doctors gave it as their considered opinions that Loeb's dangerous fantasies, carried into his years of adolescence, had so completely taken possession of him that they had swallowed up whatever urges to a normal life he may have had; that he had developed a dual personality—on the one side the apparent friendly, pleasant, well-mannered boy; on the other, the liar, cheat, thief, mischief-maker and plotting criminal. He was termed "a disintegrating personality," inevitably headed for a complete mental breakdown. The doctors found a close relationship—largely of endocrine origin—between his physical abnormalities and mental condition.

Leopold, too, according to the physicians, gave evidence of a dual or split personality. One of them said: "This will develop more and more and eventually he will not know which world he is living in—the fantasy or the real. By the use of his intellect he has built up a successful fantasy defense of superiority against a complex of inferiority which might otherwise cause the breakdown toward which Loeb is headed." Added the doctor: "His intellectual drive is of endocrine origin." There was no reason in Leopold's mind, the doctors agreed, why he should not commit what the law regarded as a crime. He was, as one of them put it, "a completely intellectual individual who might experiment with ideas of right and wrong, of conscience and God."

Leopold, agreed the experts, had no natural criminal tendencies and, had he not come into association with Loeb, would probably never have committed a serious crime. Likewise, Loeb, while possessed of dangerous criminal tendencies, would probably never have undertaken the commission of a major felony without the presence and aid of an intelligent and devoted accomplice. "There was no one serious defect in either which would account for the crime—it was all in combination," stated one of the doctors. The crime was made possible by Loeb's consuming desire to commit the perfect crime and Leopold's willingness, because of their compact, to aid in its execution. "The compact," in one psychiatrist's words, "made the crime inevitable."

The crime, all of the experts agreed, was without normal motivation or was the result of diseased motivation. The pose as kidnapers demanding ransom was but an incident, an "extra kick," in the perfectly planned crime of murder. Both of the defendants, in the unanimous opinion of the experts, were "mentally diseased."

The cross-examination of the defense's medical experts was not particularly fruitful. They admitted their findings were in large part based on what the defendants had told them; that both, and particularly Loeb, were admittedly notorious liars; that they might have fabricated the contents of many of the answers which they had made, but that the experts didn't think they had. The experts readily admitted that both boys knew that murder was prohibited by law, and that they undoubtedly would not have committed the crime had they thought they would be discovered.

The prosecutor in a series of direct, leading questions procured admissions which indicated that the details of the crime had been carefully and shrewdly planned. The witnesses denied, however, that there was any inconsistency between this and the opinions they had expressed as to the defendants' mental conditions. To questions containing assumptions that the defendants had exhibited consternation when confronted with evidence of the discovery of Leopold's glasses, the experts replied that such an exhibition was not at all at variance with their findings and opinions. The cross-examiner scoffed at the acceptance by the doctors of the "compact" story; but the doctors, in reiterating their direct testimony, fortified it by reference to two letters—written by Leopold to Loeb several months before the tragedy—which contained veiled but unmistakable allusions to the claimed relationships.

The defense supplemented the evidence of the psychiatrists with the testimony of a dozen or more witnesses. Classmates and associates of Loeb testified that he drank heavily, that he was nervous, and that the muscles of his face twitched. They were a unit in declaring that many of his actions were childish; that he would laugh uproariously at nothing; that he drove recklessly and seemed to get a kick out of scaring people; and, in general, he played the buffoon. Some declared that at times, in and out of class, he would become belligerent without provocation and, in argument, grow excited and frequently lose the main point and drift off into surprising irrelevancies. Many of them had witnessed his frequent fainting spells. One, a doctor from Charlevoix, Michigan, where the Loebs had a summer home, testified to having attended him for these spells. He said he knew Loeb had had as many as six in a single day. At such times, said the doctor, his body appeared rigid, his eyes glassy and he frothed at the mouth. He was variously characterized as "immature," "lacking in judgment," "unbalanced" and "irresponsible."

Classmates of Leopold at the University of Chicago told of his having discussed with them his beliefs in atheism, nihilism and Nietzscheism. They said he repeatedly argued that the so-called rules of law and ethics did not exist for the superman, who could by his philosophy justify any destruction of life or property. He was characterized as "argumentative," "egocentric" and "conceited." One of the witnesses, a tutor in the law school, testified that in his observation of him, Leopold had manifested no evidence of heightened emotion either before or after the crime.

Five witnesses, with short stories, completed the case for the defense. Loeb's uncle testified to finding three Liberty bonds in young Loeb's desk shortly after the confessions. The principal of one and the interest on all of them were overdue. A brother testified to having found one of the letters written by Leopold to "Dickie." A secretary of Loeb's father testified she was authorized to write checks for such amounts as young Loeb should ask up to $250, and that she had written one such check in February and another in March.

A brother of Leopold testified that Nathan received a monthly allowance of $125 from his father and such other sums of money as he from time to time asked for. He said he paid no board. His father paid his tuition and bought his schoolbooks and his clothes. His father also paid for the upkeep of his automobile and had arranged to give him $3,000 for his contemplated vacation in Europe.

The Loeb family chauffeur testified that the route taken by the defendants after they had picked up the Franks boy lay through much-traveled, closely built-up public streets.

On August 12 the defense rested and the State commenced the production of its rebuttal.

The State called as its first rebuttal witness the state's attorney's secretary who testified that when Loeb was told that Leopold's glasses had been found near the place where the Franks boy's body was discovered "his face lost color, he gave a violent start and was terribly agitated." When Loeb was told that the Leopold family chauffeur had smashed their alibi—by stating that the family car was in the Leopold garage all of the afternoon and evening of the murder—the secretary said Loeb "was agitated, his hands shook and his face lost color." Then Loeb slid back in his chair and seemed about to faint. Someone brought him a glass of water, and the witness heard him exclaim, "My God!"

Other rebuttal witnesses added their testimony to the record. The chief of the state's attorney's detective force testified that when he, in company with Loeb and Leopold, visited the lunchroom where the boys said they had stopped on the day of the murder, Loeb fainted and fell to the floor. The professor of criminal law at the University of Chicago who had previously testified in the State's direct case was recalled. He testified he remembered nothing out of the ordinary about Leopold except that he was extremely bright. A former associate of Leopold testified that he had always considered him a normal person. It was brought out on the cross-examination of this witness that he had frequently heard Leopold express his belief in the philosophy of Nietzsche.

To meet the expert medical testimony offered by the defense, the State called five doctors. Four of them were alienists. All were men of high standing, with extensive experience in the observation and treatment of mentally disordered persons. Under direct examination, by hypothetical questions which purported to sum up the evidence of the defense, the doctors testified there was nothing in the physical findings in either boy to indicate mental abnormality.

The findings of glandular abnormalities were dismissed as of little significance. "The tendency of modern science," said one doctor, "has been to place altogether too much emphasis on such distortions." In the opinions of the State's experts, a recital of the boys' histories and conduct before and after the murder disclosed no abnormality except a lack of appreciation of the enormity of their crime. "Unless it could be assumed that every man who commits a deliberate, cold-blooded murder must, by that fact, be deemed mentally diseased," they all declared, "there was no evidence in this case of any mental disease."

While the opportunities of the State's witnesses to examine, question and study the defendants were confined to an interrogation and observation of the boys immediately after the confessions, or while they were sitting in the courtroom, they refuted the testimony of the defense experts by testifying to definite, and in their opinions, normal emotional reactions in both boys. They testified, particularly, to the defendants' pronounced agitation when they were asked to describe their actions and feelings. One witness said that when he asked Leopold, "Why in Heaven's name did you do such a thing?" the boy's face trembled and he almost broke into tears.

The cross-examinations of the State's experts by Darrow and Benjamin Bachrach elicited several admissions helpful to the defense: Children are born without any inhibitions. Ethical ideas have to be instilled into them by teaching, precept and example, so that a habit of thought and conduct can be formed. What we call moral education is a question of habit fixed deep enough to withstand temptation. If the teaching is deep enough and the resulting habit strong enough, the individual will fit into a moral groove. If, however, the emotions are strong and the teaching weak, he will leap over it. One's beliefs and theories of life tend to fix one's habits and puberty and adolesence are the most trying stages in the life of a young man. Changes in their emotional life come during that period. Insanity is more apt to develop in boys between the ages of twelve and twenty than during their earlier or later years. Suicide is also more likely to occur in those years.

The State concluded its rebuttal on August 19 and the summations began. Marshall and Savage presented the opening argument for the State. Marshall's assignment had been to collect the legal authorities on the responsibility of minors for their crimes and precedents for the infliction of the death penalty upon their conviction for murder.

Marshall was a scholarly, painstaking and industrious lawyer with extensive experience as principal assistant in the prosecutor's office. The result of his effort was a long memorandum of excerpts from the ancient writings of Blackstone and other highly regarded writers and commentators on criminal law, together with dozens of legal precedents for the execution of convicted murderers between the ages of fourteen and nineteen. The texts and cases cited were unimpeachable. They would not be successfully answered by denial or the opposition of contradictory authority. Later it will appear how nimbly Darrow confessed and avoided them.

Savage followed Marshall. He had been in intimate contact with the case since its inception and had every detail of the evidence at his fingers' ends. He was a comparatively young man—vigorous, enthusiastic and ambitious. As an assistant state's attorney, he had prosecuted a number of important cases and had an impressive record of convictions. He was a gifted speaker and his experience had given him a poise and assurance which belied his years. He recalled every detail of the crime, emphasizing its premeditation, its careful planning and its ruthless and cold-blooded execution. He made no attempt to analyze or discuss the medical testimony, and, except for a general denunciation of the defense experts, he confined himself to a restatement of the testimony of the State's doctors and other witnesses. He declared the emotional reactions of the defendants, when they were caught in the mesh of their lies and contradictions, were not different from those of ordinary trapped criminals.

Savage was dramatic, impassioned and vehement, and his argument was studded with extravagant characterizations and declarations: "This is the coldest-blooded murder that the civilized world ever saw. . . . The defense had plead the defendants guilty because they were afraid to do anything else. . . . No one would strike a dog the way these murderers had beat the life out of poor little Bobbie Franks with a cold chisel. . . . If there ever was a case in history in which the most severe punishment was justified, this is the case. . . . If these two escape the gallows, no jury in Cook County could thereafter be expected to inflict upon any defendant, no matter how depraved, the extreme penalty for murder and kidnaping."

Walter and Benjamin Bachrach preceded Darrow in the summations for the defense. They laid particular stress on the time and opportunity afforded the defense psychiatrists for accurate study and extended observation, and their resulting complete knowledge of the defendants as the basis of their considered and scientifically supported conclusions respecting their mental condition. Such opinions, so arrived at, the defense argued, were entitled to vastly greater weight than the opinions of the State's alienists which were negative in character and drawn from "superficial and farcical" examinations. The arguments of the Bachrachs provided the essential background for the emotional appeal of Darrow which followed.

Darrow began his argument on August 22. It was the high point in this sensational trial. He talked for more than twelve hours. The courtroom was jammed to suffocation, with hundreds of men and women rioting in the corridors outside. Word that Darrow was about to speak had brought to the courthouse hundreds more than all the courtrooms in the building could have held.

"The setting," as one of the newspapers reported, "could not have been bettered—the noisy, milling crowd giving point to his argument that the court was the only thing standing between the boys and the bloodthirsty mob."

Darrow knew that the pressure of public opinion was the real force he had to fight. At the outset and throughout his long plea, he sought to keep constantly before the Court that it was this pressure alone, operating consciously or unconsciously, which would prevent any judge from following the usual, and almost routine, procedure of imposing a sentence of life imprisonment on a plea of guilty to first-degree murder, especially where the defendants were minors and their mental condition had been brought into serious question. He began his plea:

Your Honor, our anxiety over this case has not been due to the facts that are connected with this most unfortunate affair, but to the almost unheard-of publicity it has received; to the fact that newspapers all over this country have been giving it space such as they have almost never before given to any case; the fact that day after day the people of Chicago have been regaled with stories of all sorts about it until almost every person has formed an opinion. And when the public is interested and demands a punishment, no matter what the offense, great or small, it thinks only of one punishment and that is death. It may not be a question that involves the taking of human life; it may be a question of pure prejudice alone; but when the public speaks as one man it thinks only of killing. . . . We have said to the public and to this Court that neither the parents, nor the friends, nor the attorneys would want these boys released. They are as they are. Unfortunate though it be true, those the closest to them know perfectly well that they should not be released, and that they should be permanently isolated from society. We have said that; and we mean it. We are asking this Court to save their lives, which is the least and the most that a judge can do.

Darrow's argument on the first day was largely a plea for consideration of the defendants because of their youth, of their pleas of guilty and the expressed willingness of their counsel to accept and abide by a sentence of life imprisonment:

Your Honor, there has never been a case in Chicago where, on a plea of guilty, a boy under twenty-one has been sentenced to death. I will raise that age and say, never has there been a case where a human being under the age of twenty-three has been sentenced to death. And yet this Court is urged, aye, threatened that he must hang two boys contrary to the precedents, contrary to the acts of every judge who ever held court in this state.

Why? Tell me what public necessity there is for this. Why need the state's attorney ask for something that never before has been demanded? Why need a judge be urged by every argument, moderate and immoderate, to hang two boys in the face of every precedent in Illinois, and in the face of progress of the last fifty years? Lawyers stand here by the day and read cases from the Dark Ages, where judges have said that if a man had a grain of sense left, and a child if he was barely out of his cradle, could be hanged because he knew the difference between right and wrong. Death sentences for eighteen, seventeen, sixteen and fourteen years have been cited.

Brother Marshall has not half done his job. He should read his beloved Blackstone again. . . . Why did not my friend, Mr. Marshall, who dug up from the relic of the buried past these precedents that would bring a blush of shame to the face of a savage, read this from Blackstone: 'Under fourteen, though an infant shall be judged incapable of guile prima facie, yet if it appear to the court and the jury that he was capable of guile, and could discern between good and evil, he may be convicted and suffer death.' Thus a girl of thirteen has been burned for killing her mistress. . . . One boy of ten, and another of nine years of age, who had killed his companion, were sentenced to death; and he of ten actually hanged. Why? He knew the difference between right and wrong. He had learned it in Sunday school. . . . Your Honor, we have raised the age of hanging, we have raised it by the humanity of the Court [and] by the progress in science which at last is reaching the law.

Darrow spent practically an entire day discussing the mental condition of his youthful clients. He first addressed himself to the lack of a rational motive for the crime—"a senseless, useless, purposeless, motiveless act of two boys." He scoffed at the idea that Loeb, who had $3,000 in a checking account, and three Liberty bonds, one of them past due, and the interest on all of them not collected for three years, and who could by his father's order get up to $250 from his father's secretary whenever he wanted it, would plan and execute a kidnaping and murder and risk his neck either to pay a bridge debt of $90, or to share in $10,000 of ransom money.

That Leopold was actuated by such motives, Darrow argued, was equally ridiculous. Leopold was in regular receipt of $125 a month. He had an automobile. He paid nothing for his board and clothes. He could get money from his father whenever he wanted it. He had arranged to go to Europe before entering Harvard Law School in the fall. His ticket had been bought, and his father was giving him $3,000 to make the trip.

The so-called Machiavellian plans of the defendants, said Darrow, so far from showing sane premeditation, as contended by the State, proved that their act was the product of diseased minds. "I say again," argued Darrow, "whatever madness and hate and frenzy may do to the human mind, there is not a single person who reasons who can believe that one of these acts was the act of men of brains that were not diseased. There is no other explanation for it. And had it not been for the wealth and the weirdness and the notoriety, they would have been sent to the psychopathic hospital for examination and been taken care of, instead of the State demanding that this Court take the last pound of flesh and the last drop of blood from two irresponsible lads."

Darrow then proceeded to review the evidence: After they had killed the boy and wrapped him in the blanket they drove for twenty miles through thickly populated streets, where everyone knew the boys and their families, on to the Midway, traveled by automobiles more than any street on the South Side, through the drives of Jackson Park. Leopold was on the front seat driving, and Loeb was on the back seat with the dead boy.

In his review Darrow declared:

The slightest accident, the slightest misfortune, a bit of curiosity, an arrest for speeding, anything would bring destruction. . . . And yet they tell me this is sanity; they tell me that the brains of these boys are not diseased. You need no experts, you need no X rays; you need no study of the endocrines. Their conduct shows exactly what it was, and shows that this Court has before him two young men who should be examined in a psychopathic hospital and treated kindly and with care.

They get through South Chicago and they take the regular automobile road down toward Hammond. There is the same situation: hundreds of machines; any accident might encompass their ruin. They stop at the forks of the road and leave little Bobbie Franks, soaked with blood, in the machine, and get their dinner, and eat it without an emotion or a qualm. . . . Your Honor, there is not a sane thing in all of this from beginning to end. There was not a normal act in any of it, from its inception in a diseased brain, until today, when they sit here awaiting their doom.

And then in a day or so we find Dick Loeb with his pockets stuffed with newspapers telling of the Franks tragedy. We find him consulting with his friends in the club, with the newspaper reporters—and my experience is that the last person that a conscious criminal associates with is a reporter. He even shuns them more than he does a detective, because they are smarter and less merciful. But he picks up a reporter, and he tells him that he has read a great many detective stories, and he knows just how this would happen and that the fellow who telephoned must have gone down 63rd Street, and the way to find him is to go down 63rd Street and visit the drugstores and he would go with him. And Dick Loeb pilots reporters around the drugstores where the telephoning was done, and he talks about it, and he takes the newspapers, and takes them with him, and he is having a glorious time. . . . Is there any question about the condition of his mind? Why was he doing it? He liked to hear about it. He had done something that he could not boast of directly, but he did want to hear other people talk about it, and he looked around there, and helped them find the place where the telephone message was sent out.

Your Honor has had experience with criminals, and you know how they act. Was any such thing as this ever heard of before on land or sea? Does not the man who knows what he is doing, who for some reason has been over-powered and commits what is called a crime, keep as far away from it as he can? Does he go to the reporters and help them hunt him out? There is not a single act in this case that is not the act of a diseased mind, not one.

With this background, Darrow entered on a discussion of the medical testimony:

Now, Your Honor, who are these two boys? Leopold, with a wonderfully brilliant mind; Loeb with an unusual intelligence—both from their early youth crowded like hot-house plants, to learn more and more. . . . But it takes something besides brains to make a human being who can adjust himself to life. In fact, as Dr. Church and Dr. Singer regretfully admitted, brains are not the chief essential in human conduct. The emotions are the urge that make us live; the urge that makes us work or play, or move along the pathways of life. They are the instinctive things. In fact, intellect is a late development of life. Long before it was evolved the emotional life kept the organism in existence until death. Whatever our action is, it comes from the emotions, and nobody is balanced without them. . . . The question of intellect means the smallest part of life. Back of this are man's nerves, muscles, heart, blood, lungs —in fact, the whole organism; the brain is the least part in human development. Without the emotion-life man is nothing.

Darrow then proceeded to review the evidence as to Loeb's escaping from the tyranny of his governess, his deceits and lies, his devouring of tales of crime, his fantasies, his developing criminal tendencies, his larcenies and destructions, and his final obsession that he must commit the "perfect crime." Darrow stated:

Dickie Loeb was a child. The books he read by day were not the books he read by night. We are all of us molded somewhat by the influences around us, and, of those of us who read, perhaps books are the greatest and the strongest influence. . . . We all know where our lives have been molded by books. The nurse, strict and jealous and watchful, gave him one kind of books; by night he would steal off and read another. Which, think you, shaped the life of Dickie Loeb? Is there any kind of question about it? . . . These books became a part of his life and as he grew up his visions grew to hallucinations. . . . There never was a time since he was old enough to move by what seemed to be from his own volition that he was not haunted with these phantasies. . . .

We may have all had the dreams and visions and built all the castles we wish but the castles of youth should be discarded with youth, and when they linger to the time when boys should think wiser things then it indicates a diseased mind. "When I was young I thought as a child, I spake as a child, I understood as a child, but now I have put off childish things," said the psalmist twenty centuries ago. It is when these dreams of boyhood, these phantasies of youth, still linger and the growing child is still a child— a child in emotion, a child in feeling, a child in hallucination—that you say it is the dreams and the hallucinations that are responsible for his conduct.

There is not an act in all of this horrible tragedy that was not the act of a child, the act of a child wandering around in the morning of life, moved by the new feelings of a boy, moved by the uncontrollable impulses which his teaching was not strong enough to take care of, moved by the dreams and hallucinations which haunt the brain of a child.

I say to Your Honor that it would be the height of cruelty, of injustice, of wrong and barbarism to visit the penalty of death upon this poor boy. . . . This boy needed more of home, more love, more directing. He needed to have his emotions awakened. He needed guiding hands along the serious road that youth must travel. Had these been given him, he would not be here today.

Darrow next turned to Leopold:

His emotional life was lacking, as every alienist and witness in this case, excepting Dr. Krohn, has told you. He was a half boy, an intellect, an intellectual machine going without balance, without a governor, seeking to find out everything there was in life intellectually, seeking to solve every philosophy but using his intellect only. . . . He took up philosophy. . . . He became enamoured of Nietzsche.

Your Honor, I have read almost everything that Nietzsche ever wrote. He was a man of wonderful intellect; the most original philosopher of the last century. A man who probably has made a deeper imprint on philosophy than any other man within a hundred years, whether right or wrong. More books have been written about him than probably all the rest of the philosophers in a hundred years. More college professors have talked about him. . . . Nietzsche believed that some time the superman would be born, that evolution was working toward the superman.

He wrote one book, *Beyond Good and Evil,* which was a criticism of all the moral codes as the world understands them; a treatise holding that the intelligent man is beyond good and evil; that the laws for good and the laws for evil do not apply to those who approach the superman. He wrote on the will to power. He wrote ten or fifteen volumes on his various philosophical ideas. Nathan Leopold is not the only boy who has read Nietzsche. He may be the only one who was influenced in the way that he was influenced.

Darrow then proceeded to quote at length from the works of Nietzsche. He dwelt on such extracts: "To be obsessed by moral considerations presupposes a very low grade of intellect. . . . The morality of the master class is irritating to the taste of the present day because of its fundamental principle that a man has obligations only to his equals; that he may act to all of lower rank and to all that are foreign as he pleases." He quoted an interpreter of Nietzsche, a professor of philosophy: "The superman-like qualities lie not in their genius, but in their freedom from scruple. They rightly felt themselves to be above the law. What they thought was right, not because sanctioned by any law beyond themselves, but because they did it. So the superman will be a law unto himself. What he does will come from the will and superabundant power within him." Darrow continued:

Now, here is a boy at sixteen or seventeen becoming obsessed with these doctrines. . . . It was not a casual bit of philosophy with him; it was his life. He believed in a superman. He and Dickie Loeb were supermen. There might have been others, but they were two, and two chums. The ordinary commands of society were not for them. . . . Here is a boy who by day and by night, in season and out, was talking of the superman owing no obligations to any-one; whatever gave him pleasure he should do, believing it just as another man might believe a religion or any phil-osophical theory. . . . You will remember that I asked Dr. Church about Nietzsche. He said he knew something of Nietzsche, something of his responsibility for the war,[4] for which perhaps he was not responsible. He said he knew something about his doctrines. I asked him what became of him, and he said he was insane for fifteen years just be-fore his death.

His very doctrine is a species of insanity! Here is a man, a wise man—perhaps not wise, but brilliant—a thoughtful man who has made his impress upon the world. Every stu-dent of philosophy knows him. His own doctrines made him a maniac. And here is a young boy, in his adolescent age, harassed by everything that harasses children, who takes this philosophy and believes it literally. It is part of his life. It is his life. Do you suppose this mad act could have been done by him in any other way? . . . He did it ob-sessed of an idea, perhaps to some extent influenced by what has not been developed publicly in this case—perver-

---

[4] Darrow is referring, of course, to World War I. The philosophy of Nietzsche, preached to the German people by the Nazi leaders, is generally credited as one of the major causes of World War II.

sions that were present in the boy. Both signs of insanity; both, together with this act, proving a diseased mind.

Is there any question about what was responsible for him? What else could be? A boy in his youth, with every promise that the world could hold out before him—wealth and position and intellect, yes, genius, scholarship, nothing that he could not obtain, and he throws it away and mounts the gallows or goes into a cell for life. Is it too foolish to talk about? Can Your Honor imagine a sane brain doing it? Can you imagine it coming from anything but a diseased mind? Can you imagine it is any part of normality? And yet, Your Honor, you are asked to hang a boy of his age, abnormal, obsessed of dreams and visions, a philosophy that destroyed his life, when there is no sort of question in the world as to what caused his downfall.

Darrow concluded his discussion of Leopold's mental condition with a reading of two letters written by Leopold to Loeb some seven months before the murder. One of them—the longer and more revealing one—was a State's exhibit. The letters, while somewhat vague, left little room for doubt as to the abnormal relationship between the two boys and of Leopold's complete obsession with Nietzschean philosophy. In regard to the letters Darrow said:

Are those the letters of a normal eighteen-year-old boy, or are they the letters of a diseased brain? Is that the letter of boys acting as boys should, or is it the letter of one whose philosophy has taken possession of him, who understands that what the world calls crime is something that the superman may do—who believes that the only crime the superman can commit is to make a mistake? He believed it. He was immature. It possessed him. It was manifest in the strange compact that the Court already knows about between these two boys, by which each was to yield something and each was to give something.

Out of that compact and out of these diseased minds grew this terrible crime. Tell me, was this compact the act of normal boys, of boys who think and feel as boys should —boys who have the thoughts and emotions and physical life that boys should have? There is nothing in all of it that corresponds with normal life. There is a weird, strange, unnatural disease in all of it which is responsible for this deed.

I submit, Your Honor, that by every law of humanity, by every law of justice, by every feeling of righteousness, by every instinct of pity, mercy and charity, Your Honor should say that because of the condition of these boys' minds it would be monstrous to visit upon them the vengeance that is asked by the State.

The last subject of Darrow's long pleas was the inhumanity, futility and evil consequences of capital punishment. It was a matter close to his heart. From young manhood he had been a serious student of criminology. He had written innumerable pamphlets and articles advocating the abolition of the death penalty as a punishment for crime. He had debated the question on platforms throughout America. He had appeared before state legislatures and legislative committees to urge the repeal of the death-penalty statutes. But in a Chicago courtroom, in the defense of two boys admittedly guilty of the atrocious murder of an innocent child, he was, through the world-wide publicity given to the case, to reach his largest audience.

One cannot judge of the persuasiveness of the argument without reading it in its entirety.[5] The excerpt given below is but one of many which might be quoted to illustrate its quality. Assistant State's Attorney Savage had been particularly bitter in his denunciation of the defendants and vehement in his demand that the Court give them "the same mercy they gave to Bobbie Franks." Darrow availed himself of this opening to introduce his argument:

Mr. Savage, in as cruel a speech as he knew how to make, says age makes no difference, and if this Court should do what every other Court in Illinois has done since its foun-

---

5 Darrow's entire argument after publication in the public press was published in pamphlet form shortly after the trial by Haldeman-Julius Company, Girard, Kansas.

dation, and refused to sentence these boys to death, no one else would ever be hanged in Illinois. Well, I can imagine some results worse than that. So long as this terrible tool is to be used as a plaything, without thought or consideration, we ought to get rid of it for the protection of human life. . . .

I marveled when I heard Mr. Savage talk. I do not criticize him. He is young and enthusiastic. But has he ever read anything? Has he ever thought? Was there ever any man who had studied science, who had read anything of criminology or philosophy—was there ever any man who knew himself who could speak with the assurance with which he speaks?

What about this matter of crime and punishment, anyhow? I may know less than the rest, but I have at least tried to find out, and I am fairly familiar with the best literature that has been written on that subject in the last hundred years. The more men study, the more men doubt the effect of severe punishment on crime. And yet Mr. Savage tells the Court that if these boys are hanged, there will be no more murder. Mr. Savage is an optimist. He says that if the defendants are hanged, there will be no more boys like these.

I would give him a sketch of punishment, punishment beginning with the brute which killed something because something hurt it; the punishment of the savage. If a person is injured in the tribe, they must injure somebody in the other tribe; it makes no difference who it is, but somebody. If one is killed, his friends or family must kill in return. You can trace it all down through the history of man. You can trace the burnings, the boilings, the drawings and quarterings, the hangings of people at the crossroads, carving them up and hanging them as examples for all to see. We can come down to the last century where nearly two hundred crimes were punishable by death, and by death in every form; not only hanging—that was too humane— but burning, boiling, cutting into pieces, torturing in all conceivable forms.

You can read the stories of the hangings on a high hill, and the populace for miles around coming out to the scene, that everybody might be awed into goodness. Hanging for picking pockets—and more pockets were picked in the crowd that went to the hanging than had been known before. Hangings for murder—and men were murdered on the way there and on the way home. Hangings for poaching, hangings for everything, and hangings in public, not shut up cruelly and brutally in a jail, out of the light of day, wakened in the nighttime and led forth and killed, but taken to the shire town on a high hill, in the presence of a multitude, so that all might see that the wages of sin were death. What happened?

I have read the life of Lord Shaftesbury, a great nobleman of England, who gave his life and his labors toward modifying the penal code. I have read of the slow, painful efforts through the ages for more humanity of man to his fellow men. I know what history says. I know what it means, and I know what flows from it, so far as we can tell, which is not with certainty. I know that every step in the progress of humanity has been met and opposed by prosecutors, and many times by Courts. I know that when poaching and petty larceny were punishable by death in England, juries refused to convict. They were too humane to obey the law; and judges refused to sentence. I know that when the delusion of witchcraft was spreading over Europe, claiming its victims by the thousands, many a judge so shaped his cases that no crime of witchcraft could be punished in his court. I know that these trials were stopped in America because juries would no longer convict. I know that every step in the progress of the world with reference to crime has come from the human feelings of man. It has come from that deep well of sympathy which, in spite of all our training and all our conventions and all our teaching, still lives in the human breast. Without it there could be no human life in this weary old world.

Gradually the laws have been changed and modified, and men look back with horror at the hangings and killings of the past. What did they find in England? That as they got rid of these barbarous statutes crimes decreased instead of increased; as the criminal law was modified and humanized, there was less crime instead of more. I will undertake to say, Your Honor, that you can scarcely find a single book written by a student—and I will include all the works on criminology of the past—that has not made the statement over and over again that as the penal code was made less terrible, crimes grew less frequent.

The infliction of the death penalty, continued the great advocate, entailed another serious consideration:

Let us take this case. If these two boys die on the scaffold —which I can never bring myself to imagine—if they do die on the scaffold, the details of this will be spread over the world. Every newspaper of Chicago will be filled with the gruesome details. It will enter every home and every family. Will it make men better or make men worse? . . . Would it make the human heart softer or would it make hearts harder? How many men would be colder and crueler for it? How many men would enjoy the details? And you cannot witness human suffering without being affected for better or for worse. Those who enjoyed it would be affected for the worse.

What influence would it have upon the millions of men who will read it? What influence would it have upon the millions of women who will read it, more sensitive, more impressionable, more imaginative than men? Would it help them if Your Honor should do what the State begs you to do? What influence would it have upon the infinite number of children who will devour its details as Dickie Loeb has enjoyed reading detective stories? Would it make them better or would it make them worse? The question needs no answer. You can answer it from the human heart. What influence, let me ask you, will it have for the unborn babies still sleeping in their mothers' wombs? And what influence will it have on the psychology of the fathers and mothers yet to come? Do I need to argue to Your Honor that cruelty only breeds cruelty?—that hatred only causes hatred; that if there is any way to soften the human heart, which is hard enough at its best, if there is any way to kill evil and hatred and all that goes with it, it is not through evil and hatred and cruelty; it is through charity and love and understanding.

How often do people need to be told this? Look back at the world. There is not a man who is pointed to as an example to the world who has not taught it. There is not a philosopher, there is not a religious leader, there is not a creed that has not taught it. This is a Christian community, so-called, at least it boasts of it, and yet they could hang these boys in a Christian community. Let me ask this Court, is there any doubt about whether these boys would be safe in the hands of the founder of the Christian religion? It would be a blasphemy to say they would not. Nobody could imagine, nobody could even think of it. And yet there are men who want to hang them for a childish, purposeless act, conceived without the slightest malice in the world. . . .

I do not know how much salvage there is in these two boys. I hate to say it in their presence, but what is there to look forward to? I do not know but that Your Honor would be merciful if you tied a rope around their necks and left them to die; merciful to them, but not merciful to civilization, and not merciful to those who would be left behind. To spend the balance of their lives in prison is mighty little to look forward to, if anything.

Is there anything? They may have the hope that as the years roll around they might be released. I do not know. I will be honest with this Court as I have tried to be from the beginning. I know that these boys are not fit to be at large. I believe they will not be until they pass through the next stage of life, at forty-five or fifty. Whether they will be then, I cannot tell. I am sure of this: that I will not be here to help them. So far as I am concerned, it is over.

I would not tell this Court that I do not hope that some time, when life and age have changed their bodies, as it does, and has changed their emotions, as it does, that they may once more return to life. I would be the last person on earth to close the door to any human being that lives, and least of all to my clients. But what have they to look forward to? Nothing. And I think here of a stanza of Housman:

> "O never fear, lads, naught's to dread,
>   Look not to left nor right:
> In all the endless road you tread
>   There's nothing but the night."

I care not, Your Honor, whether the march begins at the gallows or when the gates of Joliet close upon them, there is nothing but the night, and that is little for any human being to expect. . . .

Now, I must say a word more and then I will leave this with you where I should have left it long ago. None of us are unmindful of the public; Courts are not; juries are not. We placed our fate in the hands of a trained Court, thinking that he would be more mindful and considerate than a jury. I cannot say how people feel. I have stood here for three months as one might stand at the ocean trying to sweep back the tide. I hope the seas are subsiding and the wind is falling, and I believe they are, but I wish to make no false pretenses to this Court.

The easy thing to do and the popular thing to do is to hang my clients. I know it. Men and women who do not think will applaud. The cruel and thoughtless will approve. It will be easy today; but in Chicago, and reaching over the length and breadth of the land, more and more fathers and mothers, the humane, the kind and the hopeful, who are gaining an understanding and asking questions not only about these poor boys, but about their own—these will join in no acclaim in the death of my clients. They would ask that the shedding of blood be stopped, and that the normal feelings of man resume their sway. And as the days and the months and the years go on, they will ask it more and more.

But, Your Honor, what they shall ask may not count. I know the easy way. I know Your Honor stands between the future and the past. I know the future is with me, and what I stand for here; not merely for the lives of these two unfortunate lads, but for all boys and all girls; for all the young; as far as possible, for all the old. I am pleading for life, understanding, charity, kindness, and the infinite mercy that considers all. I am pleading that we overcome cruelty with kindness and hatred with love. I know the future is on my side. Your Honor stands between the past and the future.

You may hang these boys; you may hang them by the neck until they are dead. But in doing it you will turn your face toward the past. In doing it you are making it harder for every other boy who in ignorance and darkness must grope his way through the mazes which only childhood knows. In doing it you will make it harder for unborn children. You may save them and make it easier for every child that sometime may stand where these boys stand. You will make it easier for every human being with an aspiration and a vision and a hope and a fate. I am pleading for the future; I am pleading for a time when hatred and cruelty will not control the hearts of men, when we can learn by reason and judgment and understanding and faith that all life is worth saving, and that mercy is the highest attribute of man. . . .

If I should succeed in saving these boys' lives and do nothing for the progress of the law, I should feel sad, indeed. If I can succeed, my greatest reward and my greatest hope will be that I have done something for the tens of thousands of other boys, for the countless unfortunates who must tread the same road in blind childhood that these poor boys have trod—that I have done something to help human understanding, to temper justice with mercy, to overcome hate with love.

I was reading last night of the aspiration of the old Persian poet, Omar Khayyám. It appealed to me as the highest that I can vision. I wish it was in my heart, and I wish it was in the hearts of all.

> "So I be written in the Book of Love,
> I do not care about the Book above;
> Erase my name or write it as you will,
> So I be written in the Book of Love."

The effect of Darrow's appeal was manifest. As a special correspondent for one paper put it: "There was scarcely any telling where his voice had finished and where silence had begun. Silence lasted a minute, two minutes. His own eyes, dimmed by years of serving the accused, the oppressed, the weak, were not the only ones that held tears." Every newspaper in Chicago, and many throughout the nation, printed the long argument in full—a tribute rarely paid to even the greatest of advocates.

State's Attorney Crowe made the final summing up for the State. He talked for the better part of two days. His argument was unrestrained, sarcastic and vituperative. In rapid-fire sequences, which one press reporter likened to the striking and clawing of a maddened panther, he assailed and belittled the defense experts, the defendants and the defendants' lawyers—Darrow, in particular. The experts, stated Crowe, with their "emotional immaturity," their "fantasies and delusions," their "glandular abnormalities," and their "split personalities" were the hired, crooked and gullible tools of a "million-dollar defense," prepared to swear to anything, no matter how fantastic.

The defendants, shouted Crowe, were ruthless killers, dangerous to society, and "as little entitled to sympathy and mercy as a couple of rattlesnakes, flushed with venom, and ready to strike." The pact between Leopold and Loeb, he declared, was a myth. Leopold "had something on Loeb" and blackmailed him into submission to his perverted practices. Both planned the crime. Both executed it. The motive was $10,000 ransom money. Darrow, repeated Crowe over and over again, was "an atheist, the same as his clients," "the exponent of a philosophy as dangerous as that of Leopold," and "a paid advocate whose profession it was to protect murder in Cook County, and concerning whose health thieves inquire before they go out to commit crime."

Crowe denied Darrow's contention that severe punishment did not deter others from committing crimes. He cited the criminal statistics of Great Britain and the American Federal courts to sustain his contention. He closed with his most telling argument: the reading of a letter written by Theodore Roosevelt while he was President, in which Roosevelt denied a plea to commute a death sentence for a particularly atrocious murder to life imprisonment. The letter read:

Among the most dangerous criminals, and especially among those prone to commit this particular kind of offense, there are plenty of a temper so fiendish or brutal as to be incompatible with any other than a brutish order of intelligence. But these men are nevertheless responsible for their acts; and nothing more tends to encourage crime among such men than the belief that through a plea of insanity or other method it is possible for them to escape paying the penalty for their crimes. The crime in question is one to the existence of which we largely owe that sort of lawlessness which takes form in lynching. It is a crime so revolting that the criminal is not entitled to one particle of sympathy from any human being.

"Now," concluded Crowe, "I submit it is safer to follow the reasoning of this state document than it is to follow the sophistries of Clarence Darrow. I submit it is safer to follow the philosophy of Theodore Roosevelt as he laid it down in this state paper when he was President of the United States, and concerned only with the enforcement of the law, than it is to follow the weird, uncanny philosophy of the paid advocate of the defense, whose business it is to make murder safe in Cook County."

After the summations were concluded the State recalled Jacob Franks to make formal proof of the kidnaping indictment. He testified to the telephone calls and identified the ransom note, which was offered in evidence. To this the defendants offered no defense.

The fate of the defendants was now in the hands of the Court. Judge Caverly announced that the cases would be continued to September 10 at which time he hoped to have reached his decision. He disclosed that during the course of the hearing he had received a number of "crank" letters, some threatening him with bodily injury if he hanged the defendants, and others suggesting consequences equally dire if he didn't. On September 10, said the judge, in order to forestall the possibility of any untoward demonstrations, no one other than the defendants, members of their families and counsel for the respective parties would be admitted to the courtroom.

On September 10, 1924, Judge Caverly was visibly nervous as he mounted the bench and stood—as did the defendants, the assembled lawyers and court attaches—while the clerk intoned the customary: "Hear ye, hear ye, hear ye, this Honorable Branch of the Criminal Court of Cook County is now in session pursuant to adjournment." There was a sharp rap of the gavel, and the clerk announced: "People of the State of Illinois versus Nathan Leopold, Jr., and Richard Loeb." Judge Caverly adjusted his glasses, arranged his papers and began: "In view of the profound and unusual interest that this case has aroused not only in this community but in the entire country and even beyond its borders, the Court feels it is his duty to state the reasons which have led him to the determination he has reached."

The case before him, the judge declared, was unlike the usual plea of guilty, made by previous arrangement with the state's attorney and accompanied with his recommendation of an appropriate punishment. Here there was no doubt of the defendants' guilt; the State possessed conclusive evidence of it, supplemented by the voluntary confessions of both defendants. The pleas of guilty, therefore, did not make a special case in favor of the defendants.

Because it was his duty under the statute, continued the Court, he had heard all of the evidence offered by both sides, of facts or circumstances aggravating or mitigating the offense. From a consideration of all of the evidence, he said, he was satisfied that the case was not one where, if the evidence as to mental condition had been submitted under a plea of guilty, it would have amounted to a legal defense of insanity; and that, while the evidence had shown the defendants to be abnormal in certain respects, he was "strongly of the opinion" that a similar study of the mental condition of many other criminals would reveal similar or equivalent abnormalities. He added that while the broad question of human responsibility for crime might well be deserving of legislative consideration, he, as an arm of the judiciary, was bound to enforce the law as he found it.

"The testimony in this case," continued the Court, "reveals a crime of singular atrocity. It is in a sense inexplicable, but it is not thereby rendered less repulsive and inhumane. It was deliberately planned and prepared for during a considerable period of time. It was executed with every feature of callousness and cruelty." The Court added that the evidence did not establish that the body had been subjected to any unnatural abuse, but "the absence of that fact did not make the crime any less revolting." Summing up his findings, the Court declared himself satisfied that neither in the act itself, nor in the lack of motive, nor in the antecedents of the defendants could he find any mitigating circumstances.

After reading the statutes defining the crimes and specifying the alternative punishments provided for murder and kidnaping, the Court declared there was no rule of law to guide him in fixing a particular punishment. It would be easy, he said, to follow the line of least resistance and impose the extreme penalty of the law; but it was within his province to choose imprisonment instead of death, and he was moved to that alternative by a consideration of the age of the defendants—boys of eighteen and nineteen years of age—and his unwillingness to impose a sentence of death on persons not of full age. Such a sentence, he concluded, was in accordance with the progress of the criminal law all over the world and all of the dictates of an enlightened humanity.

The Court then proceeded to pass formal sentence upon each defendant; imprisonment for life on the indictment for murder; imprisonment for the term of ninety-nine years on the indictment for kidnaping.

The relief of the defendants, their kin and counsel was manifest. The long strain was over. The shadow of the gallows within which they had stood for nearly four months had disappeared. The state's attorney and his assistants appeared stunned. The early paragraphs of the Court's decision, finding that the pleas entitled the defendants to no special consideration, and that there were no mitigating circumstances, had pointed unmistakably to a sentence of death. The reversal in the concluding paragraphs had come as suddenly and unexpectedly as a flash of lightning out of a clear sky.

The prisoners were led out of the courtroom, and back to their cells. The most sensational trial in Chicago's history was ended.

AFTERMATH

Leopold and Loeb were immediately taken to the Joliet penitentiary. They were subjected to the usual entrance routine, given prison clothes and numbers. After the inevitable follow-up stories in two or three issues of the daily papers, Leopold and Loeb ceased to be news.

Eleven years went by. Then tragedy once more turned the spotlight upon the two convicts. On January 28, 1936, another prison inmate—one James Day—in a fight with Loeb so cut him with a razor that Loeb died. There were opposing versions as to what happened. The prison authorities claimed that Day deliberately sought Loeb out and without provocation assaulted and killed him. Day claimed that Loeb possessed a special influence with the prison authorities; that he had pretended a friendship and interest in Day and had procured an easy office job for him; that he then commenced to hound him and threaten to take the job away unless Day became "broadminded" and submitted to Loeb's perversions.

According to Day, on the day of the fatal quarrel, Loeb accosted him in a shower bathroom in the prison. He had a razor in his hand and, by threatening to kill Day, caused him to disrobe. When the opportunity offered, Day said, he kicked Loeb in the groin, causing him to fall and drop the razor, but Loeb continued to struggle with Day and beat him with his fists. Day said he managed to get possession of the razor and, in resisting Loeb's attack, struck him with it repeatedly until Loeb's body went limp and fell to the floor.

Day was indicted for murder. He pleaded not guilty, was tried by a jury and acquitted.

Leopold, on entering the penitentiary, became a part-time teacher in the prison school. Later he was assigned to the hospital as a nurse. In June of 1945 he was one of a small number of convicts to volunteer for inoculation with malaria germs and subsequent treatment with experimental sera. As a result he was made seriously ill, but in a matter of a few weeks he made a complete recovery. In January 1948 he made an application for executive clemency, and on June 22, 1949, his ninety-nine-year sentence on the kidnaping charge was commuted by Governor Stevenson to eighty-five years. Under Illinois law,[6] this made him eligible for a definite sentence parole in December 1952.

For Leopold the "night," which Darrow so eloquently predicted, while it has lasted for more than twenty-five years, may not be eternal.

---

[6] A life-term convict is eligible for consideration for parole after having served twenty years; a term-of-years convict at the expiration of one-third of his sentence.

IV

The Trial of

BRUNO HAUPTMANN

for the Murder of

CHARLES LINDBERGH, JR.
(1935)

4

The Bruno Hauptmann Case

THE KIDNAPING AND KILLING *of the Lindbergh baby stirred the emotions of the American public as no other crime has done in the last fifty years. From one end of the country to the other, fathers and mothers shared the anxiety of the beloved and distracted parents during the supposed negotiations for their child's safe return. Anxiety became horror when the body of the dead baby was found. With an outpouring of sympathy from every home in the land came a demand for the apprehension and punishment of the perpetrator and a strengthening of laws to halt the incidence of this terrifying crime. When, after more than two years, the culprit was discovered and put on trial, the day-to-day proceedings in the little old courthouse at Flemington, New Jersey, claimed top priority in every newspaper and news radio program in the nation.*

The discovery, as the result of one of the most amazing investigations in criminal history, of an incredible concatenation of incriminatory facts and circumstances, the intelligent and forceful presentation of the technical and unusual aspects of the case to a lay jury, and the celerity with which the appeal from the judgment of conviction was fully and dispassionately considered and disposed of by the court of last resort increased public confidence in the effectiveness of the judicial process. As a consequence of the spotlight of publicity focused on the Lindbergh case, the laws against kidnaping, both state and Federal, were strengthened. This and the revelation of the power and ability of the state to deal with the crime, the judgment of death for Hauptmann and his execution served for the future as a deterrent to the criminally minded from embarking hastily on this particular criminal adventure. Kidnaping became an infrequent, rather than common, crime.

For the trial lawyer particularly the case possesses unusual interest. In no reported case involving the identity of disputed handwritings has there been assembled such a galaxy of scientific talent. Solution of the problems presented involved the application of all the usual techniques employed by these experts. The shorthand transcript of the record of the case—available in the office of the clerk of the Court of Errors and Appeals of New Jersey and in the New York Association of the Bar, the Chicago Bar Association and other law libraries—affords the interested practitioner an invaluable source of preparation in a case involving questions of handwriting identity and comparison. The extraordinary expert testimony of Arthur Koehler, the "expert on wood," is not only fascinating for its own interest and merit, but also for its suggestion to the practitioner of the growing importance and possibilities of the application of the results of scientific research to trial problems.

KIDNAPING is a terrifying crime—terrifying to the victim, who suddenly finds himself the prisoner of ruthless criminals, potential murderers; terrifying to the family of the victim, who must needs live in mortal suspense and know no peace unless and until he is safely returned. When the victim is an infant of tender years the agony of the parents is increased by fear that the child, regardless of the intention of the kidnapers, may die of ill-treatment or neglect.

While the crime of abduction or kidnaping for ransom is not indigenous to any single community, it is unquestionable that during the late twenties and early thirties this particular crime became more prevalent in the United States than in any other country of the world. There were several reasons for this. In no other country are the wealth and family and living habits of its more fortunate citizens more widely advertised. In no other country do organized gangs of racketeers and lawbreakers, prepared for any criminal undertaking, exist and operate with less molestation. In no other country are crimes and the exploits, successful and unsuccessful, of criminals given greater publicity.[1] To the alert criminal, kidnaping for ransom in 1932 promised a larger and more certain return, with no greater risk of failure or detection, than highjacking a liquor convoy, holding up a wayfarer on the highway, or blowing up a safe. The penalty in any case, unless unfortunately complicated by incidental murder, was a term of imprisonment.

In the United States in the five years preceding 1932 there were more than 300 reported kidnapings for ransom. Many of these had been successfully executed. The ransom money—sometimes as much as $100,000—had been paid, the victim had been safely returned, and the perpetrators remained unapprehended. Fear of detection in the attempt to collect the ransom money had caused some of the less bold and case-hardened to abandon their plans and free their victims. In a few cases the abductors were caught, convicted and sentenced to prison terms; but the incidence of the crime increased rather than diminished.

The peak of the epidemic of kidnaping was reached on March 1, 1932. On the evening of that day the twenty-month-old son of Charles A. and Anne Morrow Lindbergh was stolen from his crib in the nursery of the Lindbergh country home in Hunterdon County, New Jersey. Public reaction was immediate and violent. The prominence of

---

1 Writers on criminology have noticed the "drift of imitation" in crime; that is, the number of similar crimes or criminal attempts that follow a widely advertised crime.

the child's parents and the general affection in which they were held brought forth a wave of universal sympathy and, with it, the demands that the perpetrators of this culminating outrage be apprehended and punished, and that if present laws were inadequate new laws be passed and enforced which would end this "reign of terror."

The Lindbergh country estate of some three hundred and fifty acres was located in a sparsely settled section of Hunterdon County, about three miles from the little town of Hopewell.[2] The property was bounded on the east by a main highway and on the south by a little-used narrow road called Featherbed Lane. The house, completed in the autumn of 1931, was set back on a natural elevation approximately one hundred yards, or more, from the main highway. It was a large two-story brick-and-stone structure, seventy or more feet long and something less than forty feet wide. The first or downstairs floor contained a garage, kitchen, dining room, library and living room. On the second or upstairs floor there were master bedrooms, a nursery, and, above the garage, servants' quarters. The nursery, directly above the library and in the southeast corner of the building, had three shuttered windows, two facing south and one facing east.

The Lindberghs' habit was to spend the week ends—Friday or Saturday until Monday—at Hopewell. The remainder of the week was usually spent with Mrs. Lindbergh's parents, Mr. and Mrs. Dwight W. Morrow, at Englewood, seventy-five miles distant. The regular servants in the Lindbergh household were Mr. and Mrs. Oliver Whately, an English couple, who served in the capacities of butler and housekeeper. They had been with the Lindberghs for about three years. Another servant, Betty Gow, a native of Scotland, twenty-eight years old, was the baby's nurse. She had been in the employ of the Lindberghs a little more than a year.

---

2 Throughout the trial the Lindbergh home was referred to as the property at Hopewell.

It was Mrs. Lindbergh's habit when at Hopewell to attend the baby herself, and Miss Gow was frequently left at Englewood. This had happened the week end preceding the kidnaping. The Lindberghs had expected to return to Englewood on Monday, but when the baby developed a slight cold Mrs. Lindbergh telephoned the nurse and told her that they would not return immediately, and that she should come to Hopewell as soon as she could. Miss Gow arrived there Tuesday afternoon. She immediately took charge of the baby and at his usual bedtime—around seven-thirty—helped Mrs. Lindbergh prepare him for the night. They removed his day clothes, and, after giving him some medicine for his cold and rubbing his chest with a mentholated salve, put on his diapers, a flannel shirt, a sleeveless overshirt—which Betty Gow had just made for him—and, over these, a one-piece sleeping suit. They "tucked" him in his crib and fastened the blankets at the top with safety pins so he could not kick them off during the night. The windows were casement-type, protected by outside shutters designed to overlap and lock with a drop catch. The weather was cold and raw and there was a high wind blowing. Mrs. Lindbergh and the nurse closed and locked the shutters on the two south windows. They were unable to lock the shutters on the east window because the frames were warped and could not be brought together. None of the windows was locked.

It was between eight and eight-fifteen when Mrs. Lindbergh and the nurse came downstairs. Colonel Lindbergh arrived at Hopewell about eight-twenty-five. Dinner was served, and it was about nine o'clock when the colonel and his wife left the table and entered the living room. While there, seated before the open fire, they were startled by a sharp cracking noise which the colonel later testified sounded like "the fall of the slats off the top of an orange crate." They concluded, however, that it must have been something someone had dropped in the kitchen and paid no further attention to it. They left the living room about nine-fifteen—Mrs. Lindbergh was going upstairs to her room, the colonel to the library, where he planned to read awhile before he retired. The east window of the library, before which he sat, was directly beneath the east window of the nursery.

Meanwhile Betty Gow was in the kitchen talking with Mr. and Mrs. Whately. At ten o'clock she glanced at her watch and said, "It's ten o'clock; I must go to the baby." According to her later testimony, she went upstairs and tiptoed into the nursery so as not to waken the child. She approached the crib and put her hands on the blankets. The crib was empty. She said she was not particularly disturbed; Mrs. Lindbergh had come upstairs and might have picked up the baby. She left the nursery to find Mrs. Lindbergh. She met her in the hall.

"Have you got the baby?" inquired the nurse.

"Why, no," replied Mrs. Lindbergh. "Isn't he in his crib?"

Betty said no and added, "Well, the colonel must have him."

Together they went downstairs. The colonel had not been near the nursery. The Lindberghs and Miss Gow were now thoroughly alarmed. The Whatelys were summoned. With the thought that the baby might have crawled out of his crib and out of the nursery, every light in the house was turned on and every room thoroughly searched. It was a vain search. The baby had disappeared.

Colonel Lindbergh, after hurried telephone calls to the local and state police, seized a rifle and ran out of the house. In the darkness he could see nothing. He returned to the nursery and looked particularly at the windows. On the floor alongside the east window leading toward the crib were some indistinct yellow-clay footprints and on the radiator grill below the window an envelope in which there was a single sheet of common white note paper on which was scrawled:

Dear Sir!
Have 50,000 $ redy 25000 $ in
20 $ bills 1.5000 in 10 $ bills and
10000 $ in 5 $ bills. After 2-4 days
we will inform you were to deliver
the Mony.
    We warn you for making
anyding public or for notify the Police
the chld is in gute care.
Indication for all letters are
singnature
    and 3 holds.

THE FIRST RANSOM NOTE
Furnished by courtesy of John F. Tyrrell and Donald Doud,
Document Examiners, Milwaukee, Wisconsin.

Opposite the words "singnature" and "and 3 holds" was a combination of peculiar markings and perforations which was to figure importantly in the search for the child and the later evidence against the kidnaper. It was made up of two overlapping circles each about the size of a quarter, with a smaller circle in the overlapped oval of the larger circles, and three small holes, one punched in the center of the smaller circle and one on the outer edge of each of the larger circles. The larger circles were edged in blue ink; the inner one was a solid blot of red ink.

Within a half hour the police arrived. Colonel Lindbergh gave them a hurried version of what had happened and showed them the ransom note and the footprints in the nursery. A systematic search of the grounds with flashlights was begun. Beside a clump of bushes some sixty feet from the southeast corner of the building they found a wooden ladder. It was made up in three sections, with each section about seven feet long. The side pieces of one section appeared to have been freshly split and broken. Footprints, evidently made by stockinged feet, started just below the nursery window and led to the place where the ladder was found. Similar prints were discovered and followed to the main road on the easterly side of the Lindbergh grounds.

Underneath the nursery window were two small sharp indentations such as might have been made by the ends of a ladder pressed into the ground. On the whitewashed brick walls, about thirty inches below the east window, were two dark marks one-and-one-half to two-and-one-half inches long, which police witnesses later characterized as ladder marks; that is, marks made by a ladder as it rested against the wall. Whitewash marks were found on the ends of the uprights of one of the sections of the ladder. In some soft mud beneath the window a small one-fourth-inch carpenter's chisel was found. There were some blurred, indistinct smudges on the nursery's east window.

These and the ransom note were all the clues. The footprints and window smudges were soon disregarded as of no value. (Later examination of the window, windowpane, chisel and ladder disclosed no identifiable fingerprints.) The note, the ladder, the ladder marks and the chisel remained important. Colonel Lindbergh at once associated the broken ladder with the clattering noise he and his wife had heard while they were in the living room.

By midnight of March 1 the news had been flashed to the world that the Lindbergh baby had been kidnaped. Wednesday morning Governor A. Harry Moore of New Jersey ordered Colonel H. Norman Schwarzkopf, superintendent of the New Jersey State Police, to take personal charge of the case. President Hoover followed with a public direction to the Federal Bureau of Investigation of the Department of Justice to lend every assistance within its power to find and punish the perpetrators of the crime.

Blocks were set up at road intersections, bridges and ferries. Thousands of automobile drivers were stopped, searched and questioned. Hospitals and nurseries within a radius of 200 miles were checked for the arrival of new infants. Police on the ground began a thorough investigation. Mr. and Mrs. Whately were questioned and quickly exonerated of any possible knowledge of or connection with the crime.

Betty Gow was examined at length. She had a boy friend, a former Norwegian sailor named Henry ("Red") Johnson. She had had a date with him in Englewood on Monday evening. Johnson was taken into custody and severely grilled. He had an unbreakable alibi accounting for all of his time on March 1 and the preceding day and was dismissed as a possible suspect. It was discovered, however, in the course of his examination that he had deserted from a Norwegian ship while it was in an American port and was in the country illegally. He was promptly deported. Betty Gow, in whom the Lindberghs expressed complete confidence, was also dismissed by the investigators as a possible suspect.[3]

The inquiry was extended to the servants in the Morrow household at Englewood. Here a serving maid named Violet Sharpe came in for close scrutiny. She was of an extremely nervous and excitable nature. When questioned immediately after the child's disappearance she became hysterical and incoherent and the police postponed her examination until a later date. It was destined never to be completed, and the mystery of Violet Sharpe continues as one of the many strange features of this remarkable case.[4]

The prominence of the Lindberghs, the spectacular nature of the crime, and the publicity given every detail of the affair brought forth a veritable flood of tips, suggestions, and "crank" letters. Practically all were anonymous. Many told of having seen the kidnapers (always plural) and the baby; others told where the baby could be found. Every such communication which gave names or places was carefully investigated. Nothing came of any of them. One bizarre touch was a letter from Al Capone, temporarily a resident of the Cook County jail in Chicago. America's "public enemy number one" said that he and his wife "felt terrible about the kidnaping," and he was sure if he were released he could be of real service in apprehending the guilty man and restoring the child to its parents. The offer was not taken seriously.

---

[3] The police, however, seemed far from satisfied; so dissatisfied indeed, that officers proceeded all the way to her old home in Scotland to check her antecedents and associations. Nothing was discovered to discredit her.

[4] The last attempt to question the girl was made on June 10. She had been questioned the day before, but her incoherent and conflicting statements and her nervous state which bordered on collapse again prompted her inquisitors to defer her examination. When the officers returned they were told she was in her room. A servant, sent to tell her that the officers wanted to talk to her, reported she was not there. A search was made for her in other parts of the house. She was finally found, on the floor of the pantry, dead. In her room the police found a small tin of potassium cyanide, and two or three tablets of the poison were still undissolved in a glass of water.

Colonel and Mrs. Lindbergh were naturally much more concerned over the safe return of the baby than in the apprehension and punishment of the abductors. Two days after the kidnaping the colonel issued an appeal which was handed to the press from the governor's office:

Mrs. Lindbergh and I desire to make personal contact with the kidnapers of our child. Our only interest is in his immediate and safe return. We feel certain that the kidnapers will realize that this interest is strong enough to justify them in having complete confidence and trust in any promise that we may make in connection with his return. We urge those who have the child to send any representatives that they may desire to meet a representative of ours who will be suitable to them at any time and at any place they may designate.

If this is accepted we promise that we will keep whatever arrangements may be made by their representatives and ours strictly confidential and we further pledge ourselves that we will not try to injure in any way those connected with the return of the child.

The frantic but hopeful mother asked the newspapers to print a story that the baby had not been well and that it was imperative that his usual diet and care be observed—"one quart of milk during the day, three tablespoons of cooked vegetables once a day, one yolk of egg daily, one baked potato or rice once a day, two tablespoons of stewed fruit daily, half a cup of orange juice on waking, half a cup of prune juice after the afternoon nap, and fourteen drops of medicine called Viosterol during the day."

The kidnaper was not slow to make cruel use of this maternal appeal to give credence to his pretensions that the baby was alive and being cared for. The first word from the kidnaper reached the Lindberghs on March 5. On the morning of that day Colonel Lindbergh received through the mail an envelope postmarked "Brooklyn, 9 P.M. March 4." In it was a note, written on both sides of a sheet of white paper, which read:

Dear Sir: We are warned you note to make
anyding Public also notify Police
now you have to take the consequences. ths
means we will holt the baby untill everyding
is quiet. We can note make any appointment
just now. We know very well what it
means to us. It is rely necessary to
make a world affair out off this, or to
get yours baby back as sun as possible.
To settle those affair in a quick way
will better for both seits. Dont by
afraid about the baby two ladys
keeping care of its day and night.
She also will feed him
according to the diet.
    Singtuere on
    all letters

In the lower right-hand corner was the strange device
which had appeared on the note left in the nursery. On
the reverse side of the paper the message continued:

We are interested to send him back in
gut health. ouer ransom was made aus
for 50000 $ but now we have to take
another person to it and probable have
to keep the baby for a longer time as we
expected So the amount will by 70,000 $
20.000 in 50 $ bills 25.000 $ in 20$ bills
15000$ in 10 $ bills and 10.000 $ in 5 $ bills.
dont mark any bills. or tacke them
from one serial nonmer. We will
inform you latter were to deliver hte
mony. but we will note do so
until the Police is out of ths case
and the Pappers are quiet.
The Kidnaping was preparet
for yeahs. so we are preparet
  for everyding

On March 7 Colonel Henry Breckinridge, a trusted
friend and attorney, whom Colonel Lindbergh had called

to his aid immediately after the child's disappearance and whose name had figured prominently in the press stories of the kidnaping, received at his New York law office a plain envelope, containing a short note, which read:

> Dear Sir.
>   Please handel inclosed letter
> to Col. Lindbergh. It is in
> Mr. Lindberg interest not to
> notify the Police.

The letter enclosed, like the one that preceded it, was written on both sides of a single sheet of cheap, white paper. The lower right-hand corner carried the same mysterious symbol which had appeared on the two previous notes. The letter read:

> Dear Sir: Dit you receive ouer letter from
> March 4. We sent the mail in one off the letter
>   pox near Burro Hall—Brooklyn. We know
> Police interfere with your privatmail; how can
> we come to any arrangements this way.
> in the future we will send ouer letters to
> Mr. Breckenridge at 25 Broadway. We belive
> Polise cupturet our letter and tit note
> forwardet to you. We will note accept
> any go-between from your seid. We will
> arrangh thiss latter. Thers is no worry
> about the boy. he is very well and will be
> feed according to the diet. Best dank for
> Information about it. We are interested to send
> your Boy back in gud Health.

On the reverse side of the paper it read:

> Is it nessisery to make a word's affair out of
> it, or to gett your Boy back as son as possible;
> Wy tit you ingnore ouer letter which we
> left in the room: the baby would be back
> long ago. You would note get any result

from Police, because this Kidnaping whas
planet for a year allredy. but we was afraid,
the boy would not bee strong enough.
and ransom was madeout for 50000 $
but now we have to but another lady to it and
propperly have to hold the baby longer as we
exspectet so it will be 70.000 $
20000 in 50 $ bills 25000 in 25 $ bills 15000
in 10 $ bills 10000 in 5 $ bill. We warn you agin
not to mark any bills or take them from one serial
No. We will inform you latter how to deliver
                the mony, but not before
        the Police is out of this cace and the
        pappers are quiet.
Please gett a short notice aboud this letter in the
                New-York American.

The next contact with the kidnaper was made on March
9, a week after the baby disappeared.[5] The circumstance

----

[5] Omitted from the text to avoid interrupting the sequence of vital occurrences are accounts of the Curtis and Means pretensions to having made
contacts with the kidnapers or their agents.
   John Hughes Curtis, said to have been a boatbuilder in Norfolk, interested two respectable but naïve citizens—Guy H. Burrage, retired admiral,
U.S.N., and the Reverend Dobson-Peacock, an Episcopal clergyman of Norfolk—in his claim that he had established contact with a criminal gang
which had the Lindbergh baby in a boat standing off the Virginia coast.
Provided it could be arranged with safety to the kidnapers, Curtis reported,
an exchange of the baby for the suggested ransom of $50,000 could be ef-
fected on the Atlantic somewhere beyond the twelve-mile limit. The trio
got in touch with Lindbergh and it is quite possible Curtis got some money
out of him for expenses. It would appear that neither the colonel nor Chief
Schwarzkopf put much faith in Curtis, but the newspapers gave wide publicity to his almost daily statements that the baby was well and would be
returned as soon as satisfactory arrangements could be made with the kidnapers. The finding of the baby's body ended Curtis' racket. He was arrested
and charged with obstructing justice. He made a full confession. From first
to last his stories had been fabricated. The only defense he offered was that
recent financial reverses had so undermined his health and mental condition
that he did not know what he was doing. He was tried, convicted, sentenced
to pay a fine of $1,000 and suffer a year's imprisonment in the county jail.
The farce was completed when an indulgent judge suspended even that sentence and Curtis was allowed to fade out of the picture.
   Another rogue who was quick to see an opportunity in the Lindbergh
kidnaping was the notorious Gaston B. Means. From the day—ten years remote—when he had serviced the notorious "Ohio gang" in the Harding administration, Means had frequently fallen afoul of the law and was no
stranger to the interior of a Federal penitentiary. The Lindbergh kidnaping suggested a chance for easy money. His target was not Lindbergh but

is a matching piece in the strange pattern of this amazing case. The intermediary was a seventy-two-year-old, eccentric schoolteacher named John Francis Condon. He had lived in the Bronx all his life and had taught in the grade schools there for nearly fifty years. At the time of the kidnaping he was a professor of education at Fordham University. "Doctor" Condon, as he was known, was a "character." He was in the forefront of every local civic and charitable movement. He was a regular contributor of both prose and poetry to *Home News,* the local Bronx paper. While regarded as something of a busybody who craved the limelight, he was widely known in his community as a well-meaning, public-spirited and trustworthy citizen.

The Lindbergh kidnaping excited and stirred him to action. On March 8 he inserted the following personal in the Bronx *Home News*:

I offer all I can scrape together so a loving mother may again have her child and Col. Lindbergh may know that the American people are grateful for the honor bestowed upon them by his pluck and daring.

Let the kidnapers know that no testimony of mine, or information coming from me, will be used against them.

I offer $1,000, which I have saved from my salary, as additional to the the suggested ransom of $50,000 which is said to have been demanded of Col. Lindbergh.

I stand ready at my own expense to go anywhere, alone, to give the kidnaper the extra money, and promise never to utter his name to any person.

If this is not agreeable, then I ask the kidnapers to go to any Catholic priest and return the child unharmed, with

---

the rich, eccentric and gullible Evalyn Walsh McLean of Washington. With a story that he, with his mysterious underworld connections, could locate the kidnapers and bring about the baby's return, he succeeded in separating Mrs. McLean from $154,000 of her money. As was the case with Curtis, Means's fictitious accounts of his activities and contacts with the kidnapers were exploded and terminated when the dead body of the Lindbergh baby was discovered. Means was arrested, indicted for obtaining money under false pretenses and sentenced to fifteen years' imprisonment. Means served his sentence in the Federal penitentiary at Leavenworth.

the knowledge that the priest must hold inviolate any
statement which may be made by the kidnapers.

John F. Condon.

On the evening of the following day Dr. Condon found
in his mailbox a rather bulky envelope on which his correct name and address were printed in ink. The envelope
enclosed a note and a smaller sealed envelope. The note,
also written in ink and unsigned, read:

> Dear Sir: If you are willing to act
> as go-between in Lindbergh cace
> pleace follow stricly instruction.
> Handel incloced letter *personaly*
> to Mr. Lindbergh. It will explain
> everyding. Don't tell anyone about
> it. as son we find out the Press
> or Police is notifyd everyding are
> cancelt and it will be a further
> delay. Affter you gett the Mony from
> Mr. Lindbergh but them 3 word's
> in the *New-York american*
>   *mony is redy.*
> affter that we will give you further
> instruction. Don't be affrait we are
> not out fore your 1000$ keep it.
> only act stricly. Be at home every
> night between 6-12 by this time
> you will hear from us.

The enclosed smaller envelope was addressed: "Mr. Col.
Lindbergh, Hopewell."

Dr. Condon lost no time in getting Colonel Lindbergh
on the telephone. The colonel told him to open the letter
addressed to him and read it over the telephone. Dr. Condon tore the envelope open and read:

> Dear Sir, Mr. Condon may act as go-
> between. You may give him the

70,000 $. make one packet. the size
will bee about

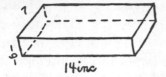

We have notifyt your allredy in
what kind of bills. We warn you
not to set any trapp in any way. If
you or someone els will notify the
Police ther will be a further delay
affter we have the mony in hand we
will tell you where to find your boy
You may have a airplain
redy it is about 150 mil.
awy. But befor telling
you the adr. a delay of 8 hours
will be between.

When he had finished reading, the doctor told Colonel
Lindbergh that the note bore no signature, but had a most
peculiar device in the lower right-hand corner—two overlapping circles with a round red blot in the center with
three small perforations, one in the exact center of the red
blot, and one on the outer edges of the two larger circles.
The device described by Dr. Condon was identical with the
markings on the earlier notes.

The doctor, at Colonel Lindbergh's request, proceeded
immediately to Hopewell. There he met Colonel Lindbergh and Colonel Breckinridge. The three sat up until
the small hours of the morning, discussing plans for future
dealings with the kidnapers. It was considered that undue
attention would be attracted if subsequent communications through the newspapers were to be signed by Dr.
Condon's full name. The resourceful professor suggested
a pseudonym—"Jafsie," a phonetic running together of
J. F. C., the doctor's initials.

On the morning of the eleventh the following appeared in the personal column of the New York *American*: "Money is ready. Jafsie."

The reply was prompt. The next evening at about eight-thirty a taxicab driver rang the front doorbell of Dr. Condon's home. The doctor answered and was handed a letter which bore his name and address, pen-printed. In the presence of Colonel Breckinridge the doctor opened the envelope and read the note enclosed:

> Mr. Condon.
> We trust you, but we will note come
> in your Haus it is to danger. even
> you cane note know if Police or
> secret servise is watching you
> follow this instrunction
> Take a car and drive to the last
> supway station from Jerome Ave
> line. 100 feet from the last station
> on the left seide is a empty frank-
> further-stand with a big open Porch
> around, you will find a notise in
> senter of the porch underneath a stone.
> this notise will tell
> you were to find uns.
> Act accordingly.
>
> after 3/4 of a houer be
> on the place. bring the mony with you.

The letter carried the now familiar circle symbol with the three perforations. The taxi driver said the letter had been handed to him by a stranger who had hailed the cab a short distance from the Condon home and given him a dollar to deliver it. The doctor took the driver's name (Joseph Perrone) and his badge and license numbers.

Although it was getting late the doctor lost no time in following the instructions contained in the letter. With a young friend, Al Reich, who owned a car he drove to the designated subway station. There they found the abandoned frankfurter stand; and, on a table on the porch, under a stone which served as a paperweight they found a note which read:

> cross the street and follow
> the fence from the cemetery.
> direction to 233 street
> I will meet you.

The note bore no signature. The interlocking circles and perforations were also missing.

Dr. Condon and his companion drove to the main gate of the Woodlawn Cemetery, where the car was stopped and Condon got out. He held up the note in his hand so that the kidnaper might see it. Quickly he espied a white handkerchief being waved by someone just inside the cemetery gate and walked over to where it was. There, in the gathering darkness, he encountered a man, referred to in his later testimony as "John."

"Have you gottet the money?" inquired the stranger.

"No," answered Condon, "I could not bring the money until I saw the baby or heard where the baby is."

At this point "John," evidently fearful he was being double-crossed, climbed over the cemetery fence and started to run. Condon followed as best he could and overtook him a short distance away in Van Courtlandt Park. There the two sat down on a bench and for more than an hour, according to Dr. Condon's story, continued their conversation. The man "John" was at first reluctant to talk; he was afraid of the "cops." He repeated "it is too dangers" and added "might be twenty years or burn."

Then, significantly, he asked Condon, "Would I burn if the baby is dead?"

"Not if you did not have something to do with it," replied the doctor.

To this the man rejoined, "I am only go-between."

He assured Dr. Condon, in response to his anxious inquiries, that the baby was alive and well taken care of. The doctor asked him how he could be sure he actually had the baby. The man answered that the symbols on the notes ought to prove that, but to satisfy him he would send him the baby's sleeping suit. Condon told him this would satisfactorily complete the identification and they parted with the understanding that the doctor would insert a personal in the Bronx *Home News* reading: "Baby alive and well. Money is ready. Call and see us. Jafsie." "John" would then contact his associates and see that the sleeping suit reached Dr. Condon promptly.

The following day, Saturday, the personal "John" had requested appeared in the Bronx *Home News*. There was no answer on Sunday, and on Monday the fourteenth the doctor followed his first personal with another: "Money is ready. No cops. No secret service. No Press. I come alone like last time. Call Jafsie."

The answer came on Wednesday in the form of a small, compactly wrapped package in the doctor's mailbox. Colonel Breckinridge was immediately notified, and in his presence the doctor opened the package. It contained a baby's sleeping suit—later positively identified by Mrs. Lindbergh and Miss Gow as the suit the baby was wearing on the night of his disappearance. With the suit was a note which bore the kidnaper's signature—the circles and the perforations. It read:

> Our man faills to collect the
> mony. There are no more confidential
> conference after the meeting from March
> 12. those arrangements to hazardous
> for us. We will not allow ouer man
> to confer in a way licke befor.
> circumstance will note allow us
> to make a transfare like you wish.
> It is impossibly for us. Wy chould we
> move the baby and face danger to

take another person to the plase is
entirerly out of question. It seems
you are afraid if we are the rigth
party and if the boy is allright. Well
you have ouer singnature. It is always
the same as the first one
specially them 3 hohls.

The message was continued on the reverse side of the
note:

Now we will send you the sleepingsuit
from the baby besides it means 3 $ extra
expenses becauce we have to pay
another one. Pleace tell Mrs. Lindbergh
note to worry the baby is well. we only
have to give him more food as the tied says
        You are willing to pay the 70000
note 50000 $ without seeing the baby first
or note. let us know about that in the
New York-american. We can't to it other ways.
becauce we don't licke to give up
ouer safty plase or to move the baby.
If you are willing to accept this deal
    put those in the paper
        I accept mony is redy
            Ouer program is:
after 8 houers we have the mony received
we will notify you where to find the
baby. If thers is any trapp, you will be
        responsible what
            will follows.

Colonel Lindbergh and the doctor lost no time in com-
plying with the kidnaper's suggestion. On March 16 the
following appeared in both the New York *American* and
the Bronx *Home News*: "I accept. Money is ready. John:
your package is delivered and is O K. Direct me. Jafsie."
Several days went by. Another advertisement was inserted in the *Home News*: "Inform me how I can get important letter to you. Urgent. Jafsie."
This last brought a quick but disturbing reply. On

Monday the twentieth the doctor's mail yielded the following:

> Dear Sir: You and Mr. Lindbergh know
> ouer Program. If you don't accept
> den we will wait untill you
> agree with ouer Deal, we know
> you have to come to us anyway
> But why shoul'd Mrs. and Mr.
> Lindbergh suffer longer as necessary
> We will note communicate with
> you or Mr. Lindbergh until you write so
> in the paper.
> We will tell you again; this kid
> naping cace whas prepared for a
> yaer already so the Police would
> have any look to find us or the child
> You only puch everyding further out
> dit you send that
> little package to
> Mr. Lindbergh? it contains
> the sleepingsuit from the
> the baby is well.   Baby.

On the reverse side the note continued:

> Mr. Lindbergh only wasting
> time with hiss search

Again there was the cryptic signature.

On Tuesday the twenty-first the *Home News* carried Dr. Condon's reply: "Thanks. That little package you sent was immediately delivered and accepted as real article. See my position. Over fifty years in business and can I pay without seeing goods? Common sense makes me trust you. Please understand my position. Jafsie."

Wednesday, Thursday and Friday went by. On Saturday another notice appeared in the *Home News*: "Money is ready. Furnish simple code for us to use in paper. Jafsie."

Sunday, Monday and Tuesday passed, but on Wednesday Dr. Condon received another communication:

> Dear Sir: It is note necessary to furnish
> any code. You and Mr. Lindbergh know
> ouer program very well. We will keep
> the child on ouer plase until we
> have the money in hand, but if the deal
> is note closed until the 8 of April we
> will ask for 30000 more—also note 70000
> -100000.
>   how can Mr. Lindbergh follow
> so many false clues he know's we
> are the right paety ouer singnature
> is still the same as on the ransom
> note. But if Mr. Lindbergh likes to
> fool around for another month—
>   we can help it.
>   once he hase to come to us anyway
> but if he keep's on waiting we will double
>   ouer amount. there is absolute no fear
> aboud the child,
> it is well.

Again there was the cryptic signature.

This time Dr. Condon's reply was prompt and unequivocal: "I accept. Money is ready. Jafsie."

Two days later the mail brought the following:

> Dear Sir: have the money ready by saturday
> evening. we will inform you where
> and how to deliver it. have the money
> in one bundle we want you to put
> it on a sertain place. Ther is
> no fear that somebody els will
> tacke it. we watch everything
> closely. pleace lett us know if
> you are agree and ready for action
> by saturday evening.—if yes—
> put in the paper
>   Yes everything O. K.

It is a very simble delivery but we
find out very sun if there is any trapp.
    after 8 houers you get the adr; from
the boy, on the place
you find two
ladies. the are
    innocence.

On the reverse side was written:

If it is to late to put it in
the New York American for saturday
evening put it in New York Journal.

Again there was the cryptic signature.

Matters seemed now to be approaching a climax. Chief Schwarzkopf had been kept informed of Dr. Condon's activities and had co-operated with Colonel Lindbergh to keep the matter secret. Now, however, with a meeting with the kidnaper imminent, both Colonel Schwarzkopf and the Federal authorities felt that plain-clothes men should cover the rendezvous—when it should be disclosed—and arrest the kidnaper or his agent when he appeared to collect the ransom. They were dissuaded by Colonel Lindbergh's plea that such a procedure might jeopardize the baby's safety.

Dr. Condon was allowed to continue his negotiation. He immediately advertised the requested reply: "Yes, everything O. K. Jafsie."

Colonel Lindbergh procured the ransom money in the denominations requested. The character of the bills and their serial numbers were duly recorded. They were placed in a specially constructed box—designed by Condon, so that it could be identified later—and given to the doctor. On April 2 a taxi driver delivered a message to the Condon residence. Dr. Condon's daughter answered the bell and let the driver get away without obtaining either his name or the cab number. This was the message:

> Dear Sir: take a car and follow
> tremont Ave to the east
> until you reach the number
> 3225 tremont Ave.
>   It is a nursery.
>   Bergen
>   Greenhauses florist
> there is a table standing
> outside right on the door, you
> find a letter undernead the table
> covert with a stone, read and
> follow imstruction.

On the reverse side of the note were further instructions
and warnings:

> don't speak to anyone on
> the way. If there is a ratio
> alarm for policecar, we
> warn you, we have the same
> equipnent. have the money
> in one bundle.
> We give you 3/4 of a houer to
> reach the place.

Again there was the cryptic signature.

It was about nine o'clock. Colonel Lindbergh and the
doctor proceeded immediately to the Bergen greenhouse.
It was directly across the street from St. Raymond's Cemetery. The colonel stayed in the car while Condon crossed
the street to the shop. There was a table near the door.
Underneath it was a white envelope weighted with a small
stone containing the promised note. It read:

> cross the street and
> walk to the next corner
> and follow *Whittemore* Ave
> to the soud
>   take the money with
> you. come alone
>   and walk
>   I will meet you.

And again there was the cryptic signature.

The doctor walked in the direction indicated. He had not got very far—not out of earshot of Colonel Lindbergh, who sat in the parked car—when, from the direction of the cemetery, he heard a raucous voice shout, "Hey, Doktor." Condon followed along the cemetery hedge in the direction of the voice.

He had gone only a few steps when he heard the voice again. This time the pitch of the man's voice was low as he called out, "Hey, Doktor, have you gottet the money?"

The doctor answered it was in the car.

The voice said, "Well, get me the money."

The doctor said he was not willing to turn over the money until he was told where the baby was. He added that all he had with him was the $50,000 demanded in the first ransom note.

The voice answered that if they could not get seventy he thought they would take fifty and that he would be back in a few minutes with exact directions where the baby could be found.

The doctor returned to the car and told the colonel what had happened. The colonel took $20,000 out of the box and handed Condon the box with the remaining $50,000. The doctor went back to the place where he had talked with the stranger. In a few minutes the man reappeared and handed Condon a note. Condon handed him the box. The man opened it to see if it actually contained money, thanked the doctor for his trouble and disappeared in the darkness. Condon was sure the man was the same "John" he had talked with earlier in Van Courtlandt Park.

Back at the car the colonel and the doctor read the final note:

> the boy is on Boad Nelly
> it is a small Boad 28 feet
>   long, two person are on the
>   Boad. the are innosent.

THE BRUNO HAUPTMANN CASE

> you will find the Boad between
> Horseneck Beach and gay Head
> near Elizabeth Island.

The note bore no signature and no markings or perforations.

About midnight Colonel Lindbergh, Colonel Breckinridge, Dr. Condon and Elmer Irey (an agent of the Bureau of Internal Revenue) left for Bridgeport, Connecticut. There, in the early dawn, they boarded an amphibian plane, which Lindbergh piloted along the Connecticut, Rhode Island and Massachusetts coasts, looking for the "Boad Nelly." All day long they flew. Keeping the plane at a low altitude they searched Horseneck Beach, Gay Head, Elizabeth Island and every nook and cove in the indented coast. No trace was found of a boat answering the description of the Nelly. Reluctantly they gave up the quest.

All the next day, hoping against hope, the colonel—alone, as he had been in his world-famous flight across the Atlantic—scoured the coast as far south as Virginia. It was all in vain. He had been victimized in as cruel a hoax as a distorted criminal mind ever contrived. He returned to Hopewell to break the news to his waiting and anxious wife. Their one and only real hope for their baby's return had been blasted.

On May 12—a little over a month later—the dead body of little Charles A. Lindbergh, Jr., was found by two truck drivers in a shallow grave which was some thirty yards back from a main road and beneath some underbrush. The place was in Mercer County, five miles from the Lindbergh home.

More than two years went by. Other news—bank crashes, Roosevelt's election, moratoriums, New Deal legislation, trouble brewing in Europe—crowded out of the press all but occasional references to the Lindbergh case. To the public it became just another unsolved crime. There were persistent forces at work, however, of which the public knew nothing. The passage of the so-called Lindbergh Kidnaping Law had made such a case a Federal crime.[6] While prosecution for the Lindbergh kidnaping under that law was impossible, this did not prevent the Federal Bureau of Investigation and other government agencies from trying to pick up the trail of the kidnapers.

In their effort they were aided by the fact that—as part of the New Deal recovery program—the United States had gone off the gold standard. The possession of gold coin had been made a crime; all previously issued gold certificates were ordered turned into the Federal Reserve Bank by May 1, 1933. By one of fate's strange quirks $35,000 of the ransom bills which had been delivered to the mysterious "John" had been gold certificates. Government agents on the lookout for the outlawed certificates were alerted to check all such bills against the listed serial numbers of the Lindbergh ransom notes. Two hundred and fifty thousand circulars containing an account of the kidnaping and the numbers of the ransom notes were printed by the government and distributed to banks and police departments in the United States, Canada and foreign countries.

Between April 1932 and May 1934 a number of gold certificates of $5, $10, and $20 denominations—in the aggregate about $1,000—came into the United States Treasury and were there identified by their serial numbers as having been part of the Lindbergh ransom money. There were, however, no other identifications on the bills, no record of who had turned them in, and no way by which they could be traced to their former holders.

On April 30, 1933, a stranger presented a deposit slip at the Federal Reserve Bank at New York City evidencing the

---

6 This statute, passed in May 1934, made kidnaping a Federal offense when a state boundary was crossed, and prescribed the death penalty if the victim of the kidnaping was not returned unharmed.

deposit of $2,980 of gold notes, for which he received other usable currency in exchange. The name on the slip was J. J. Faulkner; the address, 557 W. 149. It was discovered too late that the deposited bills were part of the Lindbergh ransom money. No trace of a J. J. Faulkner at the address given, or any other place, was ever found.[7]

On November 26, 1933, a cashier of a moving-picture theater in Greenwich Village took in as part of her receipts a five-dollar gold certificate. It was deposited in regular course in the owner's bank account. In due time it came under the scrutiny of the Federal authorities. It was one of the Lindbergh ransom bills. The cashier was interviewed. She remembered the customer. What was more, she was able to give a helpful description of him—helpful because it mentioned distinctive peculiarities. He had a pointed chin and peculiar wide-open, staring blue eyes. The description tallied with that given by Dr. Condon and Joseph Perrone of the mysterious "John."

Almost a year later, September 15, 1934, a blue Dodge sedan pulled up at a gasoline filling station at Lexington and 125th Street in New York. The driver asked for five gallons of gas and tendered a ten-dollar bill in payment. The attendant recognized the bill as an old gold certificate and because he thought it was a "gold-hoarding case" wrote the license number of the car—4U 13-41—on the margin of the bill. The bill was deposited in a neighborhood bank and checked against the serial numbers of the Lindbergh ransom notes. It was one of the listed bills.

Now the police had something definite to work with. It was simple through the license number to trace the name and address of the applicant. The record disclosed that the license had been applied for by, and issued to, one Richard Hauptmann; address, 1279 E. 222nd Street, Bronx; age, 34.

The police knew nothing of the man they were dealing

---

[7] According to all the handwriting experts who later were called into the case, this deposit slip was not in the handwriting of Hauptmann.

with. They took no chances. It has been estimated that anywhere from fifty to seventy-five New Jersey, New York and Federal officers covered the Hauptmann residence and the immediate neighborhood. They were on foot and in cars. They waited until he came out of his house, went to the near-by garage and took out the Dodge sedan that bore the license number 4U 13-41. After he had driven a couple of blocks they crowded him against the curb and arrested him. They searched him and found a $20 gold certificate which also turned out to be one of the missing ransom notes. In his garage was found hidden $14,500 more of the ransom money; $840 of it had been rolled tightly and stuffed into augur holes bored in a two-by-four timber. On the inside jamb of one of the closet doors in the Hauptmann apartment they discovered a pencil notation of Dr. Condon's street address and telephone number. They also located a chest of carpenter's tools.

Police checks to determine Hauptmann's previous record proceeded rapidly. He talked freely. His first story, glibly told, was that he had been born in Germany, had come to America in 1923, had worked at his trade as a carpenter, saved his money, gone into the stock market, and through lucky speculations had accumulated the money which the police had found. He denied that he had ever before been charged with a criminal act. A hurried examination of the readily available sources disclosed that he had no criminal record in New York or New Jersey. Cables to Germany, however, brought the information that he was an extremely clever criminal and had a prison record—had been convicted and served time for robbery, had escaped jail, and after two failures had succeeded in concealing himself on a German liner and making an illegal entry into the United States. Perrone, the taxicab driver, identified him as the man who had given him the letter to deliver to Dr. Condon. The cashier of the Greenwich Village motion-picture theater was equally positive he was the man who had bought a ticket from her and given her the five-dollar gold certificate. The employees of the Lexington Avenue filling station readily identified him as the man to whom they had sold gas and who had given them the ten-dollar gold certificate a few days before. Dr. Condon was not so positive, but he said Hauptmann looked more like the mysterious "John" than any man he had theretofore seen.

On September 26 a New York grand jury indicted Hauptmann for the extortion of $50,000 from Colonel Lindbergh. A Hunterdon, New Jersey, grand jury followed almost immediately with an indictment for murder. Governor Moore of New Jersey requested his extradition on the more serious charge, and on October 11 Governor Lehman of New York signed the necessary papers. A writ of habeas corpus sued out by an attorney for Hauptmann to test the legality of the extradition proceedings failed, and on October 19 the accused kidnaper was lodged in the Hunterdon County jail at Flemington, New Jersey, there to await trial on a charge of first-degree murder.

The case of the State of New Jersey *versus* Bruno Richard Hauptmann came on for trial in the old Hunterdon County courthouse at Flemington on January 2, 1935.

Presiding as judge was the Honorable Thomas W. Trenchard, a veteran jurist of unimpeachable integrity, with a reputation for strict impartiality. Appearing for the State were David T. Wilentz, the state's attorney general, Anthony M. Hauck, Jr., prosecutor of the pleas for Hunterdon County, and four assistants to the attorney general: George K. Large, Joseph Lanigan, Robert Peacock and Richard Stockton. The burden of the defense was carried by Edward J. Reilly of the New York bar. Assisting him were C. Lloyd Fisher, Frederick A. Pope and Egbert Rosencrans.

Wilentz, who led for the State, was an experienced trial lawyer[8]—meticulous in preparation, a persistent and relentless cross-examiner and a dynamic and convincing orator.

---

8 His experience, however, had been almost exclusively on the civil side.

All of Hauptmann's lawyers were competent and experienced practitioners. Reilly had attained a considerable reputation as a defender of difficult causes.

A day and a half was consumed in getting a jury. As finally sworn, it consisted of eight men and four women. They were solid citizens. Five of the men were over fifty-five years of age. All but two of the jurors had children.

Attorney General Wilentz made a full opening for the State. None of the dramatic appeal with which the case abounded was overlooked. He left no doubt of the State's position. "It is the law, men and women," he solemnly began, "that where the death of anyone ensues in the commission of a burglary, the killing is murder—murder in the first degree."

He told how the kidnaping had been planned—in Hauptmann's own words "for a year allredy"; how the kidnaper had stolen into the Lindbergh estate; how he had put the ladder against the house under the nursery window; how, with crime in his mind and heart, he had opened the shutters and crawled through the east window; how he had seized the baby; how, with the baby in his arms, when he went down the ladder it broke under their combined weight; how in the fall the baby had been instantly killed; how Hauptmann, in his panic, had abandoned the ladder; how he had ripped off the child's sleeping suit; how he had "scooped out a hastily improvised and shallow grave" and buried the body face downward; and how he then "went on his way to complete the rest of his plans in this horrible criminal endeavor."

Wilentz detailed the search for the kidnaper, Dr. Condon's contact with the mysterious "John" (whom he would prove was Hauptmann), the payment of the ransom money, the discovery of the baby's body, the tracing of the ransom bills, the arrest of Hauptmann and the discoveries made after his arrest. The State, continued the prosecutor, would prove beyond peradventure that Hauptmann wrote the ransom note found on the window sill and all the subsequent notes to Colonel Lindbergh, Colonel Breckinridge and Dr. Condon which bore the strange signature.

Coming back to the ladder, he revealed a startling piece of previously undisclosed evidence. Hauptmann, declared Wilentz, now had the ladder "right around his neck. One side of that ladder comes right from his attic, put on there with his own tools, and we will prove it to you." His conclusion, uttered with all the intensity and passion he could put into it, sent a shudder through the crowded courtroom: "The State will not compromise with murder or murderers. We will demand the penalty of first-degree murder."

The prosecution's first witness was a county surveyor who produced and identified a map on which he located the Lindbergh estate.

Mrs. Lindbergh was the next witness called. In a low, tense voice, she described the occurrences on the fateful evening of March 1, 1932. She was shown and identified pieces of the baby's clothing, particularly the sleeping suit. Reilly, with a protestation of sympathy for the apparent distress of the witness, waived cross-examination.

Colonel Lindbergh, who followed his wife, covered much the same ground. He, however, added testimony of importance: the entry of Dr. Condon into the case, his obtaining the demanded ransom and the visit to the cemetery with Dr. Condon on April 2. He told of hearing the harsh voice "in a foreign accent" calling from behind the cemetery hedge, "Hey, Doktor." He had heard the same voice since. He was positive it was the voice of Bruno Richard Hauptmann.

Reilly subjected the colonel to a long and searching cross-examination. He questioned him as to his servants—what he had known of them before they were hired, what credentials they had, their associations. He tried particularly to cast suspicion on Oliver Whately and Violet Sharpe—both dead. He even suggested that Dr. Condon might have been the "mastermind" of the kidnaping plot. The result was negligible. Lindbergh declared positively that all the servants were trustworthy. Any suspicion of Dr. Condon was "inconceivable." Despite the fact that two years had elapsed between the time he had heard the unknown voice in the cemetery and the known voice of Hauptmann, he was convinced they were the same. Reilly did bring out one fact of which he made much in his later argument: that the Lindberghs had a dog and at no time between eight and ten o'clock had the dog barked.

On Monday morning, after the week-end adjournment, Betty Gow and Elsie Whately took the stand. Miss Gow had voluntarily returned from Scotland to testify. Both women corroborated the colonel and Mrs. Lindbergh as to events on the evening of the baby's disappearance. They told also of finding the baby's thumb guard about a month after the kidnaping. It was near the front gate some 100 yards or more from the house. The nurse, on the verge of tears, identified the scraps of the baby's shirt and the sleeping suit. Her cross-examination, while suggestive and at times sarcastic, failed to impeach her direct testimony.

Numerous police officers were called to testify to their findings on the premises after they had been notified of the kidnaping. They located the footprints and ladder marks and told where they had found the chisel and the various parts of the ladder. The ladder sections were identified and the foundation laid for their introduction later as State's exhibits.

There was a stir in the crowded courtroom as the attorney general called Dr. John F. Condon[9] to the stand. Here was the star witness—the much-publicized "Jafsie." This was the man who had paid over the $50,000 ransom money; the man whom Reilly had advertised to the attending newspaper reporters as holding the key to the true

9 The narrative does not observe the precise order in which the witnesses were called.

story of the baby's kidnaping and death. The school-teacher told his story, graphically and dramatically. Despite his odd mannerisms, quaint expressions, and numerous digressions, he made an appealing, believable witness.

Reilly subjected him to a rapid, grilling cross-examination. The doctor seemed to enjoy it. The only headway defendant's counsel made was his development of the old gentleman's uncertainty and hesitation when he was first asked to identify Hauptmann as the mysterious "John" of the cemeteries. Even here the doctor scored with his explanation that while from the first he had no doubt in his mind of the identity, he would not express that conviction until he had subjected his recollection to a consideration of every detail and was absolutely certain.

Dr. Condon was corroborated by two witnesses who testified they drove him to the Lindbergh home at Hopewell on the evening of March 9—the day the doctor received the first communication from the kidnaper—by Colonel Breckinridge, who was present at Hopewell with Colonel Lindbergh when the doctor arrived and was at the doctor's home in the Bronx when the package from the kidnaper containing the sleeping suit had been opened, and by Al Reich, who testified he drove the doctor to the Woodlawn Cemetery on the occasion of his first meeting with the mysterious "John."

The two truckmen told of finding the baby's body. Other witnesses described the place where the body was found, its condition and the clothes which were still on it. The county coroner testified to the removal of the body to the morgue, where it had been identified by Colonel Lindbergh and Betty Gow. This was followed by the testimony of the coroner's physician: that he had performed an autopsy and that the cause of death was a multiple skull fracture suffered by the baby while it was yet alive.

Employees of the banking house with which Colonel Lindbergh arranged for the ransom money testified to the denominations of the various bills and the listing of their serial numbers.

The manager of the filling station at Lexington and 125th Street told of Hauptmann's driving up to his station and buying five gallons of gas. It was some time in September of 1934. Hauptmann, testified the witness, tendered a ten-dollar gold certificate in payment. The manager recognized it and remarked, "You don't see many more of these," to which Hauptmann answered, "No, I only have about a hundred left." The witness said he gave Hauptmann his change and, "because he thought it was a gold-hoarding case," wrote the make of the car—a Dodge—and the license number—4U 13-41—on the margin of the bill. The bill itself he turned over to one of his employees in part payment of his wages and directed him to take it to the bank and exchange it for other currency.

The employee corroborated the manager's story. Employees of a neighborhood bank described the presentation of gold certificate number 73976634, their discovery that it was one of the Lindbergh ransom notes and their notification of the Federal authorities.

A special agent of the Department of Justice testified he interviewed the bank employees and filling-station attendants, had them identify the bill and, through the State Motor Vehicle License Division, obtained the name, residence and description of the applicant for license number 4U 13-41.

A number of the police officers who participated told of Hauptmann's arrest. Others described the search of his apartment and garage, the finding of the ransom loot and their conversations with Hauptmann as to where he had got the money.

A police inspector testified to finding in a desk in Hauptmann's home a piece of cheap, white, watermarked paper identical with that used for some of the ransom notes. The sheet was produced, identified and received in evidence.

He also identified a board as the inside doorjamb of a closet opening in the Hauptmann apartment, on which was written in lead pencil Dr. Condon's address and telephone number—2974, "Decatur," "3-7154," "s" "d" "g" (Sedgwick). The witness said Hauptmann admitted the board came from his home and that the figures "2974" were in his writing; and, when asked how he came to write it, he replied that the newspapers were filled with the story of the kidnaping and he just wrote it down because he was interested. Reilly put the inspector through a vicious cross-examination, implying, as he afterward argued, that the writing on the board was a frame-up put on by some of the police officers after Hauptmann had been arrested.

If there was any shock in this not too original contention, it was short-lived. The next witness was a court stenographer from the Bronx district attorney's office who had taken down in shorthand a conversation on the same subject matter between Hauptmann and the district attorney. His testimony and his notes completely sustained the inspector.

A number of Federal investigators and accountants were called to show Hauptmann's financial condition before and after April 2, 1932. From their testimony it appeared that for a number of years before 1932 both Hauptmann and his wife had worked steadily and, by frugal living, had accumulated about $4,000 or $5,000. Some of this they deposited in savings banks; some of it they used to speculate in the stock market. According to one of the government's accountants their net loss from these stock operations before April 2, 1932, was slightly over $3,400. Between April 2, 1932, and September 19, 1934, the various brokerage house and bank records showed that Hauptmann deposited in his own and his wife's brokerage accounts $16,942.75 and in various banks $9,073.25, and that he also bought and paid cash for a real-estate mortgage of $3,750. His wife did not work at all during this period and Hauptmann's total earnings from his labor were $1,167.81. His stock-market losses from April 2, 1932, to the time of his arrest—September 19, 1934—were $5,728.63.

An accountant from the Intelligence Unit of the United States Treasury Department produced an exhibit to sum-marize the evidence as to the improvement in the state of Hauptmann's finances after April 2, 1932. According to this summary, Hauptmann's known assets on April 1 were $4,941.40. Between April of 1932 and September of 1934 he had known earnings of $1,167.81, making a total of as-sets and earnings of $6,109.21. On September 19, 1934, Hauptmann had known assets of $40,529.02. Between April 2, 1932, and September 19, 1934, his known expendi-tures, including stock-market losses of $5,728.63, were $15,530.63. This gave a total of assets and expenditures as of September 19, 1934, of $56,059.65. Subtracting from this large sum the item of $6,109.21 (assets as of April 2, 1932, plus earnings to September 1934) left a balance of $49,950.44 unaccounted for—presumably the ransom money.

A line of witnesses were called to "put the finger" on Hauptmann. Joseph Perrone, the taxi driver who de-livered one of the ransom notes to Dr. Condon on March 12, 1932, positively identified Hauptmann as the man who hailed his cab and gave him Condon's address and a dollar bill and told him to deliver the message. Hauptmann vented his mounting wrath by shouting at the witness, "You're a liar!" Neither this nor Reilly's noisy cross-exam-ination affected the witness. He stuck to his story. He was corroborated by another taxi driver to whom he had shown the letter.

A Miss Alexander, who lived in the Bronx and knew Dr. Condon, told of seeing him at the Fordham railroad sta-tion of the New York Central Railroad some time in March of 1932 and noticing particularly another man who was very evidently watching the doctor and following his move-ments. She identified this person as Hauptmann.

Cecile M. Barr, cashier of Loew's Greenwich Sheridan Theatre and an employee of the theater company for more than twenty-five years, declared unhesitatingly that Hauptmann was the man who purchased the theater ticket from her on November 26, 1933, and presented the five-dollar gold note in payment. While her testimony may have been weakened by the circumstance, brought out on cross-examination, of the unlikelihood that she would pay any particular attention to one of the hundreds of customers who paused momentarily at a ticket booth to buy a ticket, the witness stoutly adhered to her story.

An eighty-seven-year-old man, Amandus Hochmuth, whose home was on the public highway close to Featherbed Lane and not far from the Lindbergh residence, testified that on the morning of March 1, 1932, from where he sat on his front porch, he had seen a "dirty green car," with a ladder sticking out of it, nearly skid into the ditch alongside the road and pass within twenty-five feet of him. He said he had had a clear view of the driver, and it was Hauptmann. The old man's testimony was badly shaken by Reilly's cross-examination. He became hopelessly confused on locations, directions, distances and by contradictory statements he had made to various persons before he took the stand.

Millard Whited, a workman employed on the estate adjacent to the Lindberghs', identified Hauptmann as a man whom he had seen in the neighborhood of the Lindbergh property twice in the two weeks preceding the kidnaping.

Charles Rossiter, a salesman, living not far away in Maplewood, identified Hauptmann as a man he had seen at Princeton Airport four days before the kidnaping. The airport was fourteen miles from Hopewell.

The testimonies of both Whited and Rossiter were seriously weakened by Reilly's slashing cross-examination.

The next witness, Ella Achenbach, provoked a storm. She was the proprietress of a restaurant where Mrs. Hauptmann had once been employed as a waitress. She swore that two days after the kidnaping Mrs. Hauptmann and her husband called at her house; that Mrs. Hauptmann told her they had "just gotten back from a trip——" At this point Mrs. Hauptmann jumped from her chair and shouted at the witness, "Mrs. Achenbach, you are lying!" Mrs. Hauptmann was cautioned by the Court to restrain herself. The attorney general seized the opportunity to declare that the whole scene was deliberate stage play and demanded that his witnesses be protected from the abuse of the defendant and his wife. Order was restored and the witness, unperturbed, proceeded with her testimony. She said that Mrs. Hauptmann had told her that her husband had "sprained his ankle pretty bad"; and that when Hauptmann left her porch he was limping and supported himself by putting his hands against the porch wall. Reilly's cross-examination emphasized rather than weakened the witness's story.

Telling testimony against Hauptmann was given by the timekeeper for a property-management company which operated the Majestic Apartments where Hauptmann was employed for a part of March and April 1932. He testified from his records and recollections that Hauptmann entered the employment of the company on March 21, 1932; that he worked every day except Sunday up to and including April 1; that he did not work on April 2; that he returned to work on April 4 (Monday) and quitted of his own accord on the evening of that day.

Attorney General Wilentz and his associates realized that it was vital to their proof to establish beyond any possibility of controversy that the so-called ransom notes were written by Hauptmann. Realizing the importance of obtaining unquestionably genuine specimens of Hauptmann's handwriting as standards for comparison with the ransom notes, the police almost immediately after Hauptmann's arrest gave him pen, ink and paper and asked him to write from their dictation. They said he made no objection and

THE BRUNO HAUPTMANN CASE

filled dozens of pages with his handwriting. Witnesses were called who identified these sheets. Another witness produced a number of automobile-license blanks which had been filled out by Hauptmann. A promissory note and an identification card of an automobile-casualty-insurance company were also identified as having been written by Hauptmann. The ransom notes and these admittedly genuine specimens of Hauptmann's handwriting furnished the basis for the opinions of the handwriting experts.

In the broad field of expert evidence there is no more convincing witness than the qualified questioned-document examiner. The members of this profession are scientists in the truest sense of that term. By comparisons, made vivid by photographic enlargements and the employment of modern photographic processes and techniques, by microscopic measurements and chemical tests, these specialists are able to demonstrate to a Court or jury similarities or dissimilarities in documents under examination, which all but compel the acceptance of their ultimate opinions. As in every other profession, there are men on the peaks, men whose abilities are known and whose integrity is unquestioned. The prosecutors of Hauptmann brought into the little courtroom at Flemington the outstanding leaders of this profession. At their head were Albert S. Osborn of New York City and John F. Tyrrell of Milwaukee—men who over a period of half a century had appeared and testified in practically every important trial in the United States which involved a question of forgery or a disputed writing. They were supported by six other men of equal eminence—Clark J. Sellers of Los Angeles, Herbert J. Walter of Chicago, Albert D. Osborn (son of Albert S.), Henry M. Cassidy of Richmond, Virginia, Elbridge W. Stein of New York City and Wilmer D. Souder, chief of the Identification Bureau of the United States Department of Commerce.

The testimony of the elder Osborn was the most exten-

sive and is typical. "Handwriting," said Osborn, "is identified exactly as a man is identified, as a motorcar is identified, as a horse is identified, by general description and
then by individual marks and scars and characteristics
which, in combination—and that is the significant part of
this matter of comparison—is the combination of characteristics so that it is not reasonable to say they would accident-
ally coincide."

Osborn declared his opinion: that while there had been
an attempt to disguise the writing in the ransom notes, they
all had been written by the same person. He testified that
the motorcar registrations and the promissory note were
natural writings. When Hauptmann wrote the specimen
writings at the request of the police officers, Osborn said,
Hauptmann had again attempted to disguise his hand, but
"the writer didn't have but one disguise" and as a result
the requested writings showed partly the style of the ransom notes and partly the style of the motorcar registrations
and the promissory note.

There was a definite connection, said Osborn, in the ransom notes. This was unmistakable because of repetitions
of subject matter and phrases, of language employed, of
peculiar spellings and misspellings, and finally because of
"the peculiar and ingenious device that appears on the
lower right-hand corner" of each of the notes. He said the
most significant feature of that device was the three holes
—referred to in one of the later ransom letters as "specially
them three holes."

"The three holes," said Osborn, "connect the eleven
letters with each other, in my opinion, unmistakably, for
this reason: They are punched through the paper so there
is a hole through the paper, . . . and in my opinion they
were all punched with the same model or pattern. . . . They
were not punched at the same time because the holes are
not exactly the same size and not exactly the same shape,
but they are all in the same relation to each other and in
the same relation to the edge of the paper, so that you can

take letter number one, put the corners together and the sides together, hold it to the light, and you can see through all three holes, and you can see through all three holes on all eleven of them. . . . The evidence," continued the witness, "of the . . . physical connection between these writings is, in my opinion, irresistible, unanswerable, and overwhelming."

The experts, in varying language, pointed out specifically the writer's repeated practice of putting the dollar sign after rather than before the numerals and the repetition of phrases in successive letters; for example, "we will inform you," "this [the kidnaping] was planned for a year allredy," and "handel encloced letter." They also directed attention to the repetition of misspellings, among them "mony" for "money," "latter" for "later," "pappers" for "papers," "anyding" for "anything," "singnature" for "signature," "redy" for "ready," "plase" for "place," "trapp" for "trap," "note" for "not," "the" for "they," "were" for "where," "by" for "be," "bee" for "be," "whas" for "was," "cane" for "can," "off" for "of," "cace" for "case," and "handel" for "handle." The witnesses emphasized the significance of so many repetitive misspellings in the ransom notes. Said one witness: "The chance of two persons spelling all those words wrong in the same way is so improbable as to be entirely negligible."

Having proved that the ransom notes were all penned by the same hand, the prosecutor's next step was to establish that they were all written by Hauptmann. This involved a comparison of words and letters in the ransom notes with the same words and letters in the admittedly genuine specimens of Hauptmann's handwriting. Selected words and letters in the ransom notes and the specimens were photographed and enlarged by many diameters so that not only the letter formation but continuity, free or cramped movement, shading, pen pressures and pen lifts could be clearly demonstrated.

Hundreds of striking similarities were pointed out by

the experts. The words "New York" appeared repeatedly in both the ransom notes and the admitted writings with a hyphen between the two words. Both the ransom notes and the admitted writings showed the writer's difficulty in arranging the letters in words in which the final letters "ght" appear. For example: "right" in one of the ransom notes is spelled "rigth" and "light" in one of the admitted writings is spelled "lihgt." The words "Dear Sir," "making," "indication," "singnature," and "holes," as written in the nursery note, appear in almost identical formation in the specimens. The words "sleeping suit," "baby," "from," and "well" in the note to Dr. Condon concerning the sending of the sleeping suit were almost perfectly duplicated in the specimens. Striking similarities were also indicated in the formation of words used in the later ransom notes and the admitted writings.

The comparison of individual letters was even more significant. By a laborious isolation and counting of letters in the specimens to get those which were typical, photographing them and placing them in apposition to correspondingly enlarged letters in the ransom notes, it was made apparent that there was a striking similarity in the form of many of the letters. There was likewise, said the witnesses, a definite similarity in the formation of the dollar sign and the numerals 1, 2, 3, 4, 5, 6, 7 and 8 which appeared in the ransom notes and the specimens.

Based on the foregoing identities and similarities in the ransom notes and the genuine specimens of Hauptmann's writings, the eight experts gave it as their well-considered and positive opinions that all of the ransom notes had been penned by Hauptmann.

Satisfied that it had established that Hauptmann wrote the ransom notes and collected the ransom money, the prosecution proceeded to its final step to prove it was Hauptmann who abducted the child. This it did by circumstantial and expert-opinion evidence—evidence that the ladder found on the premises after the baby's disappearance had been made by Hauptmann from lumber a part of which he had purchased and a part of which he had taken from the attic floor of his house.

The State's chief witness to establish that the ladder found on the Lindbergh premises the night of the kidnaping had belonged to and had been built by Hauptmann was an employee of the United States Forest Products Laboratory at Madison, Wisconsin, Arthur Koehler. Koehler was qualified by the prosecutor as an "expert on wood," despite the protest of Defense Counsel Pope that "there was no such animal known among men."

Koehler was a graduate of the University of Michigan, where he majored in forestry, and by postgraduate work in the same field at the University of Wisconsin he had won a degree of Master of Science. In the fifteen years of his government employment, he had handled annually between 2,000 and 3,000 specimens of wood to determine their identity, age, conditions in growth, strength, peculiarities and adaptability for various uses. His education and experience had also familiarized him with timber locations, timber growth and cutting and mill machinery and its operation. He had written and published over fifty books and pamphlets on forestry, wood and related subjects.

Earlier witnesses had identified the ladder found on the premises, the carpenter's tools found in Hauptmann's possession, as well as pieces of wood taken from the attic floor above the apartment he occupied and from a bracket in his garage.

Attorney General Wilentz first directed Koehler's attention to two pieces of wood. One had been identified as the side rail of the upper section of the ladder;[10] the other as

---

10 The ladder was in three sections which could be tied together and extended by the use of dowel pins. Each section was about six feet long. Koehler testified that when these three sections were "nested together" they could be contained in Hauptmann's automobile. The ladder would then stretch from the top of the rear seat and across the top of the front seat and miss the front windshield by five or six inches.

part of a board taken out of the flooring in Hauptmann's attic. Koehler testified that the ladder rail had been part of a longer floor board in the attic;[11] that this board had been pried away from the rafters and the ladder rail sawed off of it. He reached this conclusion, he said, for a number of reasons: First, when the ladder was placed over the attic rafters, the nail holes which had been in the original attic board corresponded perfectly with the nail holes in the rafters. Second, when the two boards were joined at the ends where they had been sawed apart, the grain of the wood connected and matched perfectly. Third, the age rings in the two pieces were the same. Fourth, sawdust was found on the upper side of the ceiling plaster just below where the saw cut had been made. Fifth, the width of the saw cut was between thirty-five and thirty-seven one-thousandths of an inch and Hauptmann had two saws in his tool chest which made just such cuts.

Koehler testified further that this same ladder rail showed it had been planed down on its narrow sides with a hand plane. The peculiar plane markings on the rail showed that the knife of the plane which had made them was nicked. A test planing on another piece of wood with the hand plane taken from Hauptmann's tool chest showed plane markings identical with those found on the ladder rail. The witness, with the Court's permission, clamped a vise to the judge's bench, secured a piece of wood in it and, in the presence of the Court and jury, planed it with Hauptmann's plane. The resulting markings were identical with the markings on the ladder rail.

Under the attorney general's examination, Koehler next called attention to the notched recesses in the ladder rails into which the rungs of the ladder had been fitted. The cuts on these, he said, showed unmistakably that they had been made with a three-quarter-inch chisel. A three-quarter-inch chisel was found in Hauptmann's tool chest.

---

11 The attic had been only partially floored, which made easy the removal of part of one of the boards.

Moreover, this three-quarter-inch chisel was of the same type and made by the same manufacturer as the one-quarter-inch chisel which was found in the mud beneath the nursery window on the night of the kidnaping.

The culminating sensation in this remarkable testimony was yet to come. Koehler's examination of the ladder rails, other than the one traced to Hauptmann's attic, had showed on their wide surfaces unmistakable evidences of machine-plane markings, with peculiarities ordinarily found in all machine-planed lumber—"because no two planes leave surfaces exactly alike." Koehler had been brought into the case in May of 1932—more than two years before Hauptmann was arrested. He set himself to the task of discovering where these machine-planed boards had been cut into finished lumber and from where they had been retailed for use. To the layman such a quest would have seemed utterly hopeless. To Koehler, with the vast facilities of the Department of Justice at his command, it was routine.

He first determined from his own education and experienced observation that the wood was North Carolina pine,[12] and that the machine through which the logs had passed in the planing of the boards was a type equipped with an eight-knife cutterhead on top and bottom and a six-knife cutterhead on its two sides. He knew that only two concerns in the East included that type of mill machine in their manufactured output. From these companies it was ascertained that 1,598 of their planing machines had been sold to Eastern and Southern saw mills. Through the mail, by telephone and by personal calls, the witness communicated with all of these purchasers. Twenty-five of them were found to have purchased machines with eight-knife cutterheads on top and bottom and six-knife cutterheads on the sides. The planing machines in each of these twen-

---

[12] The term "North Carolina pine" is applied to a common type of shortleaf pine found not only in North Carolina but also in Virginia, South Carolina and Georgia.

ty-five mills were carefully examined to find the one machine which left the individual markings found on the ladder rails. That machine was found in the mill of M. G. and J. J. Dorn at McCormick, South Carolina.

The next step was to find where the lumber planed by that particular machine had been shipped. The records of the Dorn mill showed that forty-five carloads of lumber containing one-by-fours—the measurements of the lumber used for the ladder rails—had been shipped to twenty-five Eastern and Southern lumberyards between October 1929[13] and March 1, 1932. There were several machine planers in the Dorn mills, and in order to locate one-by-fours which showed the peculiar plane markings similar to those which appeared on the ladder rails each shipment had to be traced. The incredible effort paid off in September 1933— a year before Hauptmann was arrested—when identical pieces of one-by-four flooring were located in the lumberyard of the Great National Millwork and Lumber Company in the Bronx.

The finishing touch to this amazing piece of detective work was the testimony of an officer of the Great National Millwork and Lumber Company that Hauptmann had worked for this company for several months in the winter of 1931—1932 and, on December 29, 1931, had bought $9.31 worth of lumber.

Pope for the defense cross-examined Koehler at length. The examination was intelligent and searching but in no way weakened the expert's testimony. There was a brief redirect, and Attorney General Wilentz announced that the State rested. With good trial technique, the attorney general had finished on a high note. He had made good the boast in his opening. He had "hung the ladder right around Hauptmann's neck."

Hauptmann's lawyers commenced his defense with a motion to discharge the defendant because of the State's fail-

13 The date the machine planer had been put in operation.

ure to prove venue as alleged in the indictment; that is, that the murder of the child had occurred in Hunterdon County. The body, it will be remembered, was discovered just over the line in Mercer County, and it was argued with force that this fact carried with it the presumption that death had occurred in Mercer County. The Court, after hearing full argument, overruled the motion, holding that the facts and circumstances proved were sufficient to justify the jury in finding that death was instantaneous and had occurred in Hunterdon County.

Fisher then proceeded to outline the evidence which would be introduced by the defendant: He had been nowhere near the Lindbergh premises on the night of the kidnaping. He had never met and did not know Dr. Condon. He had been at his home in the Bronx, enjoying a "musical evening" with friends on April 2, the date on which the State claimed Dr. Condon paid over the ransom money to the mysterious "John." Hauptmann, declared Fisher, would take the stand in his own defense, and he and other witnesses would refute every charge that had been made against him.

Bruno Richard Hauptmann was called to the stand. A uniformed sheriff's guard stood at his back during the entire seventeen hours of his examination.

Under the skillful management of Chief Counsel Reilly, Hauptmann faced the jury with amazing assurance and told his story. He was born in Saxony and had eight years' common schooling and two years in an industrial academy where he studied and practiced the carpenter's and machinist's trades. He was taken into the German Army when he was seventeen and one-half years old and served not quite two years. He testified he was unable to get work after the armistice and, because of his financial distress, got into trouble and was convicted for "an offense" for which he suffered imprisonment. He was paroled in March of 1923 and almost immediately tried to enter the United

States. After two unsuccessful attempts he succeeded in September of 1923 in making an illegal entry at the port of New York. He worked at various jobs: in a restaurant as a dishwasher, in a dyeing and cleaning establishment as a clothes dyer and as a machinist and carpenter. In 1925 he met and married Anna Schoeffler, a waitress. Both continued to work regularly until April 1932.

Hauptmann claimed to have been quite steadily employed after 1924 at wages ranging from $20 to $50 a week; sometimes overtime made it more. His wife worked steadily and, with wages and tips, earned between $30 and $35 a week. They were frugal, saved their money and at the end of 1929 owned a mortgage of $3,750, had $700 or $800 in the bank and, according to Hauptmann's testimony, had something in the neighborhood of $4,000 cash in the house. Hauptmann said he "went into Wall Street" in 1929 and, in spite of the record to the contrary, insisted he made some money. On April 2, 1932, he claimed he had fifty shares of Warner Brothers common stock (market value $200), $202.26 in a bank account, a mortgage of $3,750 and about $4,000 in a trunk in his home. He also owned a 1930 Dodge automobile which had cost him $700.[14]

Hauptmann testified he met a man named Isidor Fisch in March or April of 1932. Fisch was in the fur business, and the two entered into a partnership: Each was to put up an equal amount of money to buy furs and to speculate in the stock market, and they were to divide equally the profits and losses of both ventures. Hauptmann was to manage the market operations; Fisch, the fur business. The fur business was carried on in the sole name of Fisch; brokerage accounts and stock purchases were in the sole name of Hauptmann. Fisch's end of the business, according to Hauptmann, returned substantial profits—there were frequent periodic divisions out of which Hauptmann sometimes obtained amounts in excess of $1,000. Fisch, testified

---

14 This was the car he was driving when he was arrested.

Hauptmann, gave him various substantial amounts with which to make purchases of stocks—items of $582.50, $860, $850, $2,787.50, $2,500, $2,575, $2,197, $2,225, $4,500 and $2,000. Hauptmann, from money he said he had, paid into various brokerage accounts between $6,500 and $8,000. He also claimed to have given cash to Fisch which the latter used to buy furs; the exact amount does not appear. The mortgage of $3,750 which was purchased after April 1932, was acquired, testified Hauptmann, with fur profits and "money he had in the house."

Fisch left the United States for Germany in December 1933. Shortly before that, according to Hauptmann, the partners had a settlement: Fisch owed him $5,500 and Hauptmann let him have an additional $2,000 cash, making his total debt $7,500. Fisch, when he left, had 400 Hudson sealskins in which Hauptmann claimed a half interest. The night before Fisch's ship sailed he called at Hauptmann's home and left with him for safekeeping two suitcases and a little cardboard box, about the size and shape of a shoe box. As to the latter, Hauptmann testified that Fisch said to him: "Take care of it and put it in a dry place." Hauptmann said he asked what was in it and Fisch replied, "Paper." Hauptmann testified he put the box on the upper shelf of a small broom closet and forgot all about it until sometime in the middle of August 1934, when he went into the closet to look for a broom and accidentally hit the box and broke it open. He then saw that it contained paper currency, which was wet from water which had leaked into the closet from the roof. He testified he "loosened up" the bills and squeezed some of the water out of them, put them in a tin pail and carried them to his garage. There he transferred them to a basket which he secured against the ceiling by nailing two strips of wood underneath it. Then he put another basket on top of the basket containing the money, and left it there. Hauptmann testified he did not count the money until later and never told his wife about the "find." Fisch, said Hauptmann, died in Germany in the latter part of April 1934.

Hauptmann denied unequivocally that he had ever been at Hopewell or on the Lindbergh premises or that he had ever seen the Lindbergh baby. He denied writing any of the ransom notes or ever having seen Dr. Condon until after his arrest, at which time the old schoolteacher had appeared to view and identify him. He disclaimed all knowledge of the baby's thumb guard, the sleeping suit, or the wrapping paper which had enclosed the suit upon its delivery to Dr. Condon. He swore he had never seen the ladder until it was offered in evidence and declared with disdain he never could have built such a ladder—*he* was a carpenter; the alleged ladder looked to him like a "moosic instrument." He denied he ever carried a ladder in his car. He also denied he had ever removed or used a board from his attic floor for building a ladder or for any other purpose. He admitted the chest and tools found in his garage were his, but he denied ever having owned or seen the chisel which was found on the Lindbergh grounds the night of the kidnaping.

Hauptmann gave the following account of his movements on March 1, 1932, the date of the kidnaping: From eight o'clock in the morning until late afternoon he was in New York looking for a job. He returned home in the early evening. About eight-thirty he drove to the Fredericksen bakery and lunchroom, where his wife worked, to bring her home. There he saw Fredericksen, had a cup of coffee and, as was his wont, took Fredericksen's police dog out for an airing. While out with the dog he met a stranger who inquired about the dog and told him it had been stolen. He drove his wife home about nine o'clock and, shortly after, retired for the night. He said he read in the paper the next morning that the Lindbergh baby had been kidnaped.

As to March 12, 1932, the date of Dr. Condon's first

meeting with the mysterious "John," Hauptmann testified that was a Saturday night and he believed he was, as usual, at his home playing cards. He vehemently denied that he was at or near the Woodlawn Cemetery—some fifty blocks distant from his home—or that he met Dr. Condon or any other person there that night or at any other time.

Hauptmann denied with equal positiveness Miss Alexander's testimony that he was at the Fordham railroad station of the New York Central Railroad in March of 1932, or at any other time, stalking Dr. Condon.

As to April 2, 1932, the date which Dr. Condon testified he paid over the ransom money to the mysterious "John" in St. Raymond's Cemetery, Hauptmann swore that on that Saturday he worked all day—from seven till twelve and from one till five. He said he took the subway and arrived home at six. His friend Hans Kloeppenburg, following an unbroken custom on the first Saturday of each month, came at seven and they had a musical evening—Kloeppenburg played the guitar; Hauptmann, the mandolin. Possibly a second friend—Jimmy, whose last name he did not remember—was there. The party did not break up until eleven-thirty, when Hauptmann drove Kloeppenburg to the subway station. St. Raymond's Cemetery, testified Hauptmann, was miles away from his house—he could remember having been by there only once and that was six years ago.

Hauptmann denied ever having been at the Greenwich Village theater where, according to the testimony of Cecile Barr, he had appeared on November 26, 1933, and purchased a ticket with one of the ransom bills. November 26, said Hauptmann, was his birthday and he was positive he was not alone at a remote theater, but that he was at home with his wife and some of his friends celebrating the event.

Hauptmann closed his testimony with an attack on the police. He had been "beaten up" and deprived of his sleep until his resistance had been broken. He had been made to write, write and write until he could hardly hold a pen. He was told what to write and what words to misspell—"note" for "not" and "singnature" for "signature." This was how the misspellings had got into the specimens of his handwriting. When he appeared before the district attorney and other examining officials, fear of a repetition of police brutality had induced him to say anything to obtain a surcease from the incessant questioning.

Attorney General Wilentz' cross-examination was merciless. Hauptmann's criminal record, touched on lightly on direct examination as "an offense," was expanded by the defendant's forced admissions to include convictions for breaking in and entering a dwelling house through a window in the nighttime, for robbery at the point of a gun of two mothers while they were wheeling their baby carriages and for receiving and selling stolen property. He had escaped from jail, been recaptured and served a four-year term of imprisonment.

Confronted with dozens of contradictory statements which he had made to the police, the district attorney, and in the Bronx court in the extradition hearing, Hauptmann replied, usually without apparent embarrassment, that his previous answers had been untrue; that he had told the truth only "to a certain extent."

Hauptmann was shown various of his memorandum books which the police had found in his home. In one of them the word "boat" was spelled "boad," as in the last ransom note. He admitted that in Saxony the German equivalent of "boat" was "boad." He denied that he had ever voluntarily spelled the word "signature" "s-i-n-g-n-a-t-u-r-e" or that he had any difficulty in properly placing the letter "n" in English words, but he was shown and admitted writing checks in which the word "seventy" was spelled "s-e-n-v-e-t-y." Similarly, he was confronted with his admitted writing of "Curtiss-Wright" in which the word "Wright" was spelled "W-r-i-h-g-t"; so, also, with the word "night," which he spelled "n-i-h-g-t." This transposition of the "g" and "h" was one of the peculiarities in the ransome notes. Hauptmann denied any similarities in the formation of individual words and letters in his admitted writings to the same words and letters in the ransom notes, but, confronted in one instance with altogether obvious similarities, he said, "It looks as though somebody had tried to copy my writing."

Hauptmann testified during the course of his cross-examination that he had been corresponding with his mother in Saxony and at the time of his arrest was contemplating a trip to Germany. Under Wilentz' rapid-fire examination, which hinted that it had been a hastily taken decision, Hauptmann answered, "Oh, that was planned for a year already." This was an exact arrangement of words which occurred twice in the ransom notes. The attorney general was quick to seize on the coincidence. Asked if that was not a characteristic of his speech, Hauptmann gave the significant answer, "How can I say it otherwise?"

Wilentz subjected Hauptmann to exhaustive questioning on his relations and dealings with Isidor Fisch. Hauptmann testified that when Fisch sailed for Germany in December 1933 he knew Fisch was a sick man, but he fully expected he would return to America. He was made to retell the story of the cardboard box which he claimed Fisch had left with him for safekeeping. The cross-examiner emphasized that Fisch had asked specifically that it be put in a dry place. Hauptmann admitted he had put it in the wettest place in the house—in the broom closet underneath a known leak in the roof. It was further developed that Fisch at that time told him he had no money—that was why he could not repay Hauptmann the $5,500, which Hauptmann claimed Fisch owed him, and had to borrow an additional $2,000 to pay the expenses of his trip to Germany. He had no answer to the attorney general's question as to why Fisch should have borrowed $2,000 cash from him to pay his expenses to Germany and left behind $14,600 in cash in a fragile cardboard box.

There was an implication in Hauptmann's testimony that Fisch had written the ransom notes. Wilentz put the question to him baldly: Was it his contention that Fisch had written the notes? Hauptmann hesitated and finally answered he "wouldn't say he had."

Hauptmann's statements on direct examination as to the amounts of money he had in March of 1932 had always included a substantial sum in cash which he said he had hidden in a trunk in his house. At the end of 1929 he said this amount was between $3,000 and $3,500; in 1932 it was $4,000. Wilentz' cross-examination seriously weakened this story. It was developed that while Hauptmann and his wife pooled their earnings, he had never told her about these secret hoards; also, that in May of 1931, with $4,000 alleged secreted cash in the house, he had begged his stock-brokers for a few days' extension on a margin call, with a threat of close-out, for $74.

Hauptmann admitted on cross-examination that neither he nor his wife did any work to speak of after April 1932; that his wife stayed at home, except for the trip she took to Germany, and he spent most of his time in the brokerage offices following security prices. He admitted various purchases and expenditures after April 1932: $400 for a radio, $126 for a pair of field glasses, $109 for a canoe and an unnamed amount for pleasure trips to Maine, the Carolinas and Florida.

Hauptmann, despite Wilentz' repeated, rapid-fire questions—some of which were deliberately assumptive—was alert to catch and deny every direct or implied suggestion that he had ever been at Hopewell or had anything to do with the kidnaping, or with the writing of the ransom notes, or with the solicitation or receipt from Condon of the ransom money. He admitted having been in his attic and of having used it to store things, but he denied he had ever tampered with any of the floor boards.

Hauptmann was shown the piece of doorjamb identified in the State's case as having come from the closet-door opening in his apartment, on which was written in lead pencil Dr. Condon's address and telephone number. He said the handwriting was not his and, while the numbers looked like his, he had no recollection of having written them. After being confronted with widely conflicting statements which he had previously made to the police, to the district attorney for the Bronx, or in the extradition hearing, he finally "guessed" he might have told District Attorney Foley that it looked like his writing. He said he must have noticed Dr. Condon's address in a newspaper article about the kidnaping and written it down; that making such notations was a habit of his. He immediately qualified this admission by saying that while he sometimes wrote such things on the kitchen wall, he was positive he never wrote anything on the inside of a dark closet. When pitilessly crowded with these contradictions and equivocations, he fell back on his direct line: The police had so abused and exhausted him that he had said anything his examiners wanted him to say in order to escape further questioning; that whatever he might have said about the writing in the closet was under duress and untrue. When the exhausting cross-examination was completed, Hauptmann's initial confidence had largely evaporated. He was a tired, discredited and beaten man.

Mrs. Hauptmann followed her husband on the stand. She told of her marriage to Hauptmann in 1925 and her successive employments up to December of 1932, when, at her husband's suggestion, she ceased her outside work to devote herself to her home. She denied the testimony of Mrs. Achenbach: She did not see Mrs. Achenbach at all in March of 1932—Mrs. Achenbach was confusing a call she and her husband made on her after their return from their California trip in July of 1931.

She corroborated Hauptmann as to his movements on March 1, 1932: He called for her at Fredericksen's bakery at seven o'clock on the evening of March 1 and stayed there until she ceased work at nine-thirty or nine-forty-five. She distinctly remembered April 2, 1932: It was a Saturday, and she and her husband were at home. Hans Kloeppenburg called shortly after seven and they played cards and "made music" until nearly midnight. She also had a distinct recollection of November 26, 1933: It was Hauptmann's birthday, a Sunday, and her husband was home all day. In the evening Paul Vetterle, Maria Muller and Isidor Fisch came in. They had coffee and music, and the party did not break up until ten o'clock.

She told of meeting Fisch at Mrs. Henkel's house "sometime in 1932," of his frequent visits to the Hauptmann home and the "farewell party" in December of 1933 just before he sailed for Germany. She testified that Fisch brought to her home two suitcases and two rather large packages containing furs, but she remembered nothing about a shoe box. She described the broom closet and said it was usually wet from a leak in the ceiling.

While given in a somewhat hesitant manner, Mrs. Hauptmann's direct testimony definitely corroborated that of her husband. It was under Wilentz' broad and relentless cross-examination that she was forced into reluctant admissions which seriously weakened her direct testimony and did the defendant incalculable harm. Hauptmann, she admitted, never told her of Fisch's shoe box which he had put on the top shelf of the broom closet, nor of his later discovery that it contained over $14,000, nor of his concealing the money in his garage. She admitted she could easily reach the top shelf of the closet, that her kitchen apron hung from a hook immediately above it, and that she had cleaned every shelf of the closet except the top one once every week. At no time, she said, had she seen a shoe box. She admitted that when the police first talked to her after Hauptmann's arrest she told them she could not remember anything as far back as March and April of 1932.

When she was questioned on the many answers she had given in her testimony in the Bronx extradition hearing which were clearly at variance with her direct testimony, her invariable reply, "I don't remember," was repeated until its monotony quite obviously irked both the jury and the Court.

The defense called six additional witnesses to testify to Hauptmann's presence at the Fredericksen restaurant on the evening of March 1, 1932, between the hours of seven and nine-thirty. Only four of these pretended to have a definite recollection of seeing Hauptmann at the time and place in question.

The first—one Carlstrom—testified that he read of Hauptmann's arrest in September of 1934 and identified a newspaper picture of him as a man he had seen in the Fredericksen restaurant about eight-thirty on the night of March 1, 1932. He was wholly discredited by Wilentz' cross-examination: He had not notified the police of his identification of Hauptmann because he "didn't want to get mixed up in the case." He had not been sure of the identification until very recently when he saw another newspaper picture of Hauptmann and Reilly together; then he had volunteered as a witness for the defense. His stated reason for being at the restaurant was unconvincing. He was uncertain of his movements before eight-thirty and declined to answer where he was and what he did after eight-thirty "for fear his answer would incriminate him."

The second of these witnesses was a Hungarian bootlegger named Kiss. He testified that he was in the neighborhood to make a delivery of liquor. He went into the restaurant about 7:45 P.M. to get a cup of coffee. There he saw a man whom he later identified from a newspaper picture as Hauptmann. He was positive the date was March 1, because he had taken his little daughter to Bellevue Hospital exactly one week before. This witness, too, was completely wrecked by the attorney general's cross-examination. He was led to repeat with great certainty that his only way of fixing the time was by the fact that he had taken his daughter to the hospital on February 22, exactly seven days before. The hospital records were produced to fix the time of his daughter's admission as 1:30 A.M., February 22. Then Wilentz sprang his trap: 1932 was a leap year; February that year had twenty-nine days. Retreat was impossible. The witness's sole basis of calculation had fixed the date not as March 1 but as February 29.

The third witness—one Van Henke—told a strange story of encountering a man outside the restaurant on the evening of March 1 who was leading a police dog on a leash. He said he had shortly before lost a police dog, and he thought this dog might be his. He asked the man his name and the man replied, "Hauptmann." He identified that man as the defendant from a newspaper picture which he saw after the arrest in September of 1934. In a brief cross-examination it was developed that the witness was a speak-easy proprietor and bookmaker. He admitted that his place of business had been frequently raided by the police and that to escape identification and arrest he had gone under numerous aliases.

The fourth witness—one Manley—testified that at seven-thirty on the evening of March 1, 1932, he had been in the Fredericksen restaurant and had seen a man at one of the tables whom he identified from a newspaper picture in September of 1934 as Hauptmann. He admitted on cross-examination that he never told anyone of his discovery until shortly before the trial started, when he gave the information to an unidentified man who relayed it to Reilly.

This was the defense corroboration of Hauptmann's March 1, 1932, alibi. It had been all but completely discredited by the State's cross-examination. It would suffer still further assaults from rebuttal impeachment.

Only one witness—Hans Kloeppenburg—corroborated Hauptmann's alibi for April 2, 1932, the day the ransom money was paid to the mysterious "John" in St. Raymond's Cemetery. He testified that he clearly remembered April 2, 1932. He came to the Hauptmann home at about seven o'clock that evening, and he and Mr. and Mrs. Hauptmann played music and sang until eleven o'clock or midnight. Then Hauptmann drove him to the White Plains subway station. He admitted on cross-examination that he was a very close friend of Mrs. Hauptmann. He said he and Hauptmann had not—as the opening statement for the defendant had indicated—got together on the first Saturday of every month, and when first questioned by the district attorney for the Bronx he had told the attorney that he could not remember where he was or what he had done on any particular day in March or April of 1932. He was put through a searching examination to test his memory on happenings on other dates and, in the face of the results, was forced to admit that his memory "was weak on dates."

Two witnesses—one a niece and the other a lifelong friend of Mrs. Hauptmann—were called to corroborate Hauptmann's alibi for November 26, 1933, the date which, according to the testimony of Cecile Barr, he had passed one of the ransom bills at the Greenwich Village movie theater. These swore that they and Isidor Fisch were at the Hauptmann home with Mr. and Mrs. Hauptmann on the day and evening in question; that it was Hauptmann's birthday, and they celebrated it with refreshments and music from four-thirty in the afternoon until ten in the evening.

The defense introduced three witnesses in an effort to prove that someone other than Hauptmann was in the neighborhood of the Lindbergh home on March 1, 1932, who had an automobile with a ladder in it. The first of these was a man named Harding, who said that on March 1 he was working as a laborer on one of the public roads of Princeton. He testified that between two and three o'clock in the afternoon two men driving a dark-blue sedan, with a New Jersey license, stopped and asked him the way to the Lindbergh estate. He was positive neither of the men in the car was Hauptmann. He said there was a large pasteboard box and a ladder in the car. On March 2 he was arrested and taken to the Lindbergh home. There, he said, he saw a ladder that "looked something like" the ladder he had seen the previous day. On cross-examination the witness admitted he had not had a very good view of the ladder in the car and could not describe it. He admitted he had paid no particular attention to the ladder he saw at the Lindbergh home. He further admitted that he had been convicted and served time for criminal assault and carnal abuse of an unnamed woman.

A second witness—one Palmer, a civil engineer, but then employed as an automobile-service-station attendant near the Princeton airport—testified as follows: At 1:15 A.M., March 1, 1932, a man and a woman drove up to his station in a green Ford coupé and bought some gas. The man was not Hauptmann. His attention was attracted to a "poor-looking ladder" in the car which looked like the ladder in evidence. He testified on cross-examination that he had never reported this to the police and had only recently made contact with a representative of the defense.

The testimony of the third witness—one Sebastian Lupica, a student at Princeton Preparatory School—proved a boomerang. He testified that he lived close by the Lindbergh estate. Sometime after 5:00 P.M. on March 1 he stopped his car at his mailbox and was reading a piece of mail when a dark-blue Dodge with a New Jersey license pulled up and stopped on the wrong side of the road. He said he noticed two sections of a ladder on top of the front seat of the car. He described the man in the car as between thirty-five and forty years of age, with thin features and wearing a dark coat and fedora. He said he could not say and never had said that the man was Hauptmann, but he saw sections of a ladder on the Lindbergh premises the following morning that "looked strikingly like" the two sections of the ladder he had seen in the strange car the day before.

On cross-examination Lupica admitted that immediately after the kidnaping he had told Prosecutor Hauck and others that the man he had seen "resembled Hauptmann." He then added, "Yes, it is the truth; I say so today." With equal frankness he admitted he had appeared before the Hunterdon County grand jury which had indicted Hauptmann and testified before it that the man he saw in the lane resembled Hauptmann. He further testified that in October of 1934 he had contributed an article to a local paper in which he wrote: "Bruno Richard Hauptmann is the same man that I saw at the foot of the lane leading to the Lindbergh home only a few hours before poor little baby Lindbergh was killed and murdered."

Another profitless effort of the defense was directed to casting suspicion upon Violet Sharpe and Fisch as the kidnapers. One Peter H. Sommer, who said he was a fingerprint expert by profession but who was presently working as a clerk in the New York Department of Public Welfare, told a weird story of having seen two men in the early morning of March 2, 1932, at the New York side of the 42nd Street—Weehauken Ferry. He testified that when they left the boat, a woman carrying a blond baby, wrapped in a blanket, appeared—he could not say from where—and was assisted onto a streetcar by the two men, and one of the men got on the car with her. He was shown a picture of Violet Sharpe and said "it looked like the lady." He was then shown a picture of Isidor Fisch and said it "strongly resembled" one of the two men whom he had seen get off the boat.

The second witness who attempted to tie Violet Sharpe into the kidnaping plot was one Anne Bonesteel. She ran a restaurant in Yonkers on the New York side of the ferry. She identified a newspaper picture shown her as that of

Violet Sharpe and testified the girl came into her place of
business at 7:30 P.M. March 1, 1932. The girl was carrying a gray blanket and appeared to be very nervous. She
said the girl remained in the restaurant until eight-thirty
and then went outside and got into an automobile which
had stopped about 200 feet away from the restaurant. She
said there were two men in the car. On cross-examination
she was shown several photographs of Violet Sharpe which
she said were not pictures of the girl she had seen on March
1. The attorney general appeared quite unconcerned over
the testimony of these two witnesses. He was fully prepared to rebut it by credible evidence which definitely accounted for the movements of Violet Sharpe and Fisch on
the evening of March 1, 1932.

The defense called two witnesses who claimed to have
been at or in the vicinity of St. Raymond's Cemetery on the
evening of April 2, 1932. One—a taxi driver named Moses
—testified that about 8:00 P.M., as he left the road which
cuts through the cemetery, he was hailed by three men who
had him drive them about two blocks beyond the cemetery to a point where a fourth man was standing alongside
a gray automobile which was stalled on the road. He said
all four men got into the gray car. He gave it a push to get
it started, and it drove away. The testimony was vague and
obviously of little or no probative value.

The second witness—one Benjamin Heier, who gave his
occupation as a lunchroom cashier and "writer"—had a
much more definite story to tell. This was his testimony:
On Saturday evening, April 2, 1932, he had called at the
home of his girl friend and drove with her in his car to St.
Raymond's Cemetery. He stopped opposite the main entrance gate and parked there for two hours. Most of the
time his lights were off, but occasionally he switched them
on. In one of these moments when his lights were on—
sometime between nine-thirty and ten—he said he saw a
man who apparently had jumped off the cemetery wall.

The man took two or three steps toward him and stopped. The automobile lights were fully on him and, from newspaper pictures and photographs he had since seen, he was convinced the man was Isidor Fisch.

The witness was subjected to one of Wilentz' bitterest cross-examinations. The young lady, said the witness, had since died, and he refused to give her name. The Court compelled him to answer. He next refused to tell where she lived and, when again forced to answer, said he could not remember. It was only under the Court's compulsion that he told where she had worked. He swore he had never told anyone of the episode and had completely forgotten about it until recently when he read in the paper that the ransom money had been paid in St. Raymond's Cemetery. He had not fixed definitely on the date as April 2 until a few days past and had then got in touch with the defense attorneys. He completed an unmistakably bad impression by a series of evasions before admitting that he had been convicted of a felony and was under a suspended sentence. Whatever doubt may have lingered as to the truth or falsity of this story was completely dispelled by the State's later rebuttal.

The defense called fifteen witnesses to prove the existence of Isidor Fisch, his activities and associations with Hauptmann. Kloeppenburg testified he had seen Fisch at the Hauptmann home between ten and twenty times—the first time in July or August of 1932. One Greta Henkel testified that Fisch and Hauptmann met at her house in July or August of 1932, but "she was sure they had known each other before that." A Mr. and Mrs. Wollenberg testified they had frequently seen Fisch in downtown New York brokerage offices. One Theron Main identified a photograph of Fisch and testified he met the man at a bar and restaurant in August of 1933, and that he saw him give the bartender a twenty-dollar gold certificate. He swore he was positive it was a gold certificate because it had a yellow back. He was completely discomfited by Wilentz' cross-examination and exhibitions of gold certificates which disclosed that such certificates did not have yellow backs. Seven witnesses testified to their presence on December 6, 1933, at a "farewell party" which the Hauptmanns gave for Fisch. According to the witnesses' testimony, Hauptmann and Fisch seemed on terms of intimate friendship, and the party lasted from early evening until the small hours of the following day. One of the witnesses—the family friend Kloeppenburg—furnished the only corroboration for Hauptmann's claim that Fisch left with him, among other things, a small cardboard shoe box. He testified that when Fisch came in, he had under his arm a package which was about fourteen inches long, five or six inches high and seven or eight inches wide; that he saw Hauptmann and Fisch go into the kitchen together, and when they came back Fisch did not have the package.

Four witnesses testified that Fisch had money. One—Augusta Hile—swore that at one time she lent him $4,350. A taxi driver identified a photograph of Fisch, and testified that he had had the man as a fare for a short trip sometime in May of 1933. When the trip was finished the man flashed a large roll of bills and gave him five dollars and told him to keep the change. George Steinweg, a steamship agent, testified that in August of 1933 Fisch purchased from him two steamship tickets for a December sailing to Germany. One of the tickets was for Fisch, the other for a Henry Uhlig. He said Fisch paid $410 for the tickets, bought $650 worth of American Express checks, and seemed to have considerable money still left in his wallet. Uhlig corroborated the steamship agent as to the purchase of the tickets but said Fisch did not pay his fare. He was simply repaying part of a loan which Uhlig had previously made to him. Uhlig claimed to be Fisch's closest friend. He said he saw him frequently when he was in the hospital in Germany and knew that he died there. Significantly, he

gave no testimony concerning Fisch's relations with Hauptmann.

The foregoing was all of the affirmative testimony offered
by the defense. Seventeen additional witnesses were called
to negate particular testimony of the State's witnesses.

Three not too impressive witnesses took the stand and
swore that the reputation of Whited, a State's witness, for
truth and veracity was bad.

A witness testified that he had experienced difficulty in
getting the correct change from Cecile Barr when he
bought a theater ticket from her, and that her memory for
faces was not good.

A half-dozen New Jersey police officers were recalled and
re-examined as to what they had done in connection with
the fingerprinting of the ladder, the window sill of the nursery, the baby's crib and the ransom note. This was supplemented by the testimony of a Dr. Erasmus Hudson, a recognized fingerprint specialist, who said the work had not
been expertly done, and that the latest techniques for processing and revealing fingerprints on unpainted wood surfaces—which he had later demonstrated to the police—had
not been employed. Dr. Hudson also testified that he had
examined the upper ladder rail, and it had only had two
nail holes in it—not four, as testified to by several of the
State's witnesses.

One John M. Trendley, qualified after considerable discussion as a handwriting expert, disputed the findings of
the State's experts, and testified that in his opinion none of
the ransom notes had been written by Hauptmann.

The defense concluded its case with three witnesses who
took the stand to answer the testimony of the State's wood
expert, Koehler. One of these testified you could not definitely recognize the work of a particular hand plane from
marks appearing on a board which had been planed with
it. It would depend altogether, he said, on how the plane
was held, and different positions assumed would produce

different results. Another witness demonstrated that the grains in two pieces of pine coming from different trees could be matched so as to make it appear they were two pieces cut off the same board. Two witnesses testified that in their opinion the upper ladder rail had not been cut off of the board taken from Hauptmann's attic.

The State's rebuttal was brief but effective. Two witnesses were called to impeach Defense Witness Carlstrom. These testified, from recollection and records, that Carlstrom was in Dunnellen, New Jersey, all of March 1, including the evening hours when he claimed to have been at the Fredericksen restaurant.

Leo Singer, who had been mentioned by Defense Witness Kiss as the man to whom he had delivered a package of liquor on the evening of March 1, testified that the delivery was made in the latter part of March or early April.

One Joseph J. Farber, a reputable insurance broker, testified that at 10:00 P.M. on the night of April 2 the automobile which he was driving collided with a car driven by Defense Witness Benjamin Heier. The place of the collision was Sixth Avenue between 54th and 55th streets in Manhattan—nearly nine miles from St. Raymond's Cemetery. Heier, he said, was alone in the car.

A New Jersey police officer testified that when he took Defense Witness Harding to the Lindbergh home on March 2 the latter made no mention of having seen a ladder in an automobile.

Three witnesses were called to refute Dr. Hudson's testimony that the upper ladder rail had only two nail holes in it. Two of these swore they had examined the ladder rail immediately after the kidnaping and pulled four nails out of it. One of them, a police photographer, produced photographs of the ladder rail which he had taken on May 8, 1932, which showed four nail holes.

Three witnesses testified that from 7:30 P.M. till midnight on March 1, 1932, Isidor Fisch was at the home of a Mr. and Mrs. Jung and was transacting some business in which he signed some promissory notes which bore that date. The notes, which bore Fisch's signature, were produced as corroboration. A Mrs. Kohl, who operated the rooming house in which Fisch lived before his departure for Germany, testified that the room Fisch rented was the cheapest in the house—$3.50 a week; that he had very few clothes, and he showed no evidences of wealth. Fisch's sister, who came from Germany to testify, swore that when her brother reached her home in Hamburg he had his return passage to America, about $500 in currency, some cheap wearing apparel and no other property. She further testified that in the five or six years Fisch had been in America he had sent home to his family about $1,000, but that in 1932 they had, at his request, sent him money.

Five witnesses established the whereabouts of Violet Sharpe on the evening of March 1. Three of them were her companions at the Orangeville Peanut Grille—which was not far from the Morrow estate—between the hours of 8:30 and 10:45 P.M. The Morrow night watchman swore that Miss Sharpe returned home around eleven o'clock. Mrs. Dwight H. Morrow testified that the girl helped serve the evening dinner, left the house at eight and returned about eleven.

The government wood expert, Koehler, was recalled. He refuted the testimony of the three defense witnesses and reaffirmed his opinion given in chief: that the upper ladder rail and the board from Hauptmann's attic had been in one piece, and that the ladder rail bore the unmistakable marks of the nicked Hauptmann plane.

On February 9 the State again rested its case. There was no surrebuttal, and the evidence was formally closed.

Prosecutor Hauck made the opening summation for the State. His argument was comparatively brief. Hunterdon

County, he told the jury, was a small, law-abiding county, unused to major crimes and ill-equipped, either with the personnel or funds, to prepare and present the evidence in a case of the complexity and importance of the Hauptmann case. That is why he had called on his superior, Attorney General Wilentz, to assume the burden of the prosecution.

The attorney general in his opening statement, said Hauck, had told the jury what the State expected to prove. He had lived up to his promises. He had proved everything he said he would prove, and more. Hauck then carefully reviewed the testimony of the State's witnesses. All of them, he declared, were honest, law-abiding, truthful citizens whose only interest in the case had been to state the facts within their knowledge. He made no reference at all to the defendant's witnesses. Wilentz, he said, would answer Reilly and make the principal summation. Hauck closed with an earnest plea that the jurors face their stern and disagreeable responsibility and return a verdict in accordance with the law and the evidence.

With an air of supreme assurance Defense Counsel Reilly approached the gigantic task of extricating Hauptmann from the net which the State had woven around him. Public clamor, he declared, always craving a victim, was demanding the life of Hauptmann regardless of the evidence, but the jurors, he was sure, realized the responsibility of taking away that which they could not give back and were big enough to stand above the blood cry of the mob. Under the law of the land, he said, Hauptmann was entitled to a fair and impartial trial "despite the prestige of the distinguished family which finds itself here in the position of being bereaved" and "despite the fact that this is a carpenter from Germany who is on trial." That is why, said Reilly, a beneficent law presumes every accused person innocent and requires proof of his guilt beyond a reasonable doubt. The State's case, continued the advocate, was all "guesswork . . . circumstantial evidence, which is no evidence."

Reilly's most telling arguments were directed to the contention that Hauptmann could not, as the indictment charged and the State claimed, have committed the crime alone. The kidnaping, he said, was the work of an inside gang—an inside gang in the Lindbergh and Morrow households. Lindbergh had been "stabbed in the back by the disloyalty of those who worked for him. . . . I don't know what was behind this kidnaping," said Reilly, "whether it was greed or gain or for spite or from vengeance. It was a horrible, horrible thing, but . . . it couldn't have been planned by one person, it had to be planned by a group."

He then proceeded in detail: How did Hauptmann in the Bronx know anything about the Lindbergh home in Hopewell, New Jersey? How could Hauptmann know that because of the baby's cold the Lindberghs would break their usual custom and stay at Hopewell on Tuesday night? Who knew the Lindberghs were extending their stay? None but the servants. How did Hauptmann know where the room was in which the baby slept? How did Hauptmann know which window had the warped and unfastened shutters? Would not the baby have awakened and cried if a stranger had picked him up? If Hauptmann had opened the shutters of the southeast window, in the gale which was blowing, and entered the room, would not the shutters have "banged back and forth against the walls" and aroused the entire household? Wouldn't Colonel Lindbergh have heard that noise? He heard the sound of what he thought might be the breaking of wood, but it was probably nothing more than the falling of a branch from one of the trees. With such a noise as the shutters banging wouldn't the dog have barked? Wasn't it significant that throughout all this supposed breaking and entering the dog never barked? There was only one person who could have kept him quiet —Whately, who was one of the conspiring gang.

Reilly supplemented this series of questions with further challenges: the difficulty of a man getting from the flimsy ladder onto the window ledge and through the window;

the unlikelihood of anyone making such an attempt without knowledge of the obstacles he might encounter on the inside; the increased difficulty of a man getting back through the window, with a thirty-pound child in his arms, and securing a foothold on the ladder. If the ladder had broken under the combined weight, as claimed by the State, would not, inquired Reilly, the mud at the bottom of the ladder have been "kicked up"? Would not the kidnaper have been killed or seriously hurt in the fall? Would there not have been marks in the mud made by the falling bodies of the kidnaper and the baby? There were no such marks, answered the advocate. There was nothing but two small indentations where a ladder might have pressed into the ground.

Hauptmann, declared Reilly, was nowhere near the Lindbergh premises on the night of March 1. No one but a "couple of halfwits and a crazy college boy" said they saw anyone in the neighborhood who resembled Hauptmann. Rossiter was a publicity seeker. Hochmuth was senile and didn't know what he was talking about. Whited was not to be believed even when he was under oath. Lupica, the college student, had said he saw a man who resembled Hauptmann, but many people resembled Hauptmann. He was a common German type. Wollenberg looked like him. So did Kloeppenburg.

Reilly viciously attacked the good faith of the prosecution and the credibility of the State's witnesses. The ladder was a "plant." It was never made by Hauptmann or any other carpenter. If it broke under the kidnaper, why should he have carried it away from the house and put it under the shrubbery? Koehler's testimony? Mere opinion, from a man who was looking for glory. The discovery of the thumb guard by Betty Gow and Mrs. Whately a month after the kidnaping, said Reilly, was another "plant," to cover up their own parts in the kidnaping plot. The writing of Dr. Condon's address and telephone number on the doorjamb of Hauptmann's closet was a "police plant . . . the New York police could be depended upon to make their own evidence." The New Jersey police, declared the lawyer, had "bobbled" the case from the start: They had shown neither intelligence nor promptness in trying to apprehend the real culprits. They should have promptly closed all roads, organized posses and, with the hunting dogs with which the section abounded, tracked down the criminals while the trail was hot. There were probably fingerprints everywhere, shouted Reilly—on the ransom note, on the window sill and on the ladder—and yet no intelligent effort had been made to preserve them for "processing."

Condon came in for Reilly's most venomous thrusts. "Condon stands behind something unholy," declared the lawyer. His boasted education was no guaranty of his veracity. Many criminals were well educated. There was much about Condon to arouse suspicion. The answer to his advertisement in an obscure Bronx paper had come altogether too quickly. When he got the first answer from the kidnaper, why hadn't he gone to the police? Who besides him said he talked to the kidnaper in the Woodlawn Cemetery? Who saw him pay over the ransom money?

All of the State's principal witnesses shared Reilly's condemnation: Betty Gow was a hypocrite who could shed crocodile tears in Court but could leave a sick child for two hours without attention. Violet Sharpe "had guilty knowledge of the kidnaping and killed herself as a way out." Whately, for the same reason, may have committed suicide. Cecile Barr was a "cheap publicity seeker." Miss Alexander was a "dizzy young girl from the Bronx looking for a movie contract." Perrone's evidence was "fishy." Why should the kidnaper give him one letter and mail all the others? The truth probably is, said Reilly, that Perrone was one of the conspirators with Condon and others to "frame" Hauptmann.

Colonel Lindbergh was treated more charitably. He was sincere, said Reilly, but mistaken. After the lapse of two years he could not possibly have identified the voice of Hauptmann as the voice of the mysterious "John."

The handwriting testimony, argued Reilly, was nothing but opinion, all "I think stuff" which the Courts for years have told juries they could disregard if they wanted to. If the jury wanted opinions, why, inquired Reilly, was not the opinion of Trendley just as good as that of Osborn? "Oh, yes," he said, "the State had more experts than the defense; but that was because of the unlimited resources of the State—the defense had no such resources." The police, said Reilly, had dictated the misspellings in the writings they compelled Hauptmann to make; it was therefore unfair to consider them as bases of comparison. He challenged the jury to make its own comparisons of the ransom notes with the admittedly genuine specimens of Hauptmann's writing made before his arrest and "third degree." The only possible identity was of one word out of hundreds—the word "is." Surely, said Reilly, no jury would convict a man on such flimsy evidence as that.

As to the discovery of the ransom money in Hauptmann's possession, that, said Reilly, had been fully explained: It had been given to him by Fisch. Fisch was a real person, a dealer in furs, a trader in stocks. Only $15,000 of the ransom money had been traced to Hauptmann. He couldn't have disposed of the other $35,000 to the stockbrokers. They, above all others, would have "spotted" the gold certificates immediately. Where was the missing $35,000? Cached away somewhere by Fisch. Someday, somewhere, it would turn up. In any event Hauptmann was not being tried for the illegal possession of the ransom money or for extortion. An extortion charge was pending against him in the New York courts. He was being tried here for murder.

It was upon this note that Reilly ended his four-hour

argument: "I believe this man is absolutely innocent of murder. This other charge against him in the Bronx will be disposed of. I don't think you are going to pick any . . . chestnuts out of the fire for the district attorney of the Bronx."

Reilly then spoke feelingly of the great sorrow that had come to the Lindberghs and the grueling ordeal of the long trial in which their memories had been recalled to the gruesome details of their loss. He concluded that Colonel Lindbergh, one of the fairest and most honorable of men, "certainly does not expect you to do anything but your duty under the law and the evidence." While there was nothing unique or spectacular about Reilly's argument, it was a sincere, capable effort to put everything forward in the light most favorable to the defendant. In the face of the case made by the State, no advocacy, however brilliant, would have availed to save Hauptmann.

Attorney General Wilentz began his closing argument for the State the following morning. One by one he took up the points made by Reilly and answered them. If there was a "public clamor" against Hauptmann—which Wilentz denied—it was not the fault of the State. An honored and respected judge had conducted the trial with perfect decorum and scrupulous fairness. Public feeling, if such there was, had resulted from the dispassionate presentation of the testimony of over a hundred "God-fearing, honest, truthful people who came here in behalf of the State of New Jersey to see justice done."

Reilly's argument that Hauptmann could not have committed the crime alone, said Wilentz, was "clearly the effort of an experienced criminal lawyer to confuse and befuddle a jury. . . . You don't have to worry about that," said the attorney general. "So far as Hauptmann is concerned, he could have had fifty people help him. If he participated in the murder that is all you have got to deal with. He can bring Violet Sharpe's corpse and lay it alongside of him, if he wants. He can bring Isidor Fisch's grave from Germany and put it alongside of him. That doesn't help the defendant in this case one bit. If he participated in this crime he is guilty, and it doesn't matter whether six, ten, or fifty helped him."

Reilly's insinuations against Violet Sharpe, Whately and Betty Gow found no justification in the evidence, said Wilentz. Violet Sharpe and Whately were dead. They could not answer for themselves. The attempt of the defense to disgrace the memory of Violet Sharpe by irresponsible and perjured testimony, declared the attorney general, had been completely frustrated by the rebuttal testimony of Mrs. Morrow, the night watchman Marshall, and the girl's three companions, which had accounted for every moment of her time between seven-thirty and eleven on the night of March 1, 1932.

Reilly's principal attack had fallen on Dr. Condon. Wilentz put up a spirited defense. He conceded Condon was "eccentric," perhaps something of a "busybody," but a more honest man never lived. Condon's reputation in the Bronx, where he had lived and taught school for fifty years, proved that. His testimony was not, as Reilly had asserted, uncorroborated. On the contrary, the old gentleman had been in continuous contact with Colonel Lindbergh, Colonel Breckinridge and, through them, with the police ever since he had received the first note from the kidnaper. True, he was alone the first time he met the kidnaper, but it had to be that way. The presence of anyone else would have frustrated the plans and hopes for the return of the baby. But that trip to the Woodlawn Cemetery was corroborated by the testimony of Al Reich and the subsequent receipt of the sleeping suit. Colonel Lindbergh was as close to Hauptmann as it was possible to be on the occasion of the second meeting with the kidnaper when the ransom money was paid.

Reilly had not "attacked" Colonel Lindbergh's credibility. As to that part of his testimony most damaging to the defendant—that he had recognized the call, "Hey, Doktor," at St. Raymond's Cemetery as the voice of Hauptmann—he had argued that the colonel must be "mistaken." This afforded Wilentz one of his best opportunities, and he took full advantage of it.

"He [Lindbergh]," declared the attorney general, "went to the cemetery with Condon to pay his money so that he could get his baby. It was the tensest moment of his life. He was close to him—straining every effort to see or hear him—and in the stillness of the night, that voice comes out, 'Hey, Doktor, hey, Doktor!' God, could you ever forget it? Would anybody ever forget it? How many nights do you think he heard that voice in his sleep? . . . And, it is not an ordinary voice. Oh, no. Why, if that man [Hauptmann] said one word in this room above a whisper, I wouldn't have to look around. I could tell you it was Hauptmann. There is a different quality, there is a different tone, there is something weird about it. And Lindbergh remembered that voice, and who is to say that he didn't? Are you going to substitute your judgment for his? He was in that automobile, in that cemetery—not you or I. Lindy's ears were trained; Lindy, whose happiness was involved, whose heart was crushed; Lindy, there with his money waiting for his child. And Reilly says, 'Why, he couldn't. . . . How could Lindy remember?' Why, that voice. God, I can't sleep after I hear it at nights myself. And he says Lindy wouldn't have remembered it."

The attorney general replied vigorously to the defense contention that Fisch and not Hauptmann had collected the ransom money. The time when Fisch and Hauptmann first met was important, said Wilentz. The State contended it was in July or August of 1932. This was what Hauptmann and Mr. and Mrs. Henkel had told the police immediately after his arrest. Why had they changed their stories to place the meeting in the preceding March or April?

Simply to account for the large deposits by Hauptmann in his brokerage accounts in April, May and June of 1932. No one, declared the prosecutor, ever saw Fisch give Hauptmann a dollar. All that had been proved about Fisch was that he was a poor man, sick unto death with tuberculosis; that he had borrowed money from his friends and relatives; that he had borrowed $2,000 from Hauptmann to get to Germany. No money of his, save $500 in traveler's checks, was found after his death. Not a single ransom bill had ever been traced to him. No one could be credulous enough to believe the concocted story of the carelessly left and forgotten shoe box.

Who wrote the ransom notes? The attorney general devoted a considerable portion of his argument to answering this question. He went carefully over the testimony of each of the State's experts. How had this testimony been met? he inquired. Fisher in his opening had suggested the defense would refute it by other experts. The names of "Meyers" and "Malone" had been mentioned by the defense. Where were they? They had not been called. Who had been called? One man—Trendley, an alleged expert who confessed to a series of previous mistaken testimonies, which utterly destroyed his credibility, and whose testimony on the stand could not be considered seriously against the testimony of the State's witnesses.

Wilentz then proceeded to show the jurors scores of similarities between words and letters in the ransom notes and the same words and letters in a promissory note and in a memorandum book written by Hauptmann long before his arrest. In the promissory note, the dollar sign was written after the numerals, exactly as in the ransom notes. The word "boad" for "boat" was written in the memorandum book the same as in the last ransom note. Hauptmann had sworn that when the police had him write specimens for them they had told him to spell "signature" "singnature." Dramatically Wilentz spread all the requested writings before the jury and asked them to examine them to see if they could find the words "signature" or "singnature" in any of them. The words nowhere appeared. Proof positive, declared Wilentz, of Hauptmann's readiness to lie about anything and everything to save his hide.

The attorney general proceeded to the handwriting on the jamb of the closet door opening. He went over the testimony of Hauptmann on the stand and his previous contradictory statements to District Attorney Foley and before the Bronx magistrate. He pointed out to the jurors the numerals on the board and the numerals on the ransom notes and asked them to compare them. Anyone, he declared, could see they had been made by the same person. Hauptmann, through more lies, was simply trying to escape the consequences of another damning piece of evidence.

Could Hauptmann deny that $14,600 of the ransom money was found in his possession? Did he not admit that he had passed a number of the ransom bills? What explanation had he given of his embarrassment when called on in December of 1931 to meet a $74 margin call? Could he dispute the records of his brokers and bankers that after April 2 he had deposited $16,942.75 in his brokerage account and $9,073.25 in his bank account and, in addition, purchased a $3,750 mortgage? Didn't he admit that the brokers' records showed him as having lost more than $5,000 in the stock market after April 1932? What about his purchases and expenditures after April 2: a trip for his wife to Europe, his purchase of a $400 radio, of field glasses, of a shotgun, and his hunting trips to Maine and Florida? Hadn't he and his wife both quit working after April 2? Where had the money come from? These, declared Wilentz, were questions neither Hauptmann nor his counsel had answered. The prosecutor added yet another question: Was it not passing strange that since the arrest of Hauptmann not a single ransom bill had turned up?

Wilentz furnished a convincing answer to Reilly's contention that the entire case against Hauptmann was built on circumstantial evidence. The testimony of Hochmuth, Rossiter, Whited and Lupica that they had seen Hauptmann or a man closely resembling him near the Lindbergh home shortly before the kidnaping was not circumstantial. The testimony of the taxi driver, Perrone, that Hauptmann had given him the letter to deliver to Dr. Condon was not circumstantial. The testimony of Dr. Condon that Hauptmann was the man to whom he talked about the sleeping suit and to whom he had delivered the ransom money was not circumstantial. The testimony of Colonel Lindbergh that the voice which shouted, "Hey, Doktor!" at St. Raymond's Cemetery was the voice of Hauptmann was not circumstantial. The mute evidence of the brokerage and bank accounts was not circumstantial. The $14,600 ransom money found hidden in Hauptmann's garage was not circumstantial. The case against Hauptmann, declared Wilentz, had been overwhelmingly established by credible direct evidence.

For the most part the attorney general's argument was a steady hammering of the direct facts proved by the State's evidence. Only on one or two occasions did he resort to inference. One of these was his argument that the kidnaper and murderer of little Charles Lindbergh, Jr., had to be an unusual criminal like Hauptmann. He had to be, argued Wilentz, "a fellow with ice water in his veins"—a bold, determined, conscienceless, secretive criminal, an egomaniac with a confidence that he "could plan and get away with anything." Hauptmann was such a man—a man so bold that when as a youthful criminal he planned a burglary in Germany he picked out as the object of his imagined skill the home of the principal man in the town, the burgomaster; a man so abandoned to all of the finer instincts of human beings that he could hold up mothers while they were wheeling their infants; a man so determined that he would stow himself away in the crowded hold of an ocean liner and subsist for days on no more food and water than he could secrete on his person and, when caught and returned to Germany, would repeat the attempt twice in the ensuing six months; a man so secretive that he hid his earnings from his wife and told her nothing of his sources of wealth after April 2, 1932. This, declared Wilentz, is the man before you for your judgment—"an animal lower than the lowest form in the animal kingdom—public enemy number one of this world." Wilentz closed his five-hour summation with a ringing demand for a verdict to fit the crime and the criminal—a verdict of first-degree murder.

In New Jersey, the trial judge, following the English and American Federal court practices, charges the jury orally on both the law and the facts. Judge Trenchard's charge as to the law followed the orthodox pattern in criminal cases. It was dispassionate and meticulously accurate. Considering that the record of testimony taken filled over 4,000 printed pages, the Court's charge as to the facts was surprisingly brief. He summarized the State's evidence as to the events preceding and following the kidnaping.

He reviewed in some detail the testimony of Dr. Condon. "It is argued," said the judge, "that Dr. Condon's testimony is inherently improbable and should be rejected by you, but you will observe that his testimony is corroborated in large part by several witnesses whose credibility has not been impeached in any manner whatsoever. If there is in the minds of the jury a reasonable doubt as to the truth of any testimony, such testimony must be rejected, but, upon the whole, is there any doubt in your minds as to the reliability of Dr. Condon?"

The most damaging part of the charge to the defendant consisted of a series of questions which went to the very heart of the case: "If you find that the defendant was the man to whom the ransom money was delivered as the result of the directions in the ransom notes bearing symbols like those on the original ransom note, the question is pertinent: Wasn't the defendant the man who left the ransom note on the window sill of the nursery and took the child from its crib after opening the closed window? . . . Does it not appear that many of the ransom notes were traced to the defendant? . . . Does it not appear that many thousands of dollars of the ransom bills were found in his garage, and others were found on his person, and that others had been passed by him from time to time? . . . The defendant says that these ransom bills . . . were left with him by one Fisch, a man now dead. Do you believe that? . . . Do you believe the testimony that the money was left with him in a shoe box and that it rested on the top shelf in his closet for several months?"

As to the defense contention that the kidnaper was one of a gang, the Court posed this question: "Now do you believe that? Is there any evidence to justify or support any such claim?"

The Court charged that the testimony of the defendant "and others" as to where he was on March 1 and April 2 should be considered by the jury "and given such weight as it is entitled to"; but, the Court added, there was the testimony of "Hochmuth and others," as to the defendant's presence at or near the scene of the crime shortly before its commission, which should be weighed. Judge Trenchard followed this with the question: "Is there any reason to doubt it?"

In conclusion the Court charged that if the death of the baby was caused by the unlawful act of the defendant in seizing the child and carrying it and its clothing away, and if the death of the child might be considered the probable consequence of such an act, then the defendant was guilty of murder; and that under the law of New Jersey a murder committed in the perpetration of a burglary was murder in the first degree regardless of whether the killing was intentional or unintentional.

The jury, charged the Court, if it found the defendant guilty of murder, might, if it saw fit, recommend as the penalty imprisonment at hard labor for life, and the Court would enter judgment accordingly; if, on the other hand, it returned a verdict of guilty of murder in the first degree and nothing else the penalty which would be decreed in that event would be death.

Taken as a whole, the Court's charge carried a strong intimation to the jury that the judge believed the defendant guilty. This is not said in criticism. In any jurisdiction where the law permits the Court in a criminal case to charge the jury on the facts as well as the law, it is almost inevitable that inferences will be drawn as to the trial judge's personal opinion of the guilt or innocence of the accused.

At 12:09 P.M., February 13, 1935, after thirty-two days of testimony and argument—the longest trial in the history of New Jersey—the fate of Bruno Richard Hauptmann was committed to the jury.

The jury deliberated for nearly eleven hours. At 10:45 P.M., twelve haggard-looking men and women filed into the courtroom. The foreman, his voice trembling and scarcely audible, read the verdict: "Guilty of murder in the first degree." There was no accompanying recommendation that the punishment be life imprisonment. Judge Trenchard immediately pronounced the formal sentence of death: execution to take place the week of March 18.

AFTERMATH

After sentence had been pronounced Hauptmann, following customary procedure, was removed from the Hunterdon County jail to the state penitentiary at Trenton and there confined in one of the death cells to await execution.

His attorneys, Fisher, Pope and Rosencrans, immediately prosecuted an appeal to the New Jersey Court of Errors and Appeals. Reilly, for reasons undisclosed, had dropped out of the case. Twenty-five separate grounds were urged for reversal and vigorously argued.

In a decision handed down on October 9, 1935, the high court of thirteen members unanimously rejected all the defendant's contentions. Speaking to the charge that the verdict was contrary to the evidence, the Court said, after a review of the record: "From the foregoing it is deducible, to a moral certainty beyond a reasonable doubt, that he [Hauptmann] collected the ransom money and was therefore the kidnaper. . . . The explanation of the source of this money [the $14,600 found in his possession and represented by his bank and brokerage accounts] offered by defendant was incredible, and we find not the slightest evidence to corroborate it. . . . Our conclusion is that the verdict is not only not contrary to the weight of the evidence, but one to which the evidence inescapably led."[15]

A petition for a writ of review was immediately filed in the Supreme Court of the United States. This was denied on December 9, 1935. Judge Trenchard resentenced Hauptmann to be executed during the week of January 13, 1936.

With the usual avenues of court review closed, recourse was next had to the New Jersey State Court of Pardons. This so-styled court was made up of eight members with the governor as chairman. During the course of the Hauptmann trial, Governor Moore had been succeeded by Governor Harold G. Hoffman.

A meeting of the court of pardons to consider Hauptmann's plea was held January 11, 1936. There was a new item to consider. Two days earlier the governor had received a letter signed "J. J. Faulkner," but with no address given. In it the writer declared that Hauptmann was not guilty of the crime for which he stood convicted. The gov-

---

15 115 N. J. L. 412.

ernor gave it out that a cursory comparison of the hand-writing in the letter with the handwriting on the deposit slip which had figured in the trial indicated they were written by the same person.[16] After a six-hour session in which this item and the evidence produced on the trial were reviewed, the court of pardons denied Hauptmann's application for clemency.

On January 14 a petition was filed with Judge J. Warren Davis of the United States Court of Appeals for a writ of habeas corpus. It was promptly rejected. An appeal to the Supreme Court of the United States to review Judge Davis' decision was denied two days later. With the ultimate mo-ment for the execution of the Court's order less than thirty hours away, Governor Hoffman granted Hauptmann a thirty-day reprieve. Contemporaneously with his official announcement, he declared the purpose of his action was to enable Colonel Schwarzkopf, head of the New Jersey state police, to reopen the investigation to determine if any others had been involved in the kidnaping. He added that this was the only reprieve he would grant. Hoffman's action caused a storm of protest. There were insistent de-mands for his impeachment. A petition for that purpose was actually presented to the legislature.[17]

Nothing came of Schwarzkopf's investigation.

On February 19, 1936, Judge Trenchard entered an order directing that Hauptmann's execution be carried out during the week of March 30. April 1 was fixed by the warden of the penitentiary as the exact date.

On March 30 the governor reconvened the court of par-dons—this time to consider the final bizarre episode in this amazing case. The day before, a story had been flashed to

---

16 J. Vreeland Haring—a handwriting expert previously engaged by the State but not called to testify on the trial—and other recognized handwrit-ing experts unhesitatingly declared that while there had been an obvious attempt at the imitation of the deposit-slip writing, the two papers had not been written by the same hand.

17 It was not pressed and, after Hauptmann's execution, was forgotten.

the world that a chief of detectives of Burlington County, New Jersey, had in custody a man who had confessed to the Lindbergh kidnaping. The accused was a disbarred lawyer of Trenton, New Jersey, named Wendell. For a considerable time previous to his arrest on a charge of embezzlement, he had been confined in public and private institutions for the treatment of the mentally afflicted. Before the court of pardons met, Wendell had repudiated his alleged confession and declared that he had been kidnaped from Brooklyn, New York, forcibly taken to Mount Holly, New Jersey, and there had been beaten and tortured by the police into signing a statement that he was the Lindbergh kidnaper. The court of pardons considered this "new evidence" and again rejected Hauptmann's plea for clemency.

It would seem this should have ended the matter, but there was to be yet another delay. A grand jury was in session in Mercer County, where the dead body of the Lindbergh baby had been found. Presumably the inquisitors thought it within their jurisdiction to consider the alleged confession of Wendell and, in the early evening of April 1, just before the start of the death march at Trenton, the warden received a telephone request from the foreman of the grand jury to "hold up the execution of Hauptmann for forty-eight hours." Either with or without the governor's added consent, the warden complied.

The forty-eight hours passed. The grand jury adjourned without taking action. The governor announced officially there would be no further reprieve. At eight-forty on the evening of April 3, 1936, Hauptmann was told to prepare for death. He made no last-minute statement, uttered no protest and approached his fate calmly. The lethal current was passed through his body and the brief but crowded career of Bruno Richard Hauptmann was at an end. His accomplices, if such he had, could breathe easier: he had not betrayed them.